Less Stress, More Success

A New Approach to Guiding Your Teen Through College Admissions and Beyond

by

Marilee Jones,
Dean of Admissions, MIT

and

Kenneth R. Ginsburg,
MD, MS Ed, FAAP

With Martha M. Jablow

American Academy of Pediatrics
Department of Marketing and Publications Staff

Maureen DeRosa, MPA
Director, Department of Marketing and Publications

Mark Grimes
Director, Division of Product Development

Eileen Glasstetter, MS
Manager, Consumer Publishing

Sandi King, MS
Director, Division of Publishing and Production Services

Kate Larson
Manager, Editorial Services

Jason Crase
Editorial Specialist

Theresa Wiener
Manager, Editorial Production

Shannan Martin
Print Production Specialist

Peg Mulcahy
Graphic Designer

Jill Ferguson
Director, Division of Marketing and Sales

Kathleen Juhl
Manager, Consumer Product Marketing and Sales

Library of Congress Control Number: 2006920980
ISBN-10: 1-58110-230-5
ISBN-13: 978-1-58110-230-7
CB0045

The information contained in this publication should not be used as a substitute for the medical care and advice of your pediatrician. There may be variations in treatment that your pediatrician may recommend based on the individual facts and circumstances.

Statements and opinions expressed are those of the authors and not necessarily those of the American Academy of Pediatrics.

9-151/0706

1 2 3 4 5 6 7 8 9 10

To my daughter Nora, always Nora, the love of my life, my greatest teacher, and my partner in this vision. If it weren't for you, I never would have known. Thank you for picking me.

~ MJ

■ ❖ ■ ❖ ■ ❖ ■ ❖ ■

With love to my wife Celia, the best mother I know, and to Ilana and Talia, my little girls who are growing up. Girls, this book is written so that your generation will be able to follow its dreams and figure out how to make the world a better place, each in his or her unique way.

~ KRG

Table of Contents

Acknowledgments

Many people have supported us in writing this book or have inspired us to feel that it should be written, but some in particular must be singled out. The Committee on Communications of the American Academy of Pediatrics (AAP) deserves special mention. Committee Chair Dr Donald Shifrin and members, Drs Michael Brody, Daniel Broughton, Susan Buttross, Alberto Gedissman, Rosario González-de-Rivas, Paul Horowitz, Regina Milteer, Deborah Mulligan, Michael Rich, and Brian Wilcox. The committed AAP staff—Carolyn Kolbaba, Veronica Noland, and Marjorie Tharp—have offered encouragement, support, and guidance. We thank the AAP for trusting us to take on this important topic. We are especially grateful to Carolyn Kolbaba and Mark Grimes for the vision to make this project happen, and Eileen Glasstetter for her skill and support in guiding the book to publication.

Each of us would like to acknowledge other individuals for the important roles they have played in our lives and work.

From Dean Jones

I want to thank the admissions staff, the administration, and all of my many friends at Massachusetts Institute of Technology (MIT), the greatest university of science and technology on earth, for supporting my efforts these past few years. I'm the person I am today because of the rigor and discipline I've learned there. Though many have been a part of shaping my ideas and the concepts described in this book, a few people have been especially critical in getting it launched by encouraging (and occasionally pushing) me, including my amazing publicist Kristen Collins, my manager and personal favorite Eric Chemi, my assistant Ellen Stordy, and my angel Martha Jablow.

I am so grateful to the men and women who taught me what it means to be a Wise Elder. I have worked for the best—Peter Richardson, Julie McLellan, Michael Behnke, Dan Langdale, Bob Redwine, Susan Hockfield, Dan Hastings, and Chuck Vest (my hero).

I'm grateful to others in my field who have risen with courage to speak out on behalf of children, especially Lloyd Thacker, founder of the Education Conservancy and all of its member schools who have chosen to do the right thing, even if it hurts their rankings.

My deepest thanks go to the key teachers of my life—Diane Englund, who saved me, got me back on my feet, and taught me how to be a good mother; Sharon Turner, the best teacher I have ever had, who came into my life just in time, taught me how to trust my own information, and who regularly reminds me who I really am; Sarah Smith, Joy Musacchio, and Cynthia Brownley, my Sacred Sisters, who love and honor me and with whom I have the most fun; Lynn McKenna, who has helped me see the deeper meaning of my mission; my wonderful friends from Sharon's New York class who have held the energy for me; my entire family, living and dead, who formed me at the core and who cheer for me, especially Mom and Dad, Pat, Kate, Peggy, and Pete; and of course my husband Steve Bussolari who has always believed in me. Thank you all from the bottom of my heart.

From Dr Ginsburg

First, I must thank Martha Jablow for her patience, commitment, and clarity of thought. This book never could have become a reality without her skill and perseverance. And I never would have had so much pleasure writing it without her support, humor, and warmth.

I thank my professional mentors, Drs Donald Schwarz and Gail B. Slap, who have demonstrated to me that physicians must remain healers and steadfastly refuse to become technicians. They have showed me through their actions that sometimes doctors have to go beyond the bedside if we are really to make a difference in our patients' lives—we must advocate for the kind of support adolescents need if they are to thrive. They have offered me much more than experience and knowledge. They have transmitted their love of youth to me. I am particularly thankful that they have always cared about me as much as they cared about my academic career.

I thank the young people and their families who have let me into their lives. I am awed by the love I see every day from parents who bring their children to me at The Children's Hospital of Philadelphia, and I am honored to pass along their wisdom to you. I am equally impressed by how well my adolescent patients are navigating an increasingly complicated world. The resilience that I have observed in them has proven to me that youth can meet and overcome almost any challenge when someone really believes in them.

I am deeply appreciative to my wife Celia, first for tolerating me and remaining consistently supportive, but also for being an authentic example of a parent who can withstand all of the messages that suggest good parents are those who "enrich" their children with an abundance of activities. She has proven to me that children thrive when offered the freedom to explore their world, the time and space to remain children, and unconditional parental love. My girls, Ilana and Talia, serve as a source of inspiration for me always. Every day their joyous nature and innate idealism remind me how special childhood is—a time that we mustn't rush our children through.

Introduction

American youth have a major problem...and we're not talking about sex, drugs, or rock and roll.

They are under such tremendous stress that it's damaging their physical health and psychological well-being. The pressure from parents and high schools to get into college is producing the most anxious, stressed, sleep-deprived generation ever. This pressure begins at an increasingly early age and threatens individual children as well as society itself. If we don't change our ways, many of today's youth may not be equipped to deal with adult challenges because we will have done real harm to their creativity, initiative, and potential to contribute and lead in the world. This problem has national implications.

Adolescents have always faced stressful experiences: coping with peer pressure, finding their own identity, breaking from parents to become more independent, and worrying about their future as adults. Such pressures affect every generation in different ways and to varying degrees. Young people have always had innate strengths and resilience, however, and most survived and even thrived despite the challenges of adolescence.

But the kind of stress on today's youth is unique. We are worried that the current trend of pressuring adolescents so intensely may undermine their natural resilience. They are driven to be perfect at everything, participate in scores of extracurricular activities to pump up their college applications, take as many advance placement (AP) courses as possible and earn As in each—all to reach the holy grail: acceptance at the best colleges...and oh, yes, they also must please adults along the way.

Kids aren't suddenly tossed into this pressure cooker on the first day of high school. Many parents are obsessed with getting children off to the swiftest academic start from birth. Toddlers are plopped in front of computers before they can talk. Parents try to enroll them in the "best" preschool to guarantee admission to the best primary school, which will ensure the best secondary school, which in turn will give them the best chance to get into an elite college. Parents don't stop with trying to provide every possible academic advantage; they also sign up their youngsters for enrichment programs throughout childhood so that they will acquire impressive credentials as young ballerinas, musicians, or artists. Athletics are good too, so their kids play at least one sport every season or—a growing trend—a single sport year-round, year after year, with the goal of becoming skilled enough between ages 7 and 17 to win an athletic scholarship.

What is this crazy pace doing to individual children and families? What is it doing to society? And what does it mean for our country's future? These questions and concerns brought us together from 2 distinct vantage points— higher education and adolescent medicine. Who are we and why do we care?

Marilee Jones, Dean of Admissions at Massachusetts Institute of Technology (MIT): Having worked in college admissions for 25 years, I have seen many changes over time, but I have recently become alarmed at the pressures we adults are collectively placing on young people to make us all happy because I see how this drive to be admitted to college is affecting them so negatively. Wanting to become part of the solution, I have begun to speak out publicly about the effects of this pressure on kids. I am now involved in a growing movement to change the way higher education handles admis-

sions so that students are seen, as I like to describe it, as human "beings" rather than human "doings."

Dr Ken Ginsburg: I have specialized in adolescent medicine for 19 years at The Children's Hospital of Philadelphia and at the University of Pennsylvania School of Medicine. My patients range from poor urban to upper-income suburban youth. I am very concerned about how young people's behaviors affect their health. It seems that every year I see more young people who are physically ill, anxious, and depressed—some of whom are turning to dangerous quick fixes, such as drugs and alcohol—as a result of constant pressure to prove they are good enough to get into college. But I've become increasingly convinced that children and teens can overcome a great deal of adversity and deal with significant stress if their resilience is given the opportunity to flourish.

■ ❖ ■ ❖ ■ ❖ ■ ❖ ■

Both of us are critically concerned about what's happening to young people and deeply committed to redirecting them from the dangerous direction in which they're headed. We share a mutual goal: to help parents support their children in becoming successful at school and in life. Truly successful young people know how to face challenges, manage stress, enjoy life, and reach their potential while remaining healthy and well balanced. Success doesn't mean being the best at everything or attending the "best" college. Success isn't determined by a fat acceptance letter from their first-choice college. Success in the college admissions process can be achieved by finding the most appropriate college for each individual student—the best match—and by using this opportunity to develop resilience, integrity, and confidence for a lifetime.

The college admissions process represents a journey of initiation into the adult world. We want young people to find their own compass, their own direction. Adolescents can gain confidence in their own capabilities as they go through this initiation rite. But the journey requires parents to become something of a travel agent—making suggestions, helping to map out the route, and monitoring some details, but standing back and letting their child embark on the journey independently.

Unfortunately that is not what's happening in many families today. It is common for parents to take over. They write their teenagers' application essays, call admissions offices to check on their status, too often demand acceptance, and occasionally threaten to sue a college when their kids are denied admission. After acceptance and enrollment, many parents are still too involved, even to the point of calling college administrators and professors about their son or daughter's grades ("I'm paying a fortune in tuition. He deserves an A. How will he get into grad school if you don't raise his grade?"). When overly involved parents take charge and increase the pressure, they send their kids the message that they aren't capable or independent. The consequences are clear: Young people are disempowered and lose out on opportunities to learn to trust their own instincts and abilities. Parents unwittingly deprive them of a chance to grow up, take chances, perhaps fail at a few things, and learn to deal with adversity and bounce back. In other words, adults are robbing the next generation of opportunities to develop their own strengths and resilience.

Often dubbed hyper-parents or helicopter parents (for their tendency to hover over their kids at all times), they are well-intentioned, loving people who only want the best for their children. But they are adding so much stress to their already over-scheduled, overburdened kids that they don't recognize the far-ranging dangers of their over-involvement. These parents never intend to put undue pressure on their children. Their only interest is preparing them for a competitive world by providing every advantage. But they get caught up in a cycle that feeds on itself and is reinforced by other parents, high schools, the media, and colleges and universities. No wonder parents have come to think, "If my child doesn't get into a good college, she'll never have a chance for a successful career. If she doesn't take 5 AP courses, some other kid will be accepted and she won't get in. If she doesn't have 12 extracurricular activities, no admissions officer will bother to read her application."

Parents' anxiety spills over onto their children. Instead of modeling how to lead a balanced life in a complex, stressful world, parents often set negative examples. Young people see parents who don't have lives of their own, don't take time for themselves, and don't deal well with stress, but live vicariously through their children. And this is not healthy for kids or parents.

This spiraling pressure and angst not only damages relationships between parents and children, but also threatens young people's physical health and psychological well-being. Health professionals today are seeing more medical problems caused by stress—everything from bellyaches and headaches to disordered eating, drug abuse, self-mutilation, depression, and suicide. Psychological support services on many college campuses are overflowing; some students' fear of failure is paralyzing their efforts to learn or acclimate to the college environment.

Character comes into play as well. If young people continue to live in this pressure cooker, we are likely to see an increase in character deficits. Parents who write teenagers' application essays model dishonesty, not integrity. The goal is to get the trophy—the acceptance letter—at all cost. Getting an A becomes more important than the knowledge acquired by studying. There's an observation on many campuses that more students are cheating to get As and are negotiating with professors to avoid the dreaded B+. As technology makes it simple for students to swipe tests and papers electronically (with cell phone cameras and pen scanners, for example) or buy a term paper through cyberspace, the ever-increasing pressure to excel academically makes cheating and plagiarism easier. The challenge then is not just about getting into college, but about becoming an adult with integrity who will work harder to turn Bs into As than to figure out how to work the system.

Taking a Deep Breath

We know that most parents reading this are not helicopter parents. We don't assume that all readers fill in their teenagers' application forms or write their essays. But many parents find themselves on a treadmill, racing along in this college application process and wondering how they got to this point. A little retrospection is useful.

College selection is hardly the first occasion when parents consider the best environment for their children. Much earlier they probably chose among several different child care, preschool, elementary, or secondary schools. They considered the entire milieu: educational, environmental, social, and emotional factors that all contribute to a child's healthy development. At that point, the trajectory toward college, or the "best" college, may or may not have been a major factor. But over the years, parents weighed all the factors because their child was too young to have real input. Now that the child is a teenager, many parents tend to follow the same pattern and continue to make most choices and decisions. They keep jogging along on the treadmill because they want to keep providing the best opportunities. But here's a key point about the college admissions process: The child, now nearing adulthood, is the one who must evaluate the milieu because he or she best understands his or her developmental needs. This is a magnificent opportunity for parents to step back and support young people to make their own decisions.

Most parents do support their kids very appropriately, but they often say they're made to feel inferior by other parents whose over-involvement seems to be the norm. They wonder whether they're letting their children down if they don't pack their schedules with enrichment activities or hire special tutors and consultants to make their teen's college application as "perfect" as possible. Many parents live with guilt or fear that they might not be doing enough. Getting off the treadmill seems risky when other families chatter on about the many activities their kids juggle, how many AP courses and SAT prep classes they take, and all the campuses they've visited.

We know that some readers may have a great deal of ambivalence. On one hand, they want nothing more than happiness for their children. They may see the harm that this hurried lifestyle is inflicting on adolescents. On the other hand, they worry that if they jump off the treadmill, their kids will be left behind in an increasingly complex, competitive world.

Rest assured that we want your children to be authentically successful. While we have no recipe to guarantee this because each young person has different needs, we hope that this book will guide you in supporting adolescents in ways that will foster their creativity, honor their ingenuity, and enhance their inborn resilience. If you can do this, your children will be models of success and will be well prepared to get the most out of the college experience. Your neighbors will be looking back at you and asking how they too can get off the treadmill.

"Yes, But…"

We are well aware that not everyone agrees with our message. Some people believe that American parents and educators should push kids *even more* so others won't outperform us in the global marketplace. Some say, "Yes, but we can't turn down the pressure on our kids. We must keep pushing them to achieve or other countries will turn out smarter students who will have better jobs and build stronger economies. We can't let our kids be left in the wake of other countries' students or America will fall behind." One of the problems with this argument is that it assumes that success only derives from the acquisition of knowledge. It ignores the role of creativity and ingenuity in driving success.

We are not suggesting that adolescents drop biochemistry and take up basket weaving. We certainly aren't advocating lower academic standards or mediocrity. We don't want parents or teachers to let students slack off. And we see nothing wrong with extracurricular activities, as long as they don't consume a child's life. But we believe that burdening young people with the unrealistic expectation that each of them must excel in multiple areas generates so much stress that their innovative potential may be crushed.

We applaud young people who work hard to get the most out of their education. We want them to do their best in school, of course. We need tomorrow's scientists, poets, and leaders to get the finest education. A college education clearly has value for individuals and society. College graduates earn more than people with high school diplomas, for example. But why is there so much pressure to attend a "top" college, as promoted by national magazine rankings? Does a graduate of an elite college earn more over time than a graduate of a less selective college? Not necessarily. One study found that equally qualified students—all accepted by the same highly selective colleges—earned about the same income 20 years later whether they attended top schools or less selective ones.* The conclusion was that the student, not the college, determines success.

Some people believe that attending an elite college gives a young person other advantages, such as entrée into a first job, a better chance at graduate school, or wider social networking. For many students, these factors are often true. But the bottom line is that individual students determine their own success far more than their college's name or reputation.

And this brings us back to our point: Success is more about the person than the college. Successful people are motivated, resilient, and committed. Success is defined in more ways than income. But if we lead teenagers to believe they can only become successful adults by attending a top college, we may undercut the very qualities that help them succeed in the long term. If they don't get into an elite school, they step into adulthood feeling like failures. Even if they are admitted to a highly selective college, they may feel too much pressure, fear failure, and therefore won't take risks.

There are hundreds of good colleges and universities—in fact, there is less difference today among good schools than ever before. If we want young people to be truly successful, we shouldn't set them up for possible failure or to feel that they are judged for life if they don't get into a top college. The important thing is the right match for each student.

We are issuing a clarion call to examine exactly what we are doing to this generation. Today's high-pressured atmosphere is making our students less resilient because it pushes them to achieve only high grades and to be "perfect" at everything. These budding perfectionists define failure as a B or B+, often become frightened of failure at all costs, and don't take those very risks that produce the greatest new ideas. They don't develop resilience to bounce back from failure because they're too scared to try in the first place.

If we continue to push them so hard, expecting perfection, our efforts will only backfire—on their individual lives and on society. They will never be able to become resilient, capable, and creative adults if we continue to pressure them to achieve high grades and well-paying careers and to satisfy adults more than their own inner dreams. As long as we focus only on a short-range goal (college admission), we undermine the real goal: creating a generation of young people who will thrive and be prepared to live productive, joyful, and satisfying adult lives. This is true success.

---

*Estimating the Payoff to Attending a More Selective College, by Princeton economist Alan Krueger and Andrew Mellon Foundation researcher Stacy Berg Dale, published by the National Bureau of Economic Research, 2000; and "Who Needs Harvard?" by Gregg Easterbrook, The Atlantic Monthly, October 2004.

Although this book focuses on young people who are burning the candle at both ends and being "enriched" to the point of their great detriment, we must recognize that millions of American youth are relatively ignored and under-resourced. Rather than being held to unrealistically high expectations, they are held to dangerously low expectations. We are not tapping into a great potential pool of intelligence, talent, and energy—the undereducated poorer youth of this country. If we're really worried about America falling behind, we must pay much greater attention to those who deserve more enrichment and resources.

On These Pages

This book is written for parents and young people themselves, although we hope it will also be helpful to educators and health care professionals who work with students and families. About three-quarters of the book is intended for parents and other adults. While adolescents are certainly welcome and encouraged to read the entire book, the final 2 sections are specifically addressed to them. In Part Three, Dean Jones offers information and advice about negotiating the college admissions process. Part Four can help teenagers manage stress in healthy ways—right now during these challenging high school days, when they are in college, and throughout their adult lives.

This is not a "how to get into college" book. We don't offer 10 steps to guarantee admission to anyone's first-choice college. We take a very different approach, one that will help adolescents find the right college match but also develop overall strategies and strengths that prepare them for a lifetime of success. In fact, if students follow our plan to build resilience, they can develop a healthy lifestyle while generating an excellent resumé for college.

We want to widen the angle of vision beyond April or May of senior year when the acceptance and rejection letters arrive. We hope that parents will read this book a few years before the college application season. Although we address the college game and its ramifications on health and well-being, we also discuss important steps to help teenagers navigate middle and late adolescence in ways that can promote their natural flexibility, resilience, and ingenuity.

We focus on managing stress because we know that even if you try your best to shield your children from unreasonable pressure, they will still be exposed to stress throughout their lives. If we use the college admissions process as a model for a stressful but exciting challenge, adolescents can gain valuable life lessons about self-advocacy, keeping things in perspective, managing time, and rebounding from inevitable disappointments.

We hope that individual parents will consider this material seriously and discuss it within the family. We also urge parents to broaden these discussions to other concerned adults: parents of their children's classmates, teachers, and high school counselors. Many people are eager to get off the treadmill but are reluctant to do so alone. The pressure on today's youth is so serious and threatening that it deserves a national conversation. We hope that the conversation will begin in your home and ripple out into your community.

PART ONE

Dean Marilee Jones:

View From the

Admissions Office

CHAPTER ONE

My Epiphany

For the last several years I have been writing about the over-involvement of parents in the college admissions process. I've spoken to nearly 150 parent and guidance counselor groups nationwide about the proper role for parents. During the question-and-answer period of each presentation, someone inevitably raises a hand to assert that we college admissions officers are to blame for encouraging and rewarding the high-pressure, whirlwind activities of their kids. Frankly, I didn't take it seriously…until the night I did an information session about MIT somewhere in the Midwest.

At the end of my talk, a young high school student approached me to ask, "Is it true that you need 10 extracurricular activities to be admitted to MIT?" I was a little annoyed because I had just spent the previous hour describing our admissions process and nowhere had I mentioned the need for 10 extra-curricular activities. I assumed he hadn't been listening.

"No, of course not. What makes you ask?" He pulled out the MIT application and showed me the actual question. Standing shoulder to shoulder with him in that conference room, I could see the world through his eyes for a few seconds, and I was horrified to see the 10 blank lines that we had set aside for extracurricular involvement.

That moment was an epiphany for me. As I saw that extracurricular question through the student's eyes, I instantly realized that we were sending the wrong message because of a simple misunderstanding. The essence of our problem was logistical: It is more efficient for us to read thousands of applications each year if the information in them is displayed in a standardized format. But we kept adding lines each year to accommodate the burgeoning extracurricular load our applicants displayed on extra pages attached to the applications. These added pages had slowed down our application reading, so adding empty lines to the form had seemed the right thing to do at the time.

But in that moment with that Midwestern student, I saw that by offering 10 lines for that question, we were signaling an expectation that we did not actually have. We do not care how many activities an applicant has as long as there is some involvement somewhere. All of those parental accusations from my previous presentations came rushing back when I realized the extent to which we were making an anxious situation worse. To paraphrase Pogo, I had met the enemy and she was *me.*

We reevaluated our admissions process at MIT based on that single exchange with a puzzled student. The process made me think deeply about the role of college admissions officers and parents alike in the increased anxiety of this young Millennial generation. And I have come to believe that in our own way, we are making them sick.

For a variety of reasons, we are raising a generation of young people trained to please adults; kids so busy with activities that they have difficulty experiencing their own inner voice. This is particularly troubling because adolescence is the period of intensive self-discovery, the time when kids are supposed to become attuned to their own uniqueness and begin to differentiate themselves from others. In our efforts to raise them in our image, we have created an emerging health problem.

My sections of this book are not meant to be a scholarly treatise on college admissions or a how-to-get-in primer. I write as both a dean of admissions and as the mother of a teenager who has just gone through a college admissions process. I've made every mistake a parent can make, and then I've changed by following the advice I'm offering here to you. I repeat myself in a few places because, if you're like me, you might skim chapters quickly and get to the advice sections. (I hope you won't do that.) I'm sharing my best understanding of the field of admissions at the moment as well as the principles I've come to rely on as a mother.

Why This Is Troubling

Some students will always function well at warp speed, but expecting such a high level of activities and distinctions from all college applicants is actually damaging to most kids. Very few applicants today have any free time, time to relax, or even time to get 8 hours of sleep each night. Because of the academic and extracurricular obligations they accept—or that are sometimes thrust on them—they function in a perpetual state of low-grade stress that creates harmful physical effects.

Over the past decade we have done a good job of teaching kids that alcohol and drugs are bad for them. Yet we seem to have no problem turning them into workaholics. Being a workaholic may be socially acceptable, but it is a true addiction. Addictions limit our ability to seize opportunities and live happy, self-actualized lives. We Baby Boomers should know better because many of us have shaken addictions ourselves. Expecting our kids to work so hard at everything with equal vigor for external awards forces an addictive pattern that will be devastating for many of them later in life.

Another serious consequence will result from training kids to look to adults and not to themselves for rewards and self-satisfaction: We are setting up an entire generation to be susceptible to social compliance, to follow leaders they do not question. If we don't reverse this approach, the creative energies of the next generation will be stifled and their potential for leadership diminished.

Many of us in college admissions are working hard to lower the flame in the admissions process, to relieve young people of the enormous pressure they bear. We know that students do not actually need so many activities to be admitted to our colleges. While we acknowledge this modern phenomenon of students working so hard to keep up with friends and adult expectations, admissions officers most often feel helpless to stop the cycle, especially when we actually get rewarded in ranking surveys for admitting the most frenzied. Parents everywhere are eager to stop over-scheduling their kids as well, as long as their children do not suffer in the selection process. So how do we all collectively step off the treadmill and reclaim some sanity? I hope that this book offers healthy alternatives to guide parents in raising the kind of children that colleges are really looking for and to teach the proper role of parenting them through the college admissions process. And you can count on the fact that we in college admissions will continue to find ways to do our part to lower students' stress.

What Colleges Really Want

It is impossible to speak on behalf of all colleges and universities in the United States. Public and private institutions are quite different in their philosophies and selection procedures. Public universities, for example, are required by their states' laws to admit their citizens in the appropriate proportions, using procedures designed to accommodate the needs of that state. Their admissions practices are generally transparent, or clearly understandable, to the taxpayers. Private universities and colleges offer a different model in which students are admitted based on the proper match of the applicant's personality, learning style, and ability to offer something to the community. That said, because of the nature of post-secondary education and all its freedoms and demands, admissions committees are searching for some fundamental characteristics in common.

First, we seek to admit students who are the right match for our school's culture. Colleges and universities differ, just as individual students differ from each other. Some colleges, for example, offer more structured curricula that require the kind of student who desires that structure. Others, like MIT, are more flexible and require students who can handle the freedom of choice they are afforded.

Second, all admissions officers want students who are motivated to succeed in college, students who are socially competent and emotionally intelligent enough to participate in college life and to contribute to its community. Independence is critical, as are curiosity and interest. And most importantly, colleges want students who are resilient and can handle adversity well. College, after all, is a new environment for young people who, having left the safety and familiarity of their high schools, must start over in the presence of many new social pressures. Resilient students respond positively when bumping up against the challenges and new ideas they will confront in college. And that positive attitude has a cascade effect on the community around them, making that school a more satisfying experience for everyone.

Colleges create admissions applications specifically to identify these characteristics. We ask essay questions that focus on what we are looking for. We ask teachers to describe the characteristics of the applicant to identify the match. Interviews are particularly effective at this, although many colleges and universities no longer offer them due to the logistics of interviewing the burgeoning applicant pools of this large generation.

What admissions officers look for most in an application is authenticity. An authentic voice is very clearly recognized by an experienced staff member who reads hundreds of applications each year. The problem, however, is that we find far fewer authentic voices now, probably because so many applicants have been coached to be something that others think the college desires, to be someone or something other than who they really are. Admissions officers everywhere tell students to be themselves in the application—and we really mean it because we have a tendency to eschew the overly packaged candidate.

Parents often do not realize that when they get overly involved in their child's application—when they help write the essays, for example, or dictate how their son or daughter should answer the questions—they can actually contaminate their child's authentic voice. Admissions officers may not see the match if the application reflects a mixture of the student and other adults pretending to be the student. It's very much like a college pretending to be different than it really is during a campus visit. There is a problem with truth in advertising.

More than interfering with the authenticity of the application document, however, parents are sending a damaging message to young people. By getting so involved, parents are overtly or covertly telling their children that their authentic self is not good enough, not valuable enough, less than. This message can be devastating to a teenager poised to leave home and ready to begin a great adventure.

Parents Need Help

I recently received a phone call from a young faculty member who sought my advice about which school would provide his son with the best chance for an eventual admittance to MIT. He and his wife were having trouble choosing between 2 local schools, and they wanted to know which one had the better record of admission to MIT. This seemed like a rather typical phone call until he mentioned the names of the schools, which I recognized as primary schools.

"How old is your son?" I asked.

"Four." This professor wanted to know which of the 2 preschools was more academic: "You know, to get him prepared faster for college."

This type of call from an anxious parent, even a smart, sophisticated one, is no longer unusual. Even more shocking, our admissions office often receives calls from parents who have not yet had children. They want advice about the track records of various school systems and their records of admission to MIT so these not-yet-parents can get the earliest possible jump on the college admissions of their unborn children. They believe that they are doing the best for their future child's future. What's going on here? What's making grown people place this kind of pressure on themselves and their children? What's making them act so frightened and almost desperate, completely overlooking the fact that their child is a child and not a miniature adult? By the way, I told the faculty caller to pick the school with the most loving staff and the best snacks.

Many parents today are completely mystified by the college admissions process. If we attended college at all, we remember a rather simple admissions process, one unaccompanied by box loads of view books, monthly e-mails and phone calls from eager admissions staffers and student interns working to establish brand loyalty earlier than the competition. A generation ago, the admissions process consisted of hearing about colleges from friends, older siblings, or adults; taking the SATs at the last possible minute with no preparation; and filling out and submitting 2 or 3 college applications. Our parents were not often involved because we Baby Boomers lived in Kid World and rarely intersected with the adults around us. We applied. We got in. We enrolled. Pretty simple. Not a lot of angst about choice of school. Most of us applied to colleges in our local areas in an era before so many colleges acquired national name-brand recognition as recruiters spread wider nets across the country.

Now we are witnessing our children receiving mail from many colleges, maybe from test-coaching businesses, years in advance. Our children might be disinterested or scared or out of the house doing extracurricular activities to get into college, too busy to even think about choosing one. We might be choking with the thought of how we'll pay the tuition bills, or how we'll live without our children around, or how fast life is moving now. Our children, in turn, are practicing growing independence and in so doing may be making life very difficult for us in characteristic teenager fashion. (Kids that age can really be a pain.) No wonder we want to take charge. Taking charge just feels better than having life happen to us.

The rules of college admission today seem confusing and even arcane. We hear stories in the media about how colleges prefer certain kinds of people (rich or legacy or minority or athletes or brainiacs, etc) to other kinds of people (our kids). We might think we need to know someone—to have pull—to be admitted. And when adults gather socially, everyone seems to know someone who had been a sure thing for College X and who was then denied admission while "less well-qualified" kids were not only accepted but admitted with hefty scholarships. "My God," parents whisper to each other in desperation, "what does it take to get into college these days? It wasn't like that for us. How can we help our child get the edge?"

This is where trouble begins and boundaries get crossed—when we feel pressure to intervene to make the process of applying to college as easy for our children as possible. We can't bear to see them hurt or anxious. We can figure out what to do, we tell ourselves, because there is always a solution, a tactic, always a means to an end.

Over-involvement in their lives and taking too much responsibility for their college application process can actually be harmful to our kids. While parents think they are helping a busy child by making all the phone calls to college admissions offices and managing the application process, the admissions personnel on the other end are drawing a range of conclusions about this child, and none of them are good. For example, when we hear only from the parent, we assume that the student isn't interested in our school (not good in this competitive climate), doesn't know how to prioritize (too busy to talk to us? not right for us), or is too passive and connected to parents (not ready for college).

By stepping in to "help," parents also communicate a belief that their children are not competent enough or mature enough to apply to college on their own. This message undermines students' confidence at the very time they need to gather their strength to move through this difficult passage. Worst of all, by taking actions that their children should be taking, parents traintheir kids to be passive when colleges are actually looking for whole, healthy young people with intellectual curiosity, drive to answer questions, and inquisitiveness to ask previously unasked questions.

When we step into teenagers' lives and dominate them by making decisions and deflecting responsibility, we actually obstruct their path into adulthood. Adolescence is the time of experimenting, when roles are tried on and discarded, values tested and changed, and when failure is a healthy option and the best teacher. Just as keeping children hidden away from the world to protect them only hurts their socialization in the end, parents' over-involvement in their college process robs them of the chance to know themselves better, have faith in their own choices, and develop the legs that must hold them in the world.

Colleges are looking for youth who are poised for success, who have already developed baseline skills to prepare them to handle a rigorous professional life, people with the emotional intelligence and social competence to work hard while having professional longevity and joy in their careers. These skills are more important than ever because many of our kids will have several careers in their lifetimes and these skills must be portable.

Sadly, we see many parents so obsessed with ensuring that their children have outstanding college applications that they miss out on some of the joy of raising children. They fear that unless their child keeps up with over-scheduled friends he will lose out in college admissions and not be admitted to a good school. The tragedy here is that not only is this untrue, but the very cornerstone of a healthy relationship between parents and children—quality time—is often dropped in the rush for perfection.

Arranging the finest opportunities for children is not a parent's best opportunity for influence, just as the nonstop shuttling of children between activities is not quality time. Nothing will create children poised for success in college and in life more than the knowledge that their parents absolutely, unconditionally love them. This love and attention is best demonstrated when parents serve as role models and family members make time to cherish one another. The most valuable and useful character traits that prepare children for success arise not from extracurricular or academic commitments, but from a firm grounding in parental love and guidance. It's about raising happy, well-adjusted adolescents who will find the right college, the best match for them personally. It's not about forcing them to become someone they are not simply to get into a college that does not suit them but that makes their parents look good.

CHAPTER TWO

Parental Behavior and Beliefs

Egregious and dramatic parental behavior has long existed in the college admissions world (the father with the bribe in hand, the mother who falls to the floor of the admissions office in tears of despair). But over the past few years those of us who work in admissions have witnessed an escalation of bad behavior from parents that has become almost as routine as it is outrageous:

- The dad who called the admissions office and passed himself off as his son's high school principal to find out what teachers had written about his son.

- The mother who complained that she has the right to write her daughter's essays because her daughter wasn't a very good writer and, after all, there was so much at stake.

- The father who flew across the country with a fistful of doctors' letters suggesting that the reason his vindictive child broke into a classmate's account, canceled his SAT scores, and changed other students' grades was because of some yet-unknown brain syndrome instead of just plain meanness. ("Punish me, Dean Jones, not my son." "Sir, if you were the applicant, I would punish you. But your son is, so his admission is canceled.")

- The mom who signed her own name to her son's application because she had written it for him. When I called her about it ("So, Susan, about your application to MIT..."), she was embarrassed but said, "He is so busy, and it just had to get done. What else can a mother do?"

- The mother, a complete stranger to me, who passed herself off as my "close friend" to get in to see me during our selection period and plead her son's case. She brought homemade cheesecake.

■ The parents who urged their son to apply early decision (ED) to one college to maximize his chances of admission and then after his admission there, insisted that he apply to other schools' regular action, thereby violating the rules of ED. When the son was discovered to have violated his ED contract, these parents begged the dean to "punish us, not our son." (Early decision rules are further explained in Chapter 7 and Part Three.)

Parents can behave badly in many ways without even realizing it. Bad behavior also includes referring to a child's application as "our" application, being the main liaison between the college and the applicant, and asking all the questions on a college tour. Often bad behavior comes down to bad manners because we parents would never treat a neighbor or friend this way. Why do we do this to our son or daughter?

"He'll Screw It Up"

A few years ago I attended a local party to celebrate the end of my daughter's middle school soccer team's season. The team had been blessed with a dedicated coach who had a gift for inspiring love of the game. The adult conversation turned from praising the players and this wonderful coach to the topic of college admissions. As a dean of admissions, my presence is often a lightning rod for people who have heard the horror stories about the upcoming college admissions process and who can't believe that it can be as competitive and unpredictable as it is.

As these parents commiserated and swapped war stories about older children's experiences and rumors about whose child was rejected from what school and why, one woman announced that the only way to get the edge for her son was to do everything for him.

"I mean, he's 17 years old. He's a kid. This is far too important for me to leave it to him. He'll screw it up!"

The surprise for me was that everyone in the group seemed to agree with her. I could just imagine these parents believing that perhaps this is how they should act—true peer pressure in action. This is how it happens, I thought. This is how we adults lose our bearings and co-opt our children's experiences. Good old-fashioned peer pressure.

"He'll screw it up." I witness this attitude all the time now. I understand it too, because as the mother of a high school senior, I feel the pressure as well. There is real peer pressure to raise great kids, perfect kids, successful kids, even though we see how our unrealistic expectations are making them anxious or even sick.

Some Big Lies

We are good people who love our children. We've tended to them carefully since birth, getting them to the doctor, the dentist, and the orthodontist in many cases. We've helped them struggle through homework we often did not understand. We've stood in the rain to watch them play their sports. We've sat for long hours watching other kids' performances just to watch ours have their 10 minutes of performing on stage. We've driven them countless miles and spent too much money on their clothes and electronics. We've marveled at their beauty, their strength, their intelligence, and their bravery.

Sometimes we've screamed in frustration ("Teenagers!"). Often we've cried both with pride and with the thought of their growing away from us. We have been grateful for the chance to raise a child and can't imagine our lives without them. As one of my dearest friends, Diane, used to say, being a parent is an act of courage and not for the faint of heart because you get to feel a wide range of intense emotions that you would never feel otherwise, and it doesn't always feel good.

The paradox is that though we pride ourselves on our parenting, we often allow ourselves to believe some Big Lies, lies that our life experiences have proven are not true. Worse, we pass them down to our kids. When parents choose to believe and teach these Big Lies, they place unrealistic expectations on their children and increase the stress level of the entire household.

You probably catch yourself passing on some Big Lies sometimes, usually when you find yourself sounding like your parents, something you swore you'd never do. Here are just a few of those lies that are particularly devastating to young people.

Lie #1: *Successful adults are good at everything. You must prove you are good at everything to demonstrate that you will be successful.*

The truth is that no one is good at everything. It is OK to be great at one or two things and focus on them. It is even OK not to be great at any one thing. It is better to remain intellectually curious and open to learning about a lot of other interesting things at which you may not excel. For example, one of my favorite people disciplines himself to learn a new skill every 5 years (studying Arabic, taking up wind surfing, learning to play the dulcimer, flying sailplanes) so he will not only stay mentally sharp and interesting, but also remember what it's like to be a student. He believes that this keeps him humble, and that keeps him grounded. He meets many different kinds of people this way, so he has a robust social life and friends of all ages. He is a happy and resilient man, unafraid of the future and of aging because he'll surely turn that into an adventure as well.

The need to be good at everything, to be perfect students, top athletes, strong leaders, and talented musicians—all at once—is making some of our children sick with anxiety because very few humans—young or old—can do all this well. How different would their lives be if the adults around them appreciated them for just who they are, not for what they do, appreciated their human "beingness" not just their human "doingness"?

Lie #2: *If you sacrifice all of your free time now and focus on studying hard for the SAT, your future will be ensured. In some important way, SAT results define your worth.*

The truth is that life is sometimes stressful, often demanding hard work during certain periods, and, yes, you must make an investment in the future. But we know that to be really happy, you must live in the now. You have to balance daily stresses with a lot of joy every day—in the present—because joy and fun provide the ballast in life, provide a kind of protection against the long-term damage of chronic stress. Living for the future only robs you of the juice of life and makes you even more anxious because you become hyper-vigilant preparing for a future not yet determined.

And about the SATs: The truth is that you are not the sum total of your SAT scores. SATs test certain coding and decoding skills. Their scores are merely numbers. We all know that SATs do not capture the essence of the person, the character, or emotional intelligence, nor do they guarantee success in life. We also know that many of us who had low SAT scores seem happier and more successful in life than others with higher scores. Many of the most sucessful people in our culture had low SAT scores. (More about SATs in Part Three.)

Lie #3: *To be successful and happy, you must go to a top-tier college. To be admitted, you must become what those colleges want, regardless of your own interests.*

The truth is that success and happiness are states of mind and have nothing to do with where one goes to college. Many of us did not go to top-tier colleges and have managed to lead happy, successful lives. Success, after all, comes in many forms over time. Colleges look for students who are the right match in attitude and talent, and not all students are suited for the top-tier schools. With more than 3,000 colleges and universities in the United States, there is a college for everyone. The trick is to find one best suited for you. (See The Cinderella Syndrome, Chapter 6.)

And last but not least...**Lie #4:** *Other students will get the edge if we do not force our children to keep up.*

Many parents believe this lie and it, more than any other myth, creates anxious behavior. The truth is that there is no evidence to suggest that students who are pushed by parents are accepted in higher numbers by "better" colleges or go farther in life. In fact, studies generally show that any advantage earned from going to a top-tier college fades over time, and that personal characteristics such as resilience, commitment, and discipline are more important in the long run to one's eventual career successes. Children who are forced to keep up by parents who believe this lie can't hide the fact that they are often just going through the motions. Colleges ultimately look for authenticity in applicants and tend to shy away from students who do not look like they are in charge of their own lives.

What if you don't push your child, the worst happens, and your child gets rejected by her favorite college? If that happens, it is important to remember that everyone gets rejected sometime in some way, and sometimes unfairly, but that life goes on and things generally work out for the best. It's far better to teach your children this lesson sooner rather than have them learn it the hard way later by themselves because putting life's disappointments in perspective is a crucial life skill. It's a good idea now, when you are reading this book, to recall your own times of disappointment and failure. Then when the moment is right, you can tell your story to your child. For example, you could say, "Yeah, that happened to me once. I failed my driver's test the first time, too, and had to go back and do it again. But it taught me to be a more careful driver in the end. So it's all good." Your children want to hear your stories and will feel relieved that you have made mistakes, too, and have survived.

CHAPTER THREE

Why Is the College Admissions Process So Stressful?

As we parents approach the college application process, even as early as the middle school years, we begin to feel the stress. Conversations with other parents about college choices can trigger an upset stomach. We get grouchy or snappish with our children. We might even feel angry with them for not preparing better, for not looking like a neighbor's child who seems to be courted by every college in America.

It's always best to be grounded in reality and know that this anxiety is not just in your head. The college admissions process has never been as stressful as it is today. Several reasons explain this phenomenon, and understanding them should help calm your anxiety as you consider strategies for parenting through this turbulent period.

The 800-Pound Gorilla in the Room

We are in the midst of a huge upswing in population growth. The current generation of teenagers, whom we will call the Millennials, is an enormous group of children; a cohort that will increase 15% over the next decade. The same size as the Baby Boom generation, the largest in US history, Millennials are currently enrolled across the education span from primary school through graduate school. More of these students are better qualified for a wider range of colleges because of the dynamic increase in the quality of American education since the 1983 "A Nation At Risk" report, issued by the National Commission on Excellence in Education, that documented failures in the US public school system by comparing American students to students in other countries.

Since that report, and as a result of the sweeping changes in public education in its aftermath, more high school students are taking more courses in
more subjects and look very desirable to a wider range of colleges. Better
technologies make it easier to apply to more colleges today, and these students
do. The bottom line is that there are larger numbers of highly qualified kids
applying to more colleges—that makes for more competition in the college
admissions process. If you do the math, you can see that with so many more
students filing more applications, any individual will have more rejection letters come spring. There is no getting around the sheer size of this generation
and the competition that it spawns.

Colleges Have Changed

The population decrease of college-bound students in the 1980s (Generation
X) forced colleges to become more resourceful in identifying and recruiting
talented prospects. For the first time, even top-tier schools had to compete
for strong students with the less well-known but more resourceful colleges.
An entire industry of consultants sprang up to help admissions officers out-
think the competition and to help parents and students get the edge. At the
same time, the media began to compare colleges' data and produce ranking
schemes to help parents (renamed "consumers" by the media in that era)
identify the "best" colleges for their money.

The *US News and World Report* ranking system is the prime example of
this phenomenon. Each August, when its "best colleges" issue is published,
colleges and universities are publicly identified, summarized by algorithm,
and then ranked in order of "best." Educators know that it is an illusion to
believe there is one best college in America because we know that every student is different and there is a college for every qualified student in this country. We feel frustrated when people believe that a college can be No. 2 one
year and No. 5 the next when nothing has fundamentally changed. But we
often feel the effects of that ranking through the form of pressure from senior
administration, alumni, students, prospective students, parents, and the media.
Even though the weighting on the individual measurements used may be
changed from year to year, either to respond to criticism or to create drama
and sell more magazines, and even though many of those individual parameters are irrelevant to the quality of an education, we in admissions still shud-
der when our ranking drops or feel a bizarre kind of pride and even exploit
it when our ranking goes up.

Recognizing the power these ranking systems have on the population at
large, many colleges have purposely changed their admissions policies, espe-

cially those regarding early admission programs, to enhance their position in the rankings. These policy changes are not designed to enhance the student experience. They are designed to create the illusion that the college in question is more prestigious than it might otherwise be to win market share. Those of us who entered the admissions business during the 1980s, when we learned marketing and fought hard for good students, simply cannot turn off the competitive drive even now when we are flush with applicants. The temptation is strong for university officials and admissions officers alike to abdicate our role as educators and become marketers, to win at all costs.

Erosion in Belief of Merit

The media love the topic of college admissions. It's a good story and a guaranteed revenue enhancer. The college admissions process is cyclical, seemingly arcane, includes the thrill of victory and the agony of defeat, and often involves the child of an editor or reporter. There are only so many ways to tell the story, however, so reporters are always looking for new angles. Each season seems to bring another wave of "why your kid was not admitted" stories with plenty of exposés focusing on the violator of the day: legacies, athletes, minorities, or poor kids. The stories follow the same pattern, describing how the kids in question get the advantage over the victimized excellent student who does not fall into that category (your child).

When this type of story is the only one we read about college admissions, we may begin to believe that admissions is no longer about the merit of the applicant, but about something else, about a special talent, skill, or connection, about whom he or she knows to get in. This belief is corrosive to a free society and to democracy itself. It is also untrue. I tell my daughter, "This is why they call it 'news,' because it doesn't usually happen."

The truth is that merit still rules in college admissions. Students who are admitted to our higher education centers deserve to be admitted there. Merit is not always recognized in one's numbers, however, but also in one's life experiences. Ideally colleges should enroll all kinds of students because campuses are stops along the modern day Silk Road, places where ideas are seeded and innovation begins.

In ancient days, the Silk Road sliced across many different nations and cultures, connecting disparate peoples around a common need—trade. Different kinds of people with different languages, religions, and customs intersected and found ways to communicate because they needed and desired to trade goods. Wherever great civilizations and diverse peoples have met and traded, there has been a cross-pollination of ideas and expression, and the greatest innovations of humankind have occurred. This is happening at our colleges and universities right now, which is why it is so important for the advancement of our civilization that diverse populations of qualified students be admitted to study together.

It's So Expensive!

The cost of education and the dire predictions of its future costs are at the very core of parental stress about the college process: "Will we be able to send our child to the college of his choice? Will we be good providers? Will we have enough money for our own retirement if we pay for our child's college education? Who is looking out for us?"

Education is expensive in the United States because of political choices and cultural traditions. There is no national university system in America as we see in other countries, and the federal government generally does not choose to fund American higher education other than through low-interest loans and small grants. Individual states have their own approaches to funding higher education, and there is variance across states, but even state school tuition now can be very high. Higher education is expensive because it is labor intensive. It costs money to pay faculty; provide appropriate classroom, library, and laboratory facilities; and re-create the home and even hometown on campuses where students will flourish and grow. A true education does not rest in a textbook or on the Internet. It occurs when people are in the same place at the same time, sharing experience.

Paying for private college tuition in particular represents the second largest financial investment parents make after home ownership. Even tuition at publicly funded institutions places an enormous financial burden on families. It is easy to understand, therefore, why parents have come to think of college as a commodity, a service, instead of what it is—an education, a process of teaching rigorous thinking and life skills, of expanding the student's worldview, that cannot be easily measured in dollar value. With such a hefty price tag, it is understandable why the cost of college is stressful to parents who want the best for their children but who worry that they cannot provide such a luxury for their child.

Generational Characteristics

One of the most important reasons why both parents and adolescents are so stressed by the college admissions process lies in understanding that our behavior is affected by the era in which we were born. I do not mean our zodiac signs. I mean our generations. Understanding our different generational characteristics is fundamental if we are to tackle today's challenge of over-stressed college-bound youth and their parents.

Here is the premise: As we grow up and move through critical developmental stages with people our own age, the values and events of society at large influence us strongly. This affects our own values and attitudes toward life as a generational group. For example, children born after September 11, 2001, will have a different worldview than children raised before that day because their childhood was indelibly affected by that event and its aftermath. It's important to note that individuals do not all respond in the same way and do not all carry the same generational values. But when we get together in a group of peers, we have a tendency to think and act in certain characteristic ways.

Much has been written about generational differences, and the consensus is that there were 4 great generations of the 20th century, each lasting approximately 20 to 25 years. Different authors use varying names, but we will call them Matures, Baby Boomers, Generation X, and Millennials.

Matures (World War II and the Silent Generation)

Born 1909 to 1945—62 Million

These combined generations survived economic depression, saved the free world, and built America as the superpower of the modern age. Growing up during turbulent times, affected by events like the Great Depression, the New Deal, World War II, the Cold War, and landmark policies like the GI Bill and the Marshall Plan, this population is characterized by teamwork, commitment, sacrifice, discipline, and financial and social conservatism. They provided the platform of security for following generations, and they believe in the concept of honor. Although the GI Bill enabled many of them to attend college, most did not. They generally did not intrude in the lives of their children and were not overly involved with them or their college admissions process. This generation is known to Baby Boomers as "the establishment."

Baby Boomers

Born 1946 to 1964—77 Million

Ah, the Boomers. The "Me" Generation. My generation.

Born into peace and prosperity after World War II to the winners of that war, we were affected by the great social movements of the day (civil rights, the Vietnam war, feminism) as well as by television; assassinations of the Kennedys and Dr Martin Luther King; Woodstock; Watergate; and "sex, drugs, and rock and roll." As a result, we tend to be intensely idealistic (We can change the world. We watched a human step foot on the moon in real time, so we learned early that anything is possible.), individualistic (Do your own thing.), narcissistic, and dedicated to self-improvement. (Many of us are still in therapy, and one of these years we'll get it right.)

The largest generation in US history, we cherish youth and have difficulty relating to authority figures or seeing ourselves as such. We've turned parenting into a sacrament and, some say, a competitive sport. We are supersensitive to issues of competition as the result of being the largest generation, very much like puppies in a large litter who learn that they must get to the food first if they are to eat. This makes us very competitive as a generation, though we don't like to admit it. We see everything through our own filter (It's always about me, after all.) and vow never to grow up or even grow old. We have high expectations of ourselves and, as an extension of ourselves, our children, which is one of the reasons they are so stressed. We can never be perfect enough. Our adult lives have been a search for meaning and happiness.

One of the biggest problems is that we Boomers live vicariously through our children. We pre-Title IX* mothers are a prime example. When we were children, there were few girls' sports teams. We couldn't choose from a plethora of high school or college teams and certainly couldn't dream of winning a college athletic scholarship. Today we're the ones cheering loudest from the bleachers when our daughters score the winning goal.

When my daughter began to play soccer in second grade, I couldn't go to her games for the first 2 years without crying on the sidelines. I was so touched by seeing little girls compete fiercely for the ball. Growing up with no sports available to me, I watched my daughter play each week and realized that "I could have been a contender." I would have loved playing, and I would have been good at it. It was very sad for me, and in the beginning I had difficulty moving past my sadness to focus on her and her own soccer experience. I suspect many other Boomer parents have similar experiences, and this contributes to over-involvement in our children's lives.

Think of how much we enjoy our kids and their friends. We want them to love us, to think of us as buddies and mentors rather than as parents. (We're not our parents, after all.) We get a lift from their exploits on the athletic field or the stage—often actually participating with them or competing against them to win. We are so involved in their lives that we cannot bear to see them fail at anything because we don't want to fail. We, who pride ourselves on knowing so much about personal boundaries, step all over our kids' as we invade their experiences.

---

*Title IX of the US Education Amendments of 1972 prohibits discrimination based on gender in education programs, including athletics.

But it was so different for us when we were kids. We were raised with stability and freedom of movement. Many of us spent much of our childhoods on bikes. We left the house early and returned when the streetlights came on. Our parents didn't know where we were all day and probably didn't care. We entertained ourselves, built our own go-carts out of scrap lumber, and made up rules for the games we invented. We created our own world with our friends, under the radar of adults, except those peering out the curtains at us, ready to scold if we got out of line. Our psychological hardwiring developed in that environment. We had bedtimes and curfews. The most modern technology we owned was the transistor radio playing under our pillow as we fell asleep.

Coming out of that environment, with plenty of playtime as our central nervous systems were growing, we can now burn our candles at both ends as adults and get away with it. But what does it mean for our children to be raised with modern pressures and stresses while their psychological hardwiring is still growing and developing?

I truly believe that we Boomers help create most of the anxiety and competitive drive in college admissions today. Because there were so many of us, we grew up sharing the same Boomers' experiences and competing for resources. Remember those large class sizes in high school? Or how hard it was to find a job because there were so many of us vying for one spot? As a result, we are especially alert to detect any whiff of decreasing resources and higher demand. The college admissions process is the perfect trigger for anxiety about our kids' futures because we have already lived the "too many strong applicants for too few spaces" experience. No wonder we are sharpening our elbows and marshaling our considerable resources to get our children ahead in the process.

Generation X

Born 1965 to 1978—52 Million

This small generation is the most misunderstood. They are also the next generation of parents of college-bound students. Gen Xers came of age after Boomers collectively tore up and rearranged the culture. They grew up in a post-Vietnam, post-Watergate nation, and in an era of tough times and disillusionment. Many Gen Xers watched their parents lose jobs when companies to which they'd been loyal downsized workforces. As children, Gen Xers were told that they would be the first American generation to have a lower standard of living than their parents. Government reports announced that they did worse in school than the Boomers before them, and they were labeled "slackers" and "cynical" because of their detached behavior. They grew up in an era of "dangerous children" movies, when the country was not very kid-friendly. Gen Xers' childhoods were marked by increasing divorce rates, MTV, PCs, the Internet, and the arrival of AIDS, the sexually transmitted disease that could actually kill you. It's no wonder they are so different from Baby Boomers.

Because Boomer mothers went into the job market in unprecedented numbers before a national infrastructure of good child care could be created, this generation of latchkey children was forced to spend their after-school hours alone while parents worked. They were often expected to take care of younger siblings as well. Whereas Boomers, with moms at home during their childhood, could afford to be idealistic, Gen Xers became pragmatic, with their feet squarely on the ground. While Boomers are drawn to the great social movements of the day, Gen Xers cleave to small groups of friends, eschew the political scene, and tend to mistrust "the system."

Gen X is the dot com generation. They are resilient and have a strong entrepreneurial spirit. They desire a high quality of life and pride themselves on their savvy and street smarts. Unlike Boomers who were raised by Matures to have loyalty to an organization, Gen Xers see themselves as their own agents in life and therefore are far more skeptical about all organizations, including college admissions. Since they were the first generation to use modern technology, they are not "9-to-5" workers because computers make their work portable. As a result of this and the fact that they don't believe they need to "pay their dues," Gen Xers are often perceived by Boomers to be disloyal or rude. But they are the most resourceful employees because they can think outside the box.

Like any middle child, Gen Xers have a tendency to resent the 2 towering superstar generations bracketing them, the Boomers and the Millennials. But this generation on the ascendancy is even more focused on their children than Boomer parents are, and they're determined to provide their children with the security and good life they never had. They believe in accountability, fairness, and transparency and have little patience for the sentimental or impractical.

Millennials

Born Since 1979—77 Million

This is our children's generation, the generation now applying to college. Until 2001, they were raised in peacetime and relative affluence by adults who adore them and live vicariously through them. Their era is characterized by multiculturalism, 24/7, technology, the Columbine school shootings, and

September 11th. By the time they were born, society had caught up with the economic impact of working mothers, and as a result this generation has had the highest percentage of its members in child care since infancy. This enormous cohort of kids, raised in groups with Boomer values about community and service, actually likes adults and works well with them. They are idealistic like their Boomer parents but trained by Boomers to work the system, so they are very effective at making things happen and getting their way. They have been the target of sophisticated marketing since they were young, and they know how marketing works. Though they always want to hear the truth, they fully expect to be courted by colleges. After all, they have always been treated as "special."

Because Millennials were raised by busy people who never taught them the glories of delayed gratification, they desire instant gratification (they've never heard a busy signal because they grew up with call-waiting), and as a result may have trouble prioritizing. Worse, they may not see or accept the consequences of their behavior because adults are always stepping in to save them from being hurt or catching them before they can fall into difficulty. We in colleges and graduate schools, as well as employers, now see parents stepping forward to argue their child's grade with a faculty member or try to negotiate a better salary for their child while that child passively observes. After all, we Boomer parents ask, "Isn't that what parents are supposed to do?"

These young Millennials have both the great advantage and disadvantage of being our children. We've taught them to be focused on community, to lead and to follow. They are group-centered, hard working, and optimistic. They hold many of the World War II generation's values, while at the same time being hardwired with technology. This is the strongest possible skills set for any generation and when their moment comes, they will be ready to save the planet. But the price they pay for such attention from us, from our high expectations and our desire for them to make us happy, is that they are also the most anxious, sleep-deprived, judged and tested, and poorly nourished generation in history, steeped in stress.

CHAPTER FOUR

Why Are Kids So Stressed?

Most middle-class families of college-bound students are headed by 2 working parents. To accommodate parents' frantic schedules, most children spend long hours away from parents in adult-supervised environments. They spend pre- and post-school hours in safe, stimulating places because their parents are working or are otherwise occupied most of the day and often into the evening. Boomer and Gen X parents seem to have rejected the latchkey situation in which children are home alone. They have created instead the "enrichment activities" solution, in which kids are enrolled in activities where adults over-see sports, music, dance, theatre, science, leadership training, tutoring, test preparation, etc. The adults leading these activities often create award mecha-nisms at logical conclusion points to reward involvement and incentivize future attendance. With competitions come trophies, medals, and plaques— one for each participant so that no one feels left out. Parents like this, espe-cially when their children are recognized with an award. The awards accumu-late and end up on college applications. The result is that children are trained not only to focus primarily on results, but also to perform to make adults happy and help adults feel as if their efforts and time have been well spent. Even when children want to stop participating in an activity, parents often discourage them from quitting because quitting is somehow a bad thing. And besides, colleges are looking for all of those activities, right?

Activity Is Rewarded in This Culture, and Colleges Want Activities

America is a complicated culture characterized by our focus on action. Action gets rewarded, and to reward action we need measurements to explain or document success and failure. Many colleges have fallen into the bad habit of expecting applicants to have participated with distinction in large numbers of extracurricular activities.

This habit developed over time as students began submitting applications with more and more activities each year. At first, longer lists of activities and awards began to dazzle admissions officers. A returning faculty member, very experienced in reading applications before taking a 5-year break, called me after reading her first pile of new applications to say, "Who are these kids, the Super Humans?" We very quickly became accustomed to the quantity and quality of activities that we were seeing and eventually began to expect them from everyone.

Over time, however, many of us admissions officers have come to see the truth—that while some students can participate fully in many extracurricular activities, most students cannot. But because the need to have many substantial activities to be admitted to college is a major driver of stress among teenagers, the temptation is strong for them to inflate their involvement to look better on paper. This inflation, exaggeration, and sometimes just plain lying about extracurricular involvement is very common now. Thankfully many admissions officers have begun to step away from the expectation of seeing so many extracurriculars and have begun to look more carefully at the applicant's personal characteristics to assess the match between the applicant and their school.

They're Different: Pressures on Kids Today

For a dean of admissions who works with teenagers all the time, even for a dean like me with a teenager at home, it is easy to think that we know what their lives are like. After all, we were that age once. We listen to their music, follow their fashion styles closely, use AOL Instant Messenger, and talk with them for hours about how they feel. But there is just no way to understand their lives completely because their world, affected by a cultural jet stream markedly different from our own, is profoundly unlike ours. Many of the differences are obvious, like their attachment to technologies that mystify many of us parents. But many of the differences are right under our radar. Take sleep, for example.

I speak with teenaged audiences all the time, and when I have the opportunity I always ask them, "How many of you sleep more than 10 hours a night?" One hand always goes up. "Eight to 10 hours?" A few more hands. "Six to 8 hours?" A few more hands. "Less than 6 hours a night?" It is typical that more than three-quarters of the students present raise their hands.

Think about that. Young people whose central nervous systems are still developing, who are in the most learning-intensive period of their lives, are sleeping less than 6 hours nightly—when the American Academy of Pediatrics states that adolescents require 9 to 10 hours of sleep each night.

Teenagers sleep so little because their world is socialized differently from ours. There are several reasons for this, the first of which is all the academic pressure on them. With the advent of the World Wide Web and the increasing knowledge set in every subject over time, they have much more to master in their 4 years of high school than we ever had to learn. They are tested on all of that material to an extreme to follow state laws, document a school's strength to the taxpayers or tuition-paying parents, or help secondary schools generate excellent records to attract top colleges. It's a lot of pressure to be judged and tested all the time. We wouldn't like it one bit if we were the ones being judged like that.

Millennials are the 24/7 generation. Another source of stress is their portable technology, the icons of their era—laptops, MP3 players, PDAs, and cell phones—which they simply cannot turn off. We parents are not always knowledgeable enough to know what it all means and how that technology affects their social structures. We don't always know when to intervene and when it's too much stimulation for our kids. We are likely to think that they need all of that technology for school. Under our radar, long after we have gone to bed, trusting that they are up doing all of that homework, they stay up through the night chatting and socializing electronically and surfing the Web, when they really need to sleep. Often in the late hours of the night, because of the limits of the medium, there are social misunderstandings online, and students cannot rest until they can work things out the next day at school. In the morning they are exhausted, and we parents have no idea what's been happening. We might just assume that adolescents are always tired in the morning.

Teenagers often feel the pressure to carry the honor for their family, their community, and their school. We adults do not always realize all of the pressure we place on them to "do" for us, to make us proud. Family pressure has always been present in the culture at large. The story of the fourth- or fifth-generation student who is expected to enroll at a certain school and pursue a certain kind of work is almost iconic in this culture. This icon has penetrated even the middle class of America now, except that instead of the child carrying on the family tradition by going to the school of his ancestors, he is expected to enroll at a college that will reflect positively on the family. That honor is broadcast by the college sticker in the rear window of the family car, not unlike designer labels on clothing. To many parents, their child's admission to the right college is a visual symbol that they are good, successful parents.

This pressure to carry our honor can be insidious. High school personnel sometimes question a student's choice to enroll at a less well-regarded college, even though it is a better choice for her, because the high school's prestige would be enhanced if she accepts the Ivy League admission offer. Graduating high school seniors sometimes let their grades drop in their final semester, sometimes even losing their valedictorian status, to "win one for the Gipper," to help their school or favorite teacher by winning a contest for the glory of the school or by helping a teacher complete the research for a grant, at the price of neglecting their own studies. Adults allow this to happen because it enhances the secondary school's image, even as the student's grade point average suffers. The student heroically carries the school's honor.

In many towns across America, including my own, the names of students who make honor and high honor rolls at the local high school are published in the local newspaper—supposedly to incentivize students by encouraging them to earn good grades and then to be recognized. But in reality, students generally don't even read the newspaper. Publishing the names is designed to reward their parents, providing them an opportunity to be identified publicly as good parents because of their child's efforts in school. Though I am always happy when a student flourishes in school, I am most concerned about the pressure this places on the students whose names are *not* in the paper, the kids who are left to feel "less than" because they did not have top grades. It's fine to do well in school for those who can, but not every citizen is a good student. This also makes those whose names are in the paper feel either "better than" others or tense about the expectation that they have to keep it up, no matter what. The point is that we are training kids to focus on the ends and not the means. Winning, performing, producing, and being perfect are the goals.

Many of us in higher education see students who have had little previous experience in failing at anything. When they get to college and experience the disappointment of not measuring up on a whole new level of competition, some fall apart because they simply do not know how to respond to disappointment. We hope that by the time they reach college, students will have developed resilience and the awareness that they are not expected to be perfect at everything. Students need to know that they will come up short at times, and when they do, they need to know how to bounce back, recover, and persevere while keeping themselves whole and balanced.

Human "Doings" Versus Human "Beings"

If you want to assess the quality of your family's life, take a step back and observe your child's. Chances are, he or she is so busy that every spare moment is taken up with homework or extracurricular activities, enrichment activities, and the Internet and instant messaging. Our kids are the busiest young people on the planet, struggling to live up to adult expectations and participating actively with adults in all aspects of planning daily life.

I call this generation human "doings" instead of human "beings" because so much of their waking time is spent *doing* things. We have taught them that we value them for the products they produce, the goals they score, the grades they earn, the attention they attract, and the colleges that accept them. We no longer value their "beingness."

This isn't surprising because in many circles, people are only as good as their last success, and success is always based on action. Because we want to help our kids get ahead, we expect them to win, win, win, and we all know that winning takes preparation time. Action is good and necessary for our overall happiness, but action without rest and reflection is not the complete human experience. And it is the reason we live such stressful lives. What is a life lived well? It always includes rest, contemplation, reverence, and fun. Are our children having that full human experience if their lives consist of nonstop activity?

Anyone who has studied physics knows that energy exists in 2 phases: potential and kinetic. The potential state is one of stillness when energies are gathered, collected, and stored. When the moment is right, the energy explodes into the kinetic state, which is characterized by action. You can't have effective kinetic energy without an equal potential state. Consider how our kids live their lives in kinetic energy, all action—producing, being tested and judged on how they produce—with no time to rest or think. The problem with constant activity is that there is no time for just being, which means no time for creativity, imagination, or even happiness. Because they can get so out of balance, it isn't long before some kids begin to get sick. If this chronic action state continues to go unchecked, it has serious consequences for our culture. What does it mean for the future of a nation when its children don't know how to dream because they just don't have the time?

The Importance of Barbie Time

I asked a group of students recently how many daydream during the day. Few raised their hands, and most rolled their eyes. Finally a boy in the back yelled out, "Dreaming? Forget it, there are no awards for that." Everyone laughed the laugh of a shared experience. No one in their young lives has ever shown them the value of dreaming time so they have no incentive or time for it.

Human beings are creators. It is our destiny. Just take a moment to look around you now. Think about the fact that every object around you (outside of living things) originated first as a thought or pulse in the imagination of a human being. Now look around to see the sheer diversity of human creations. In one quick scan around the room you will find hundreds of examples of the products of human imagination: your coffee cup, a light bulb, the pen you write with, your computer, every stitch of clothing you wear. I like to think of the imagination as the sixth sense, an organ—not unlike the skin—that picks up information and translates it into ways that can be examined, manipulated, inverted, and reordered. As far as we know, imagination is a uniquely human sense. It is our secret weapon for creating what we want in life. The blueprints for anything to be created in the 3-dimensional world, for all of human advancement, are formed there. Imagination is the thing that makes us unique, for within it lies that little pilot light of individuality that reminds us who we really are.

Yet adults constantly tell kids to stop daydreaming and get back to work. This is particularly troubling because adolescence is the period of intensive self-discovery, the time when kids are supposed to become attuned to their own uniqueness, the time when they begin to differentiate themselves from others. They need a healthy imagination to do that. In college admissions, we now see students who excel in group work, in teams, but over time, we've seen decreasing evidence of individual creativity. So most importantly, what does it mean for the future of our culture, especially American culture built on innovation, when our children have no time to play around in their imagination?

When my daughter was little, she loved Barbie dolls. At first I struggled to accept that because I never played with dolls as a child, and as a feminist I believed that Barbie dolls brainwashed little girls into focusing only on their looks. But as I watched my daughter script and direct complicated community plays throughout our house, I gave up my resistance and got over it. She was expressing a well-developed imagination.

One morning when she was 5 years old, Nora was with me as I ran too many errands for the amount of time I had free. After visiting the fourth store, she begged me to go home for a while. "C'mon, Nora, we'll have a girls' day out. We can go to lunch and then do some shopping at the mall. We'll have fun. We'll rest after lunch."

"No," she cried, "I need my Barbie time." I reluctantly returned home, and she ran upstairs to her room to play with her Barbies. Feeling resentful that my day's plan had fallen apart, I collapsed on the couch. Forty-five minutes later, she came back downstairs, refreshed and ready for the mall. I had lost all of my energy and had to work hard to rally myself and finish the day.

Not long after that, I participated in the Myers Briggs test and learned how different people recharge their energy. Some, like me, need to be outside in an

external environment to reenergize, to be around people, light, and action—
the mall. Others, like Nora, need to be alone for a while to recharge
in their own internal way. I came to see that she was using her Barbie time to
refresh and reenergize herself. She was also using 100% imagination with no
real point, just pure pleasure. In other words, she was playing.

One of the most serious problems in our culture today is how we adults
curtail our kids' Barbie time. We expect them always to do something that
leads to an external reward or that is at least socially responsible. A good
friend recently bemoaned the fact that her daughter was having trouble fitting
in at her new school. When she came home from school, she just wanted
to go to her room and rest for the afternoon. My friend was frantic because
"resting is not achieving." She kept urging her daughter to study, read, write,
or practice her musical instrument after school like the other kids. She worried that her daughter wouldn't be competitive enough to get admitted to a
top school. Her daughter was in seventh grade, the most difficult time of
all in Girl World. No wonder her daughter wanted to come home and rest—
she was fighting her emotions all day at school. She needed her Barbie time,
her imagination's recharging time, to get through another day of catty, bratty
girl behavior.

True play, undirected and bubbling up from the imagination, is nature's
way of protecting children from the stresses of growing. Play buffers, teaches,
and soothes them. Play keeps them healthy. To play, kids need free time, with
no rules, not more assignments.

It's hard to access imagination and creativity when you are working all
the time. While we have done a good job of educating kids about the dangers
of drugs and alcohol, we expect and reward workaholic behavior. And in so
doing we are interfering with our children's natural urge to create, which is
ultimately interfering with their destiny.

The Need to Be Perfect

If the hallmark of the Boomer generation is the focus on "me" and the hallmark of Gen X is the need to control their own lives, the hallmark of the
Millennials is the need to be perfect. They have been the most protected,
experienced, exposed, and pressured generation in history. Yet no one in
their lives tells them that being themselves is good enough. Instead, we've
handed them a template of behavior by which they will know they are OK:
They must always make good grades; they must avoid drugs, alcohol, and
sex because all are dangerous; they should take chances and show initiative,
but they must always succeed. They should develop a "passion" to appeal to

college admissions officers; they must keep smiling; and they should love us. Perfection is the goal because perfect is good.

Obviously, this is not as nature intended. Everyone has individual DNA and has unique talents, desires, and dreams. People are meant to be different from one another. Just as the natural world is characterized by diversity, and not a monoculture, our human cultures need all of us. Many young people are hurting because they are made to feel "less than" if they don't fit the conventional pattern. When the coin of the realm is action and activity, what happens to the dreamers in this culture? The visionaries? The healers? The thinkers? The artists? The hermits? The loners?

Perfectionism is not only silly (we all know that no one is perfect), but it is also undesirable because perfectionists do not take risks. Taking risks advances civilization and is our birthright as humans. To teach young people, even covertly, that they must be perfect is very damaging to their spirits and is a setup for a lifetime of pain. Dr Ginsburg writes eloquently about the devastating effects of perfectionism in Chapter 8.

CHAPTER FIVE

Why Do Parents Act the Way We Do?

We know from the moment of their birth that our children will grow up and away from us. We experience their childhood as a series of gains and losses. Just when we're thrilled about their progress and how they are growing, we feel twinges of pain, even panic, with the thought that they will move out of our house in just a few years. Our family as we know it will be reconfigured, maybe even dissolved. As the senior year of high school approaches, the dread, the mixed feelings, become stronger.

I am convinced that much of the emotion underlying parental behavior during these years is actually grief. I know something about the grieving process from my earlier experience as a grief counselor at a very fine hospice center near Boston. Throughout the years, no training has prepared me better to be a college admissions officer than the training I received about the nature and effects of grief.

Parents are often surprised when I discuss grief because they have never seen the connection between their teenagers' lives and their own turbulent emotions. Yes, we grieve about our babies growing up, no longer needing us to love and comfort them through the night. We grieve about the loss of our family life and traditions that most often revolve around the children. But more importantly, we grieve the loss of our own dreams when it is clear that our children are taking another path, that they will never follow the route we had so carefully planned for them. Rarely speaking aloud about this, we fear that we are selfish or cruel, or just bad parents to admit this to ourselves. But it is a common experience to have moments of disappointment when our children do not grow to be the people we dreamt they'd be when we held them as babies, when their futures were laced with potential. Sometimes thoughts with their requisite sadness pop up: "I guess she'll never become

a doctor." "I guess he'll never play baseball." Unless we accept this in ourselves and realize that what we are feeling is grief and a normal part of the
process of transition, we are likely to turn that grief into something else and
then risk alienating our children or our spouse. In short, the old adage about
"feeling your feelings" is applicable here. When those feelings of sadness
bubble up, we need to recognize them, and then feel and accept them. Once
felt, these emotions quickly subside and move on. This is the healthy way of
approaching the coming process of our children moving on to college and
away from us.

The "Expert" Trap

Why do we feel the pressure to intervene in the college admissions process
when our parents never did it for us? While there are many possible explanations, I like to think of our behavior as an artifact of our generations—Baby
Boomers and increasingly
Gen Xers. I've described the
generational differences earlier, but it is worth examining
a few points in greater depth
as they apply to the college
application process.

Boomers and Gen Xers
have some things in common
as parents. First, we don't
trust authority, but we love
experts. And experts are
generally anyone we pay. As
members of these generations,
we grew up pushing back at
authority and rejecting anyone

"Don't cry, Mom. Lots of parents have children who didn't get into their
first-choice college, and they went on to live happy, fulfilled lives."

who tried to tell us what to do. Many of us see our children's guidance counselors, teachers, coaches, and principals as authority figures who must be
questioned or even resisted to help our kids. We designate the safe authority
figures in our children's lives by paying for their services. We'll buy all the
books, pay for the test prep, hire a consultant to help our children write the
college essay, hire a coach for our athletic children, hire anyone who will
promise to give our children the leg up. The problem is that our kids are often
left to feel that they are not good enough to be admitted to college as they
are—without the support of these experts. That message, that they aren't good

enough, is devastating to a teenager, especially one about to leave the safety of home.

In the college admissions world, we hear about highly paid consultants with very little college admissions experience who charge 5 figures to run "admissions boot camps" designed to offer students an advantage in the admissions process. I know of a case where one family paid a consultant $25,000 to package their daughter for college acceptance. He advised them to move from their top school system to a worse school district in a poorer part of town where their daughter would be considered an ethnic minority and, as a good student, would be at the top of her class. (They did move.) The consultant also advised her to drop all her activities that were considered to be characteristic of her ethnic group and take up totally different ones. (She did this.) Worst of all, the consultant urged them to change their last name from an ethnic to an Anglo name to fool the admissions officers. (And yes, they did that too.)

Think about this for a second. In their zeal to help their daughter secure a place in a top college, what were these parents really saying to her? Their message was that no top school would want her as she was, that she had to become someone very different and leave her friends and her interests behind, just to make her parents happy because they so desperately wanted her to be admitted to a top-tier college. What was this young woman to make of her own self-image? What lessons has she learned from this experience?

If you are tempted to hire someone to help your child in the admissions process, stop and ask yourself if this is just the Boomer or Gen Xer in you or if your child really needs this person. Are you doing this for your child or for yourself? And most importantly, ask yourself this, "What message am I sending my child?"

Living Vicariously Through Our Kids

One recent April after the decision letters were mailed, I received a phone call from a father who ranted about how special his son was and what a mistake we made by not admitting him, all of which I'm sure was true. But then he ended the conversation by saying, "Dean Jones, you turn down my son, you turn me down. You'll rue the day!" I think of that man as the poster boy for the concept of living vicariously through one's child.

It's easy to understand why parents do this. Our children seem to have great lives filled with endless opportunities. They like adults and so are easy to be around. We have the resources to try new things with them and this keeps us feeling young. But we must remind ourselves that we are the parents. We are not our children, and we are not the ones who are going to college.

We are living very different lives from our own parents. How does this fact enlighten the role we take on with our children? Chances are, we created our lives through our own interests, courage, and initiative. Along the way we learned to apologize and not ask permission. And we learned that sometimes rules are meant to be broken. It's been an effective style for our generation, but acting this way in the college process can actually hurt our children's chances of admission to college. Going around the rules with admissions officers is a bad idea because it signals that parents think that something is lacking with their child and they need to compensate. And admissions officers notice this.

Parent-as-Manager

Parent-as-manager of a child's life is a new role in our society. It has resulted from our busy, complicated family schedules and the fact that many of us actually are managers in our professional lives. Sometimes it's difficult to step out of the manager's shoes when we come home at the end of the day, so it's easy to see how parents can just step seamlessly into managing their children's college application process, especially when children are so occupied with schoolwork, extracurricular activities, and friends.

The problem is that when we take over the management of their lives, our children do not acquire the independence they will need for college. They do not develop the initiative and resilience that will be required. When we are chronically pressed for time, we don't make the effort to teach them the importance of delayed gratification, an important skill they will need throughout their lives. And we are signaling to them that they are not ready to manage themselves.

CHAPTER SIX

A Better Way to Look at College Admissions

In this most competitive era of college admissions in history, parents cannot control or guarantee outcomes. Parents cannot completely control their children's anxiety about it either, although they can help kids manage stress and diminish its harmful effects, as Dr Ginsburg discusses in Chapter 18. As a solid beginning, we would suggest a different and better way to look at the college admissions process.

Parents can go through this process the hard way or the less hard way. The hard way: They can do what most people do now, listen to everyone with an opinion about the topic, feel depressed, get upset with their children for not being more proactive, get more depressed, feel as if they have to fight for their children's very survival, get really depressed. The less hard way: They can see this for what it really is—an initiation into adulthood, a rite of passage.

Many religious traditions have initiations, but our secular society does not. Secular society needs a formal way to allow children to grow up and join the adult world. The college admissions process is the closest thing to an initiation that we have in this secular society.

So what is an initiation? It is a process and not an event. An initiation is genuinely hard because it is the process by which teenagers declare to the world that they are ready to be recognized as adults, that they are ready to be accepted or not ("This is who I am. Take me or leave me."). Applying to college may be the hardest thing these young people will ever do. Think about it. They must describe themselves succinctly through the written word, often reducing their human complexity into a 500-word essay. They must submit their application to strangers to be judged by rules they will never understand. Then they will have to wait for weeks or even months to learn if they're accepted or rejected. And often these results are made very public. It doesn't get any scarier than that in life.

An initiation always carries an element of anxiety and fear, so no matter how hard we try, we cannot take that away from our children. An initiation calls on all the skills previously learned and, most importantly, it can only be done by the initiate. In the initiation process, young people are granted permission to show adults what they can do, how they can manage anxiety and still function successfully—that they are indeed ready for adulthood.

We parents have a real role to play in our children's initiation, and we can do that well or we can easily and unintentionally screw it up. For example, at the very moment that we should be cheering them on and helping them through this initiation process, some of us actually cripple them by not trusting them to write their own college essays, interview well, or make the best choice of colleges. We send overt and covert signals that can make our children believe they are not ready and not truly capable of applying to college in our absence or without our input. We see it as helping out—assisting them with editing or even writing their essay, helping them connect with the "right" people who can get them in, taking over the planning and management of the process.

But our actions often make kids feel as if they are not good enough, smart enough, mature enough, or ready to go through the process on their own at the very time when they must prove that they are ready to be adults. By jumping in to help them in this way, we are essentially tackling them at the knees at the very moment they need to stand the straightest. We are actually hurting them in their moment of glory.

The Myth of the Soul Mate

Many of us were raised to believe that there is just one person out there in the world for each of us—our soul mate. And our goal in life (when we're not earning a living, of course) is to find that person and live happily ever after. This belief is scary, self-limiting, and totally fictitious. Who knows how many potential mates may exist for each of us on a planet of 6 billion humans? If we believed there are endless possibilities in life, we might feel freer somehow and make better choices.

It's the same with choice of colleges. With so many colleges and universities in the United States (more than 3,000 4-year schools alone, as well as many more 2-year and professional schools), we can conclude there are many good matches for each applicant if only we are open to countless possibilities and reject the notion of a single soul mate. For parents, this means that some choices may be schools that we aren't familiar with; they may not be in the top tier of colleges nationally. But many could be the right match for our individual child.

In our role as parent in our child's initiation, we must challenge our assumptions about what makes a good college and what makes a college a good match for our child. Be open-minded about schools you've never heard of. While you've been busy raising your children, colleges have been growing and changing. Just because you are unfamiliar with a school doesn't mean it's not good enough for your child.

The Cinderella Syndrome

You will recall the story of Cinderella. Cinderella was raised by a jealous stepmother and treated dreadfully by her family because she was beautiful. As in all good fairy tales, her fairy godmother intervened with some miracles so that Cinderella could secretly attend the ball where a handsome prince was looking for a bride. Her ugly stepsisters hoped that he would pick one of them, but magic struck when he saw our heroine. They danced until midnight and, in her haste to leave before turning back into her original raggedy self, she lost her glass slipper. Afterward the love-struck Prince frantically tried to find her by taking the slipper to every house in the kingdom and forcing every female to try it on for size, which brings us to the point of the story: When approached to try on the slipper, the ugly stepsisters tried to jam their feet into it, desperately attempting to become someone they were not. The slipper did not fit them, and they ended up frustrated and angry when Prince Charming slipped the shoe on Cinderella's foot (a perfect fit) and ran off with her to live happily ever after.

I see this phenomenon in college admissions all the time. In their applications, students try to be who they think we want them to be. They attempt to jam their feet into someone else's glass slipper. They try so hard to be picked as "the one," when in reality they simply need to be who they are: perfect for their right prince. The whole point of the college admissions process is to identify the right match between student and school, between Cinderella and Prince Charming. The good news is that there are several Prince Charmings for every Cinderella, several colleges for every applicant. The glass slipper will fit when applicants identify the right schools for their needs and then make every effort to be themselves throughout the process. It's our job as parents to remind our children who they really are, that who they are is just right, and that there are colleges that will want them for just who they are. It's not OK to insist that your child become someone else to please a particular school. What a tragedy to turn your Cinderella into an ugly stepsister.

The Importance of Standing Behind the Sidelines

The best way to parent your children through the college admissions process can be best described through the following analogy. You are going to act the way you do when you watch their athletic events. (I use soccer as my analogy because this is my daughter's sport.) What do you do? You make sure their uniforms are clean and that they have eaten a meal. You drive them to the field where they jump out of the car and run off to join their team. You park the car and join the other parents on the sidelines, behind the field's white line.

Your job during the game is to cheer for your children and their team, never to coach from the sidelines. (Only the really rude parents of the opposing team coach their kids from the sidelines.) As a cheerleader, you hold your children in their highest light, assuming the best from them, cheering their triumphs and managing your disappointment when they do not perform as you had expected. But here is the point: You NEVER run out onto the field and kick the ball into the net because you can, because you always wanted to and never had the chance, or because "our" team must win.

Yet parents step over the white line all the time in the college admissions process as they try to get their children any and all advantages. Here are some examples of white line violations that I see too often.

- **Pronoun Abuse:** The first and most ubiquitous white line violation is pronoun abuse—referring to your child's application as yours, using "our" instead of "his" or "her," as in "I'm calling to check up on *our* application." "Do *we* need to have an interview as part of the application?" Or my personal favorite, "*We're* going to sue you for not admitting *us*." When parents refer to their children's things as their own, they rob their children of their moment and co-opt their experience. These parents send a strong signal that they own the child, that the child is not strong or powerful enough to get admitted on his own and that he needs his mother or father's advocacy. For any young person undergoing an initiation, this can be devastating.

- **Asking All the Questions on the Tour:** If you've toured a college campus lately, you've undoubtedly observed parents asking all of the questions while their children hang back, content to let their parents do all the work. On one tour I took with my daughter last year, when the student tour guide asked, "Who is planning on majoring in music?" several parents raised their hands! When we visited a dorm, moms and dads pushed my daughter and other high school students aside to jam into the sample dorm room while the students who might eventually live in those rooms chatted in the hallway. Two definite white line violations.

■ **Writing and Editing the College Admissions Essay**: A faculty friend showed me an e-mail from a faculty member at another university: "Tim (her son and future applicant) has written his college essay, but Jim and I don't think it works. So we have written our own. We'd like you to read both essays and then please write and tell Tim that ours is more effective and would be the better choice to submit with his application. He'll listen to you."

Though we are seeking authenticity, admissions officers today assume that students have a lot of help with their essays because the stakes seem so high and so many adults in their world are more than happy to help them. I understand the urge to micromanage this. I have fought this urge myself with my own daughter's application process. But the essay is the only chance for the student's voice to be heard in an entire application that is dominated by the voices of others speaking on the student's behalf.

It is an important opportunity for students really to be themselves and for the college to see the match. By jumping in to help their children with the essay, parents contaminate that authentic voice. Parents also signal to their child that she doesn't write well, didn't pick a worthy topic, or in some other way just isn't ready. Most importantly, to take away a child's voice is to make him feel as if he is not ready for the initiation into adult life.

So what can you do? When teenagers are preparing an application, it's fine to look it over if they ask you. It's fine to read it for spelling or grammatical errors. Do only that. Don't rewrite it. If you think they've omitted something important, you might ask something like, "Did you consider mentioning A, B, or C? I think a college might like to know that about you." Simply point out the positive; don't attempt to package your child into a product you hope the college will buy.

■ **Picking a College Based on Your Own Desire**: This is a common sideline violation. Some parents want their child to pick the school that they wanted to attend or one that has come to their attention as a top institution. If your child wants that school, great. But chances are, he or she does not, and you must back off because you are not the one who's going to college. Your child's life is not yours. Your child has a different life path, different genes, a different destiny, and the wisest parents know that they cannot interfere with this. Young people must apply to schools they actually want to attend, and parents should respect and support that.

■ **Reading Your Child's Mail**: This is a major violation. Unless your children give you prior permission, never read their incoming or outgoing mail. It sends the message that you own their life, that they are your property.

They need their privacy now, especially when they are communicating with colleges. They need to project who they are to schools, and you want them to be themselves no matter what. So no peeking, unless you have their permission.

I'm not advocating a completely hands-off disinterest. When they open the view books or spread college catalogs and application forms all over the kitchen table, it's fine to take an interest. You can ask what they like about a particular college. You can be a sounding board. Just resist the temptation to open the envelopes before they do or edit their mail in any way. A caring and thoughtful mother told me that she discards material from colleges she finds "unacceptable" before her son can see it to limit his choices. While her intention sounds good, by tampering with her son's mail (it's addressed to him, not her), she is way over the sideline, on the playing field, and heading for the goal.

Dean Jones' 4 Rules of the Game for Parents

Here are 4 basic rules of the game to help guide you through your child's initiation process, also known as the college admissions process. They seem simple, but like all Zen-like principles, they are actually quite challenging. If you follow these 4 guidelines, however, you will not only model good adult behavior for your child—the main point of the exercise—but you will also maintain an excellent relationship with your child that will last for years to come. Keep in mind that you are modeling how an adult should act during this stressful process. Your children are watching you to see how it's done.

1. **Watch Your Language:** Vow that you will never again refer to your child's application or college choices in the first person plural, as in *"our"* application. (Remember pronoun abuse.) Be clear about your language and the fact that your son or daughter is applying to college, not you.

It's very easy to say "our" and "we." I still find myself doing it occasionally. But stop yourself every time you hear yourself say it, back up, and rephrase the sentence aloud. Instead of "We will be applying to 5 schools," try "My daughter will be applying to 5 schools." Language is very important. And your child will notice.

2. **Watch Your Attitude:** Teenagers need to vent sometimes, so thank your lucky stars if yours do that with you. But when they complain about their teachers and guidance counselors or how unfairly they are being treated, shift into neutral and follow my mother's lead. As she was cooking at the stove, I'd vent. She would nod and utter, "Umhum, umhum." She'd keep stirring the pot and just listen. She never engaged in helping me solve my problem because all I really wanted was a sounding board.

Now I do the same thing with my daughter except, when she finishes talking, I add, "I know everything will work out for you because everything always works out for you." This is a big improvement over my old style, which was to engage and try to solve her problems. I would even pick up the phone and try to intervene where I thought appropriate. But that always backfired because first, I'd learned there were always 2 sides to every story, and second, she just wanted to talk and wanted me to listen, not solve her problems. I'm sure I embarrassed her many times by trying to solve her problems for her. Thank God I changed my behavior.

It's so important that parents keep their attitudes about a situation in check because parents' opinions can contaminate their children's experiences. We can ask how we might help them, but otherwise we should be modeling the old phrase, "been there, done that, life goes on, and life is good." The next time your child complains about something, try to remember a similar event in your own life and at the right time, tell the story. Describe what happened, how you reacted, how life went on, and how life is good.

In other words, no matter what happens, everything will be fine. Stay in neutral. For example, when my daughter was upset once about getting a low B on an exam, I told her that in my first year of college I earned 4 As and a D. I explained that the D should have really been an F, but that I wrote the professor a note on my final exam begging him not to fail me, which I had actually richly deserved. It was a stupid, immature thing to do, and I later apologized to the professor, never repeating that behavior again. But, I told her, even with that situation, I went on to become the dean of admissions at the world's best university of science and technology. Been there, done that, life goes on, and life is good. She quickly got over feeling like a failure because she earned a low B on a test.

3. **Watch Your Behavior:** Behavior often follows attitude. Vow never to do your children's work for them—ever. Vow never to threaten to sue anyone, ever, or act in any way foolish, because you'll only regret it later and you will have missed the chance to model good adult behavior for your children. Remember to follow the golden rule of good adult behavior: Feel your feelings but don't always act on them.

4. **Celebrate No Matter What:** Parents frequently cut their kids down by publicly criticizing the admissions decisions or their child's final choice of college after she has been admitted. Many parents simply can't hold their disappointment in check, which can be humiliating for their child.

    I was on the sidelines as my daughter played soccer one season when a woman I didn't know approached me.

    "You work in admissions, right?" she asked.

    "Yes, how can I help you?"

    "My son was not admitted to Duke. Who do I complain to? The president, the chairman of the board of trustees, the dean of admissions? This decision simply cannot stand."

    "Wait," I said. "Where is he planning to enroll?"

    "Williams."

    "Is he happy about that?"

    "Yes, very happy. He likes Williams, but it's not the best school for him. It's not Duke."

    Perhaps because she was interrupting me as I was trying to watch my daughter play, or maybe I was just annoyed with this woman's attitude, but I quickly said, "No, wait. It's a good thing the universe intervened and he was turned down at Duke. Whew, that was a close one. No, he needs to be at Williams because he'll find his best friends for life there, and maybe even his future spouse. No, good thing he got into Williams and was turned down by Duke."

    She stared at me for a full 5 seconds before saying, "You're from MIT?" before turning on her heel and walking away quickly. I had been dissed. She must have thought I was a nut.

    At the end of the game, however, she caught up with me and apologized for her rude behavior. Tears were streaming down her face as she said, "I was thinking about what you said. I was not admitted to my first-choice college, but I came to love the college I attended. My best friend today was my college roommate. And, yes, I met my husband there and we're still married. Maybe Williams is the right choice for him."

The moral of the story is to find a way to make peace with the results of the college admissions process. Remember that the main point is not for children to get into X, Y, Z college, but to pass through the hardest initiation of their lives. When the letters come in, both the acceptances and the rejections, take your children out and celebrate their bravery, their ability to tolerate the anxiety of not knowing the results for months, their uniqueness.

Now is the perfect time to tell them how proud you are of them. Find things you admire about them and speak about that freely. For example, you could tell your son what an excellent friend he is and how you wish you were as good a friend to your friends as he is to his. Or tell your daughter how much you admire her organization and stamina and how you want to be more like her that way. Speak what is authentic and true. If you cannot talk this way, write a letter and ask them to read it after you celebrate the decisions. It's not about the college that admitted them, it's about how they traveled through the fire walk of initiation. Do your best to focus on the successful completion of their initiation. So be proud of your children no matter what.

CHAPTER SEVEN

Dos and Don'ts for Parents in the Admissions Process

Now that you understand the context of college admissions and your child's place within it, and you see this as an initiation for your child, we'd like to offer some specific things you can do to be most helpful as your son or daughter applies to college.

Stay Behind the Line: Remember those white line violations. Keep thinking about your role as a fan cheering from the sidelines, not a player on the field.

Manage the Timeline: Managers have to manage, so I encourage parents to ask their child's high school guidance counselor what a parent can actually manage. Counselors usually suggest keeping an eye on the various deadlines that students need to meet. Parents can make sure kids are registered for standardized tests on time, that they have their applications filed on time, and that they sign up for interviews as required. Remind them of the schedule and prompt them with plenty of time. I like to use the 3-week rule.

1. "Nora, your application filing deadline is in 3 weeks. Are you working on it?"

2. "Nora, your application filing deadline is in 2 weeks. Are you working on it?"

3. "Nora, your application filing deadline is in 1 week. Are you ready? Let me know when you've filed your application so I can relax."

Then I get out of the way.

Manage Your Own Anxiety: You do not want to share your worries— about your child leaving home, family finances, the thought of an empty nest—with your child because it will only make her feel worse. Now is the time to talk to a friend, preferably a friend whose child has already been through this process and who has some distance from it. If you don't have such a friend, buy one. Now is a great time to see a counselor to work through your grief and the constellation of emotions that you are experiencing. Do not share your anxieties with your children (not even the younger ones who aren't applying to college yet). Your college-bound children need to focus on their own initiation process, not help you manage your grief. And your younger children don't need a stormy forecast of your anxiety about their junior and senior years of high school.

Be Their Shoreline: My dear friend Diane Englund taught me how to be a good mother. When I asked her about her philosophy on child rearing, she gave me this analogy, which I have depended on and used countless times throughout the years.

Diane said that parents are the shoreline and the children are little boats. Sometimes when they're learning to sail, the boats tip over. Sometimes they run aground. Sometimes they get lost in the fog. But they always use the shoreline to navigate against, and the shoreline never changes. The shoreline is stable, calm, secure, and unflappable.

When we rush to fight our children's battles for them, write their college essays, or share our anxiety with them about how we'll pay for college, how we'll be able to tolerate their leaving, or in some cases, how happy we are to see them go, we jump into their boat and are no longer their shoreline.

It's often difficult, however, not to jump into our child's boat and try to steer it in another direction. For example, as her senior year began, my daughter Nora decided to drop varsity soccer. She announced this fact to me in a restaurant, a neutral spot where she knew I couldn't lose my cool. My immediate reaction was anxious: "Oh, no, you have to stick with soccer! You're so good at it and you've been playing since second grade." And then, "You can't quit varsity soccer in the fall of your senior year. What will the colleges think?" At that point, she held her hand up and asked me to stop in a very firm voice. Sitting across the table from me in that noisy French restaurant in Manhattan, Nora explained that she had lost her love of soccer because the league she was playing in became increasingly competitive and the drive to win overruled the fun of the game. Turns out that she had been yearning to try new things anyway, so after careful thought she decided that she wanted to sing in the chorus and study yoga instead. "And any school that would reject me based on that is a school I wouldn't want to attend any-way," she said, summarizing her position.

As she spoke, I could clearly see that my response at this moment would affect our relationship and set the tone between us as she entered her last year of high school. It was a rubber-on-the-road moment for me, and I struggled for a minute to regain my composure, wondering, "How do I remain the shoreline now? What would the shoreline do?"

When it was my turn to respond, I took a deep breath and told her the truth—that I thought she was very brave to reclaim her life and that, yes, any college that would turn her down because she wanted to explore new talents and broaden her life experiences didn't deserve her anyway. I told her how much I admired her maturity and willingness to step away from the crowd when she knew what they were doing was no longer working for her. And I assured her that everything would turn out fine because everything always works out for her. "No pushback then, Mom?" "Nope. No pushback."

That was a magical moment that could've turned into war if I hadn't remembered my role as the shoreline. As a result of her decision, she has earned better grades with a tougher course load, experienced new activities, made new friends, and enjoyed a much happier senior year.

It is very difficult to always be the shoreline for someone. But if we don't serve in that role, who else will our children use to navigate against as they struggle to find their way into adulthood?

Health Comes First: Insist that your children sleep at least 8 hours per night, and make sure they eat 3 meals per day, including lunch. And remember that protein bars are not food—they are a quick energy source but not food for growing bodies.

Stop Talking and Watch Their Faces: When I was on a college tour with my daughter, I watched the behavior of other families in our large group. One mother talked constantly to the tour guide, asked questions, tried to project enthusiasm on her daughter's behalf, and spoke on behalf of her daughter who was obviously bored by the school.

At the tour's end and out of earshot of the student guide, the mother snapped at her daughter, "What's wrong with you? Why aren't you enjoying this school? It's perfect for you." Her daughter responded that she hated it and never wanted to come in the first place. The mother expressed shock, but it was obvious to the strangers observing them that the student didn't want to be there.

If we want to know how our children are doing, all we have to do is stop talking and watch their faces. We know their faces so well that if we can stop thinking about our own experience of the moment and realize that we are there to support their choices, we will quickly recognize what works for them and what does not.

I experienced this with Nora even before the college application process began. She had been asking me to let her attend private secondary school for several years. When I finally relented, we toured several. She seemed bored or turned off until the last one. When we walked into the great hall to wait for her interview, Nora turned to me, her eyes glowing with her spirit, and said, "Mom, this is my school." I hadn't seen that look in her eyes for the whole previous year, and I knew at once that we'd found the right school for her. Although I knew this to be an excellent school, I didn't need to see the magazine ratings or read any guidebooks to decide anything. All it took was for me to watch my daughter's face and that was good enough for me.

Encourage Free Time: Promise yourself right now to encourage your children to pare down their extracurricular activities if they are so busy that they have no downtime or if they sleep fewer than 8 hours per night. Remember how important downtime is to their overall health and creativity. Give them permission to drop any activity that they are doing out of obligation or that no longer interests them. That one activity is not the one that would have gotten them into college anyway. Activities should be regenerative, not draining. Colleges do not want to admit human "doings." We are looking for the "being" in the human. (Dr Ginsburg also discusses the value of free time in Chapter 13.)

Insist on Integrity: Each year I become aware of several students who violate the early decision (ED) rules of other colleges by continuing to apply to MIT (and I assume other schools) after having been admitted to an ED program. I am alerted by someone at the ED school who calls to verify that the applicant in question was admitted to MIT. Most often the student's ED application was actually signed by parents who, by signing, promised to help their child follow the rules. In most of these cases, the parents themselves actually encourage the child to break the rules.

Afraid that I would cancel his son's admission for lying to another school, one father flew halfway across the country and hid in a doorway to pounce on me when I arrived at my office. He begged me not to punish his son for lying to the ED school. He went on to blame his wife who was hard at work at her business back home. "She is the bad one, not my son." (Strangely, I usually find that the parent in my presence almost always blames the one who isn't there.)

Unfortunately the students are the ones who must bear the consequences of breaking the rules, so it is always best to insist that they maintain integrity. That is what healthy adults do. What behavior are parents modeling for children if they urge them—and even conspire—to violate the rules? Do we really want to teach them that it is OK to lie, cheat, or steal to get ahead in life? Remember that your kids are always watching you.

Help Them Protect Their Privacy: We Boomers have a latent fear of Big Brother, so we guard our privacy jealously. Some of our children, on the other hand, pour out their deepest secrets and fears for the world to read on their blogs (Web logs, electronic diaries posted on the World Wide Web). They have a completely different view of privacy that can sometimes hurt them. Urge them to keep information about their college choices to themselves— where they are applying to college is no one else's business—and especially to open their admissions decisions (paper and electronic) when they are alone. Other students, even friends, can be insensitive in the moment. If the admissions decision is not a positive one, your child could be hurt by peers' reactions.

What Parents Should Not Do

If you do nothing else:

Don't Live Vicariously Through Your Children: Every time you want to live your children's lives for them, step back. Enjoy your own life. If you don't enjoy your own, now is the time to find ways to juice it up. Remeber that adults keep growing too, and maybe some well-needed change is in the offing for you.

Don't Do Your Children's Work: I really mean it! I don't care how busy they are. Never, ever do their work for them because you'll only hurt them if you do. You will train them to be passive, frightened, or dependent, and they will make you miserable when they move back into your home after college. (You'll wonder, "Who raised this person?")

"We want you to have fun, as long as it's fun that enhances a college-admission application."

Don't Take Admissions Advice From Friends: How many times have you heard neighbors and friends talk with authority about how certain colleges admit students? They seem to have the inside scoop on why a particular student was not admitted to a particular school. Think about it—what could they possibly know about something they do not do for a living?

This chatter among adults always has a pulse of competitiveness buried in it someplace. Whenever these conversations begin, as soon as your stomach starts to hurt or you begin wringing your hands, step away from the conversation and detach. You will miss nothing but gossip, and you'll quickly regain your composure while those you left behind will lose sleep that night. Remember to take admissions advice from the real experts—your child's guidance counselor and admissions officers themselves.

Never Disrespect Young Staffers: One April, during the Angry Season after decision letters were mailed, one of the best admissions officers I've ever worked with appeared at my office door. Lorelle was a beautiful 30-year-old Californian with a young-sounding voice.

"Parents are out of control!" she cried, stamping her foot. She went on to describe a phone conversation with an angry mother. "She asked why we didn't admit her son. I told her this, then she said that. Then I told her this, and she said that. Then I told her this, and she said, "Excuse me, may I please speak with an adult?"

Lorelle burst into tears. I burst into that nervous laughter that bubbles up when you've been busted because I realized that I'd done something similar the previous month. Impatient with a young sales woman, I had joked, "What are you, thirteen? May I please talk with your supervisor?" I'd thought I was being funny, but seeing the situation through the eyes of this exceptional professional, I felt shame and remorse and silently vowed to change my ways. I called the woman who spoke to Lorelle, and we had a long chat about how to treat young professionals.

After that epiphany, I began asking young staff everywhere—guidance counselors and admissions staffers—if they were treated with disrespect by Baby Boomers. The answer was always a resounding YES. These young professionals are regularly waved off by Boomer parents who are afraid that their children will be ill served by someone with such a youthful appearance and apparent inexperience, or at least better served by someone older and seemingly wiser.

Most parents do not realize the possible repercussions of crossing swords with a 20- or 30-something. The truth is, young staff members hold enormous power in their admissions work. They are closer to Kid Culture, know more about the cultures of their schools, and certainly understand applicants better than their 40- or 50-something colleagues. They often have the power to advance an application case or stop it cold. I strongly advise parents to treat young staffers with the respect they deserve and see them as your child's best advocate.

This Is Our Initiation Too

When parents accept that the college admissions experience is an initiation for our children, and when we fill our rightful role in that initiation by staying on the sidelines, we also will come to see that this is an initiation for us too.

It hurts to stand on the sidelines, watch our children struggle through difficulty, and all the while cheer and hold them in their highest light. We are unable to step in to save the day. We're helpless as we watch their stumbles and setbacks. It's painful to let them skin their knees, even if they do heal in record time. But it's critical to understand that taking the appropriate parental role in this phase of their lives, as painful as that is, actually serves as our own initiation into the next phase of our adult development. Neither parenthood nor initiation is for the faint of heart.

As they move through the college admissions process, I urge parents to repeat this mantra every day: "What behavior am I modeling for my children? Am I living what I am teaching them about how adults behave in stressful situations? How do I want my child to act as an adult?"

These questions will keep us focused on what really matters, and we will make wise choices about our own behavior during stressful times ahead. Even better, we will stay behind the white line, and our children will have the whole field to themselves, as they should.

"We Are the Ones We've Been Waiting For"

As a Boomer, I have long rejected the thought that I was an adult. An adult was my mother, and I was not like her. I was hip, cool, self-determined, the personification of youth and style. But as my daughter has grown and I've been confronted with having to function as a mother, I've come to embrace the term "elder." To me the word connotes wisdom and experience, both of which I like to think I have by the boatload. It conjures up an image of the wise elders (my friends and me) chatting around the fire with a relaxed but careful eye out for the younger ones who are playing in the distance. We let them play, we let them make their mistakes and then recover from them, but we are quick to step in if things begin to look perilous. We provide the invisible safety net while we allow our young to experience their youth, oblivious to us and our watchfulness. We are the substrate, the matrix, on which the community grows.

The Hopi Elders have a rather revolutionary saying, "We are the ones we've been waiting for." Believing this will help us finally assume our roles as elders of this nation. It is time for Boomers to accept responsibility for our earlier dream to change the world by first changing our own internal viewpoints. It is time for Gen Xers, even at their young age, to accept their rightful role as elders and to look to the welfare of all children and not just their own. To be "the ones we've been waiting for" we must first become wise elders in our own families by giving our children back their childhoods, by encouraging them to dream big dreams. Becoming an elder begins by ensuring their safety, making sure they sleep enough and eat 3 good meals a day, and making sure they have plenty of downtime when they are not judged but are free to be themselves. It begins by getting the technology out of their bedrooms—their TVs, computers, cell phones, PDAs—so they can sleep at night and have a mandatory 8 hours of non-socializing time. And it begins with us reclaiming our own lives so we do not desire or need to live theirs. If we don't do this, if we don't become the ones we've been waiting for, who will? It begins now, today, this moment.

This is one of my favorite definitions of success. It hangs on the bulletin board behind my computer in my office where I can see it every day. I share it with you in the hope that you will share it with your children and your friends.

> To laugh often and love much;
> To win the respect of other people
> And the affection of children;
> To earn the approbation of honest critics
> And endure the betrayal of false friends;
> To appreciate beauty;
> To find the best in others;
> To give of one's self;
> To leave the world a little better;
> Whether by a healthy child
> A garden patch,
> Or a redeemed social condition;
> To have played and laughed with enthusiasm
> And sung with exultation;
> To know that even one life has breathed easier
> Because you have lived....
> This is to have succeeded.
> —*Adapted from the poem "Success" by Bessie Stanley*
> (commonly attributed to Ralph Waldo Emerson)

PART TWO

Dr Ken Ginsburg:

What Can Parents Do?

CHAPTER EIGHT

The Problem With Perfectionism

Today's teenagers have more impressive college applications than a decade ago, and far more impressive ones than their parents had. Many teenagers seem to be entering this admissions process perfectly prepared. On paper they look almost too good to be true—dream candidates for any college—socially committed and brilliant, widely experienced in summer jobs, internships, and community service projects. Their resumés suggest their teeth glimmer whenever they smile and their hair blows in the wind even as they stand still.

As we prepare these paper-perfect students for higher education, are we undermining their ability to succeed in life? As we mold them to be so well balanced, are we actually making them feel unsure of their own footing? Are they so committed to being "perfect" that they fear being anything less? The most worrisome thing about this generation of driven students may be the fear of imperfection that's being instilled in their psyches. This fear will stifle their creativity, impede their ability to experience joy, and ultimately interfere with their success.

When we speak to parents nationwide, we hear 2 very distinct views. Some parents see their kids' jam-packed lives as a wonderful sign that they are poised for success. Others notice that their adolescents seem burdened, and they worry that their kids are missing opportunities for happiness during a time that is supposed to be carefree, a time before they have to earn a living and support families of their own.

The first group of parents shows justified pride that their children are driven to succeed and relish their accomplishments. They recognize that successful people always put in the extra effort. They've held their kids to high expectations and arranged the finest opportunities, and their active parenting style seems to have paid off. Some of their children seem to have garnered all of this success while remaining joyous and self-confident. If other kids exhibit signs of weariness or stress, these parents see it as the price to be paid for success. As long as their grades remain high and they continue to be involved in many extracurricular activities, their parents believe they must be doing well, regardless of outward or inward signs of stress.

The second set of parents has equal pride in their children's accomplishments, but they are concerned that their children are too stretched, too pressured. They notice the signs of fatigue and pressure. They fear that happiness has been sacrificed in the name of accomplishment.

All parents want the same thing—that young people become happy, successful adults. To evaluate whether they are moving toward genuine success, we need to look less at accomplishments and more at kids themselves. The process of producing students who are perfect on paper may be working for some and seriously harming others. Those who seem to be thriving may be budding perfectionists who are headed for elite colleges as a reward for their accomplishments. But they may not be headed toward a lifetime of success and are unlikely to achieve a lifetime of happiness, satisfaction, and contentment.

Chapter 2 mentioned "Big Lies" that parents shouldn't project on the next generation. The first Big Lie—that successful adults are good at everything—is applicable here in a discussion of perfectionism. When was the last time any of us was good at everything? Probably in second grade—we got gold stars on our spelling papers; we were told we were great artists when we made construction paper Thanksgiving turkeys; on the playground everyone was an athlete and got a chance at bat.

Since those halcyon days, how many adults can say, "I'm good at everything"? Most of us do quite well at one or two things and are less talented in many more. Successful people usually excel in one or two areas. Interesting people excel in a couple areas but also enjoy exposure to several fields even if they can't be a star in all.

So why do we push the Big Lie on teenagers that they must be good at math, science, foreign languages, English, history, the arts, and athletics? Doesn't this unrealistic expectation only foster the drive toward a perfectionism that is bound to crash land?

Not All High Achievers Are Perfectionists

The world is run by high achievers. Many might describe themselves as perfectionists because they aren't satisfied until they have done their best. Healthy high achievers get genuine pleasure from putting every effort into producing the finest quality product—an effective business plan, a work of art, or a well-designed computer program. Healthy high achievers enjoy the process and excitement that bubbles up from within them as they work their hardest. They react to deadlines by generating just enough anxiety to stay energized. Healthy high achievers see mistakes as opportunities for personal growth and as an impetus to learn to do better the next time. They see failures as temporary setbacks from which they will rebound. They appreciate constructive criticism because it informs them about how to improve. Healthy high achievers may lightheartedly label themselves as perfectionists, but they are resilient when they fall short of perfection.

Unlike resilient healthy high achievers, perfectionists reject anything less than a flawless performance. Though what they produce may be of the highest quality, they may not experience the satisfaction of a job well done. They don't enjoy the process of creating because they worry endlessly about not performing as well as they should. They have a fear of failure that is greater than the joy they experience with success. When they do well, they may not notice because they are too worried about the mistakes they might have made or how they could have done better. The perfectionist soccer star scores 3 goals, but as he is carried off the field on his teammates' shoulders he laments the penalty kick that went wide. The perfectionist gets a 96 on an exam, but is frustrated that she didn't get a 100.

Perfectionists see every mistake as evidence that they are unworthy or not good enough. When others praise their successes, they do not trust it because they see themselves as imposters whose faults are waiting to be discovered. When directly criticized, they become defensive, embarrassed, or ashamed. They see even constructive criticism as reinforcement of their ineptitude.

Perfectionists fear adversity. They lack the flexibility to rebound from difficulty because challenges paralyze them. The thought of not doing something well prevents them from taking the chances that successful people need to take to reach their greatest potential. They may be graced with creativity, but are hesitant to tap into it for fear that doing something outside of the box will disappoint others. Healthy high achievers are driven by the joy of doing, but perfectionists become paralyzed if what they are doing would disappoint the harshest of critics (who are usually themselves).

We want our children to be successful now and in the future. As they build the achievements required for a college admission—grades and extra-curricular activities—we must ask ourselves how they are experiencing the process. If they seem genuinely to enjoy their commitments and if the drive emanates from within them, they are destined for long-term success because they will be able to draw on that energy throughout their careers. But if they are driven to achieve to please others, to gain acceptance, or from fear of failing, they may not be poised for a lifetime of success and happiness. Both the perfectionist and the healthy high achiever will attain the prestigious college slot, but parents should do their best to nurture a healthy high achiever rather than a perfectionist.

The "product" certainly does not distinguish the healthy high achiever from the perfectionist. Both might achieve top SAT scores and participate in many activities, and both might be accepted into top universities. But consider the process: A maestro who writes the finest symphony could have been driven by a healthy desire to achieve or by an inability to accept anything less than a masterpiece. The difference is in how much he enjoyed the process, how much he will celebrate versus disparage his symphony, and how quickly he will burn out. The end product might be the same, but the process was either tortured or exhilarating.

People Who Don't "Live Up to Their Potential" Aren't Always Lazy

We usually think of perfectionists as high producers, but their fear of failure often prevents them from initiating or completing tasks. They might not attempt to take on a project for fear that they can't do it adequately. They might pretend they just don't care, or they might feign laziness, because it is too hard for them to confess the depths of their anxiety about failing. They may procrastinate because starting a project that they fear will have flaws is too overwhelming.

We recognize that parents reading this book may have children who are not high-scoring super students. If they aren't doing as well in school, or don't seem as driven to make the honor roll or even take a college tour, keep in mind that all kids are different, particularly in the same family. Your less-than-enthusiastic child may be reacting to an older sibling's achievement and may fear being unable to live up to that reputation.

Perfectionism as an Impediment to Success Beyond the Admissions Process

A person destined for success has passion, creativity, and flexibility. Every new venture is flavored by past experience because every disappointment was used as a learning experience to build skills. A successful person knows that she excels at something, but maintains other interests. A successful person sees interactions with others as a potential to learn and experiences constructive criticism as an opportunity to improve. She will always be open to looking outside of the box for the solutions or strategies not yet tried. She will propel her colleagues forward through her enthusiasm, love of the process, and willingness to take healthy risks.

Perfectionists fear failure more than they desire success. They will be so self-critical that they will not be buoyant when times get hard. They will not encourage their colleagues and may more likely become hypercritical of them, further damaging the team spirit needed to thrive. They will not look for creative solutions because the risk of getting the B+ is too great.

What Did We Do Wrong?

As we discuss the pressures on adolescents with parents around the country, many openly express their concern that their children are too hard on themselves. Usually one or two brave parents sheepishly insist, barely concealing their defensiveness, that the pressure is not coming from them. They explain that they keep telling their child that grades "just don't matter." We don't doubt the sincerity or their honesty for a moment.

Some young people do put an enormous amount of pressure on themselves. But many kids who say they're pushing themselves, and may even think they're internally driven, are really pressured from elsewhere. Even when the pressure is entirely self-driven, it remains unhealthy if the adolescent takes on traits of perfectionism.

So how do parents know if a child is self-driven, or if it is the parents' fault? That was a trick question. Give yourself a break and erase the word "fault." If a child is experiencing too much pressure and some of it came from you, certainly you applied that pressure with the best of intentions. What may feel like helpful encouragement to one child may be experienced as overwhelming pressure to another. In fact, what feels like encouragement to one person may feel like pressure to the same person at a different time when he is in a different mood. This is why we need to take the scrutiny off ourselves and look at our children. Are they thriving or struggling? Do they relish their achievements or fear their inadequacy? Whether parents are part of the problem, we certainly can be part of the solution.

We are willing, however, to be clear about some common parental behaviors that are wrong. If your child has tried her hardest and comes home with a C, you should be proud. Children need to be encouraged to do their best, not to strive for unattainable goals. If you show dissatisfaction with any grade or project when your child has tried her best, you are setting her up never to be satisfied with her efforts. If your child sees a B+ as adversity, how will she ever know how to face real challenges? Above all, do not lead the battle for higher grades for your child. If your child comes home with a B and you think she deserves an A, or worse *needs* an A to get into Prestige U, and you go to battle with her teacher, you will be harming her in 3 ways. First, you have made clear that nothing short of perfection is acceptable. Second, you have communicated that it is not how the game is played but the prize that matters most. Third, you have impaired her ability to be successful later in her career. When she is 37 years old, will you call her boss and demand that her evaluation be changed? In the real world, grades don't get changed. People work harder to attain greater successes. And they find the resilience to do this by using their creativity, ingenuity, and tenacity—all driven by passion for what they do. Fear of a B+ stifles passion and creativity. People with a fear of failure are not tenacious. They give up and stick with those strategies and patterns they know will get them the A, or at least not rock the boat.

What Fuels Perfectionism?

Perfectionists lack self-acceptance, a very basic ingredient that we all need if we value ourselves. We accept that we are still basically good, even when we don't hit the ball out of the park. We remain worthy of others' love even when we are in a foul mood. We feel good about our efforts even when the guy across the hall scored higher, produced more, or received more recognition. We are OK because we see ourselves as more than a package of achievements. We accept and may even cherish our complexity. We don't have to be a superstar all of the time, and we are comfortable that no one can be a star on every stage.

Perfectionists have learned somehow that they are not acceptable unless they meet a certain standard. Certain character traits make people susceptible to messages that they aren't good enough unless they are flawless. But to become a driving force in a person's life, those inherent traits have to be reinforced from somewhere. Generally, perfectionists have a global insecurity that they will not be accepted. Of course, they might have gained this insecurity somehow from their parents, but they also may have acquired it at school: "We expect our students to exemplify the high standards of this institution," from friends' expectations: "To fit in, you need to…," and even through the media: "To be successful you need to look this way, talk this way, own this, dress this way."

We live in a culture that reveres success and barely notices regular people doing their darndest. When we know the names of sports stars and great actors but forget to acknowledge the generous acts of our neighbors, are we teaching children that to be noticed you have to be a star? Certainly the college admissions process is a big offender here by generating the folklore of the perfect, well-balanced, brilliant candidates who prove it with thick applications with high SAT scores, grade point averages, and class rankings.

Most parents firmly believe that they've never said anything directly to their child that implied they expected perfection. Many are adamant that their words always reinforce the importance of happiness. Certainly most parents do send the right verbal message of unconditional acceptance. For many children, perfectionism may derive from the other forces in their lives. But we want parents to consider the possibility that children can pick up parental signals that reinforce their need to be perfect, despite the words parents are speaking.

Please ask yourself the following questions, but be gentle on yourself if some of the answers make you realize that you might be part of the problem:

- Are you a perfectionist yourself? Are you highly self-critical? Has your child seen you accept your own flaws?

- Do you judge people easily? Your other children? Neighbors? Other kids? Teachers? Might you have inadvertently communicated that you can be highly critical? Is it possible that your child will do anything not to become a subject of your judgment?

- If you and your spouse or ex-spouse fight about your children, might they do absolutely anything—being as perfect as possible—to prevent the two of you from fighting?

- Are you so busy that you forget to notice your children's achievements unless they get a trophy, a ribbon, or an A?

- Are people in your home uncomfortable with expressing emotions? Does anger freak you or your spouse out? Or do people recover easily, even have healthier relationships after heated expressions of emotion? Is the only way to achieve harmony in your house to suppress problems and pretend that everything is just wonderful?

- Do you only notice champions, or do you acknowledge other players who have played a good, fair game?

Fostering Healthy High Achievers

If we accept the premise that perfectionists worry they will not be fully accepted unless they are flawless, our job becomes clear. Unconditional acceptance is the antidote to perfectionism. The most essential ingredient in raising resilient children is an adult who loves or accepts them unconditionally and holds them to high expectation. High expectation is not about grades or performance. It's about integrity, generosity, empathy, and the traits we need our children to have if they are to contribute to the world. Of course, it is also reasonable to expect children to put in a real effort to learn. We also want them to discover their talents, interests, and passions; if we nurture their passion—usually from a distance—they will be motivated to succeed.

Parents need to accept children for themselves, not compare them to siblings, neighbors, or the kid who won a full scholarship to Hotshot College. Such comparisons are toxic to children feeling comfortable about themselves. When you believe you should comment about how your children could do better, base your statements on the fact that they already have done better. Use an example of past successes to remind your children that they are already equipped with the talent, experience, and resources to address this new challenge.

Parents must be cheerleaders. We get excited when our kids "win," but we have to learn to encourage and praise more effectively. The difference lies in what we get excited about. We tend to praise an outcome or accomplishment. "I am so proud of you for scoring that goal, getting a blue ribbon in the art show, or getting an A on your chemistry test." The hidden message is "I wouldn't be as proud if you hadn't come home with the prize." Instead we have to encourage *the process* and show our pride about the fact that they are playing the game of life with integrity, genuine effort and, yes, joy. "I love watching you paint—you seem to care so much about expressing yourself. You are practicing lacrosse a lot—you must love this game. It is good to see you so happy. I know you are struggling with your physics lab, but you sure are hanging in there and trying your best. I am so pleased that you can ask Mr Hannigan for some extra help."

One of the best things parents can do is to model for children that no one gets the prize every time. As you put in great effort at work, let your children know how you are trying a new strategy. And when you don't succeed the first, second, or eighth time, model for them how you learned from each effort and keep plugging. You are not destroyed or worthless, you do not become paralyzed, you become energized! You take disappointment with grace and good humor. Your B+ at work is not a catastrophe. They will see that their B+ in Spanish isn't either.

Kids' self-acceptance is fostered when they trust they are competent. If they believe in their ability to manage their own problems, trust their own decision-making capability, and develop their own solutions, they needn't catastrophize their mistakes. We nurture their competence by getting out of the way (by staying behind the line, as Dean Jones says), and by encouraging them to take control of their own lives. We want them to recognize that they each have a compass and can follow its direction.

Dealing With Perfectionism

When parents reject anything less than the perfect college application, they're promoting perfectionism. When they suggest that their children "just beef up" their activities a bit, they are making a statement that their children are not good enough as they are. If a parent treats a rejection letter from Ivy Walls U as an unmitigated disaster, how will a child feel about being accepted "only" by Creeping Ivy U? Won't she feel that she has failed this initiation rite? She will feel rejected (unaccepted) not only by the school of her choice, but by the people whose acceptance really matters most: her parents.

You may be reading this when your children are still quite young and you can prevent perfectionism. But if your child is already a perfectionist, it is not too late to change course, offer unconditional acceptance, and become a cheerleader whose megaphone is encouragement. Your active effort may be enough to make a big difference to your child.

Changing a perfectionist's style is not easy. A perfectionist has a lot invested in being flawless. Giving up that style brings the risk of failure or a conflict that the perfectionist is trying so desperately to avoid. It is the parent's job to let perfectionist children know that you adore them, regardless of their accomplishments or easy manner. If you directly criticize how hard they are on themselves, rather than absorbing the lesson you hope to convey, they may just use it as more fuel to reinforce their sense of inadequacy. It is OK to notice that they seem uncomfortable or are struggling more than they should: "Darling, I see that you're really worried about your grade in English in a way that seems really uncomfortable." Or, "I notice you seem disturbed that Ms Shulamay gave you a B on your history project. It makes me sad to see you this upset. Can we talk?"

A child's perfectionism may make him so uncomfortable that he deserves professional help to unlearn his catastrophic thinking patterns and to replace them with healthier ones. (More about this in Chapter 14.) Professional therapists can be very helpful in this regard; an investment now in his emotional health will pay dividends of happiness, contentment, and success throughout his life. Ask your child's school counselor or pediatrician for a possible referral.

Students Who Learn Differently Aren't Broken

In the 21st century we seek perfection and quick fixes to make every child fit into an idealized mold. When a child doesn't fit into that mold, we look for a label and a solution. Some parents worry, "But my child has a learning difference. Can he do college work? Will college admissions officers understand his talents and abilities?"

We have made considerable progress in diagnosis and early intervention for youngsters with learning differences, but many kids are still judged as not performing as well as they should, or they have social and school adjustment difficulties. I fear that too often they are seen as somehow "broken" or in need of fixing.

We forget that there are different kinds of thinkers and learners. Some people learn best visually, others through listening, and still others by tackling a problem with their hands. Most are flexible and can learn fairly well by using a combination of senses. Some students focus well despite a lot of distractions, and others lose focus on the task at hand and concentrate instead on the distractions. Different styles of thinking, different ways of being.

Each learning style may be balanced by enormous strengths. Young people with learning differences in one area are often gifted in another. Some people who don't do well in school are masterful with their hands, and others who are brilliant in the classroom can't use a screwdriver. An individual who is too fidgety to read a book can have inspirational talent and passion for the creative arts.

For every child's well-being, it is important to be able to function in school because school is where society teaches children. The problem is that schools are generally designed for people of a particular mold, those who can sit still and focus for hours and learn by hearing and seeing. But it wasn't always this way. In our ancestors' time, people cherished differences and, in fact, relied on them. Generations ago, before people could go to a supermarket and peer through cellophane for the best cuts of meat, they had to rely on each other for survival. Some tribe members foraged shrubs and fields for berries, herbs, and roots. Others hunted game. Intent on finding a herd of deer, they entered the forest with the knowledge that they couldn't survive the winter unless they bagged a deer. But the forest was a dangerous haven of lions, tigers, bears, and snakes. If all the hunters focused only on the deer, they would not have survived these perils. Some of them needed to be lookouts to prevent the other hunters from becoming prey themselves.

Generations later we still need lookouts, people who are easily distracted by a distant sound or an unusual smell. We should help students who have trouble learning in traditional ways to learn more effectively in school. But we dare not see them as broken because it may be precisely their differences that ensure our survival. The lookouts may have trouble focusing on the blackboard or textbook, but their distractibility and their great attention to their environment can be an important strength.

There is a full life ahead for students who are now labeled "distractible" or have other learning differences. If this speaks to your child, I suggest that you get extra tutoring, consider medicines, explore early interventions, and ask your pediatrician to join you in maximizing your child's chances of learning as much as he can in his own way. But trust in your child's wisdom that he will find a career path that uses his strengths.

Children with learning differences are not broken. They are different. If parents primarily view them as broken and in need of fixing, their learning difference will hold them back. If parents find appropriate interventions while reveling in and supporting their children's strengths, they will be just fine. If you refuse to see your child as broken—if you recognize and build on his strengths—you will help him overcome hurdles and become more resilient.

Many colleges have special programs and tutoring supports for students with learning differences. If your child's high school guidance counselors haven't already suggested some, ask them to investigate these possibilities. As with all students, it's all about finding the right match for each individual child.

Parents of young people with chronic diseases also worry whether their children will be prepared to make the transition to college. For children with learning differences or chronic medical conditions, the situation may be more tense for them and their parents if they have been particularly dependent on parents. Parents worry, "Are they ready to go to college? Can they survive without me?" The young person may have similar concerns or may desire to break away and assert independence, especially if parents have been doting and protective for years. In either case, it's wise for parents and teens to talk these issues through together—not on graduation eve, but much earlier. In the best-case scenario, parents offer ongoing support but gradually step back and encourage more independence for the teenager from one year of high school to the next.

When parents recognize their kids' strengths (and contain their own anxieties about the learning difference or chronic condition), children learn to view their situation as a challenge to overcome. Many of them are deeply resilient and have character traits that often surpass their chronological age. They often have a well-honed sense of what really matters. They've often developed tremendous competencies to compensate for challenges in their lives. This gives them the experience of their own abilities that builds confidence to meet other, unrelated challenges. They are certainly not broken. They may be particularly well poised for success.

CHAPTER NINE

Look at Your Child

Our kids' stress levels increase because of what they are doing and what they are not doing. They are overstretched and overcommitted, doing all the academic and enrichment activities that our spiraling expectations have imposed. At the same time, they have lost the recovery time—downtime, free time with no agenda—when they would naturally reflect and regenerate.

As we travel the country sounding this alarm, parents generally agree. Many parents readily acknowledge that their kids are stretched thin, over-worked, and often exhausted, but they believe this is the short-term road to success and that, if their child just keeps plugging long enough to "get into a good college," lifelong success will be guaranteed. Other parents swear that their children love all the activities and insist that their kids, not they, are driving the process. They ask, "What should we do—insist they stop?" Others wonder, "How do we know when there are enough activities to broaden their horizons but not too many to smother them? What is enough?"

No "expert" can tell you how much your child can handle, although one basic guideline holds true from toddlerhood through high school: All kids need unscheduled time to figure things out, relax, and reboot—to play. Even when your children seem to thrive on an abundance of activities, they will begin to burn out if they have no time for themselves. (More about this in Chapter 13.)

Short of that fact, we do not feel comfortable offering a prescription on just how much "enrichment" is enough. We don't know your kids. You do. *Look at them* and notice whether they are thriving or seem burdened. But don't be satisfied by simply asking them. They have a lot invested in telling you that they love everything. After all, you are not asking whether they wish to give up gruel or porridge. Who wants to decide whether to give up ballet or tennis? Art or music? Given those choices, you can expect the answer, "I love them both, I'm just a bit tired this week, but I'll get more sleep." Sure they will.

Listen to their answers. Maybe they will have the insight to tell you they are stretched too far and the foresight to pull back. But look at them, watch their behavior closely, and evaluate their mood. You'll know. You're their parent; you know them best.

Is It Flowing?

The real question is, how is your son or daughter doing? Does she love what she is doing? Do her activities rejuvenate her? Does she seem to lose herself in her activities, almost as if she is on vacation? Does she look forward to the next lesson, the next game, the next class? Does she relish her achievements? Does time seem to stand still for her when she is most involved in the activity she cherishes? Does the desire to participate seem to be bubbling up from deep within her?

In his books, *Flow: The Psychology of Optimal Experience* and *Finding Flow,* Mihaly Csikszentmihalyi describes the "flow" phenomenon. Flow is the process of total involvement with something that leads to genuine enjoyment and optimal experience. Flow bubbles up from inside; it's not acquired. Csikszentmihalyi states, "The best moments usually occur when a person's body or mind is stretched to its limits in a voluntary effort to accomplish something difficult and worthwhile."

If a child is experiencing flow from his activities, he is just fine. The fact that he is pushing himself might be precisely why he is deriving so much satisfaction. But 2 cautionary notes: First, while someone can certainly achieve flow in an activity that intensely interests him, it is unlikely he can achieve flow in each of many activities. Second, we want to underscore the phrase "voluntary effort." When we give young people free time to play and unscheduled time to "chill," they are likely to find their passion, the interest that is so engaging that the joy of participation bubbles up from within them. Without free time, young people may not discover their passion as they flit from activity to activity. When activities are imposed on them, when participation is primarily to meet someone else's expectations or to put on a college application, the effort is not voluntary. If your child's life is filled with activities, encourage him to drop those that do not inspire him and allow him to pursue those that engage his interest and passion. A further note on passion: Remember that adolescents are still young and may not have a passion yet. That's OK. They're kids; they have time. It is good enough if they're enjoying life and developing interests in what surrounds them. Learn to see what they like without always searching for that passion.

Parents sometimes tell me that their children are self-driven in avidly pursuing a sport or other activity, but this may not always be flow. When the drive truly comes from within a child, it is wonderful and should be supported. On the other hand, if a child's drive is motivated more by a desire to please parents than by self-satisfaction or joy, this drive can become one more stressor in the child's life. It is far better to let children explore their interests freely, discover their own flow, and follow it without imposing too much structure on their activities. We can put a little wind behind children's sails to support them, but the direction should come from within them.

Is It a Burden?

If your child doesn't seem to be in "flow," how does she seem to be managing her load? If she does not love what she is doing, does she resent her activities or commitments? Do her activities exhaust her? Does she look toward the next lesson, the next game, or the next class with dread? Does she tell you she's enjoying herself, but her body language suggests that she is at her rope's end?

Make sure your children have the capability to relax. It is not a good sign if they only feel useful or alive when they are busy. Even the greatest athlete who experiences flow during the peak of performance takes a well-deserved rest.

Does your child define herself by her achievements? Is she worried about not meeting others' approval or acceptance? Does she seem to fear failure or disappointing others if she can't "do it all"? Does she seem worried, anxious, or depressed?

How Do I Know When My Child Is Really in Trouble?

Many reasons can explain why young people reach their limits of resilience, including being overstretched or overcommitted by school and extracurricular activities. Overstretching is not always a major cause of anxiety or depression, but for many young people it is a significant contributing factor. It isn't a sign of weakness on their part or a sign of poor parenting on our part when they show their human limitations.

When they are no longer coping well, they may come to their parents silently with telltale signs like tears or a furrowed brow. At other times, they may verbalize their feelings clearly and express exactly why they are troubled and what they need. But usually, parents have to remain alert to subtle indications of trouble.

Adolescents might have the kind of tantrums they haven't had since they were 2 years old—anything to let their parents know they are scared or out of control. They experience stress through their bodies, just as we do. They get bellyaches, headaches, muscle strains, fatigue, and even chest pain and dizziness when they're stressed. Don't assume they are faking to avoid school or get out of responsibilities. If you approach them as if they are faking, they will feel ashamed. It is likely that they do not yet understand the connection between their emotions and their bodies' response. In these situations, it is important to have them examined by a medical professional to be sure there is not an illness that needs treatment. But it is equally important to consider that frequent aches and pains, which cannot be explained by a virus or other illness, may be manifestations of stress.

Pay attention when your children have frequent physical complaints that prevent them from going to school. Notice if symptoms are less frequent on weekends or vacations. That will be helpful information for your doctor or nurse, who will consider the possibility that academics is a major stressor for your child.

Many teens who are troubled also have signs of sleep disturbances— sleeping too much or having trouble falling asleep. Sometimes they don't even know that they are having trouble sleeping. Look for signs of fatigue or difficulty waking up in time for school.

Young people often reveal their level of stress through their school performance. Remember, school is an adolescent's job. Just as adults' job performance declines with increasing stress, youth find it difficult to focus on schoolwork when they're under stress. Anytime grades are slipping significantly, it should be a red flag that alerts you to explore whether your adolescent is burdened.

Look for changes in your teenager's behavior. A new circle of friends or a radical change in dress style is certainly a sign that merits a supportive conversation. Any suspicion that your adolescent may be turning to substance use, including cigarettes, deserves your intensive involvement as well as professional guidance.

Many parents are very attentive to signs of depression but mistakenly believe that adolescent depression presents the same symptoms as adult depression. Depressed adults tend to have sleep disturbances, become withdrawn, lack energy, have a lower capacity to experience pleasure, and often express hopelessness. This is true of some adolescents, but nearly half of depressed adolescents are irritable instead of withdrawn. They may have boundless energy or act out with rage. Many loving, attentive parents miss signs of depression because it is sometimes difficult to tell a normal teenager from a depressed one. Normal teenagers have phases where they are irritable at home and have occasional outrageous outbursts. Because parents may have adjusted to this moodiness, they can miss seeing rage and irritability as signals of emotional turmoil or depression. This is a critical reason that parents need to feel comfortable turning to a professional for an evaluation.

If your teenager shows any need to "overcontrol" her life, it is a sign that she feels out of control. That is a high-flying red flag that she has too much to handle. Perfectionism, as discussed in the previous chapter, is one sign of a need to be fully in control. Whereas list making and organization are hallmarks of successful people, obsession with schedule or order is a serious warning sign. Two of our greatest concerns about teenagers—eating disorders and self-mutilation—are harmful attempts at taking control of a life that seems to be spinning out of control.

Finding Help

When adolescents reach their limits, they usually experience a sense of inadequacy. It is important that they don't also have to deal with the feeling of somehow letting their parents down. If you want to make sure that this doesn't happen in your family, let go of the fantasy that your children will be able to handle everything as long as you do everything right. If you view your children's problems as a reflection on you, you won't be able to help them through the toughest of times because you'll have to work through your own feelings of failure.

Whenever your teenager does seem to be troubled, the first step is always to reinforce that you are there to be fully supportive. Listen, be a sounding board, perhaps even offer advice, but certainly offer assurance that the most important source of security, you, remains constant. But because teenagers seek and need independence, it is likely that your adolescent may be more receptive to help from another adult or a professional.

At this point, most parents have to work through their own disappointment that their children need something more than they can give. But think of it as an act of love, not of failure. You love your children so much that you will get whatever help they need to be able to thrive. Accept that they may need to turn to another adult from whom they don't need to gain independence.

It may be tough to guide a teenager to agree to seek professional guidance. Adolescents may feel ashamed that they can't handle their own problems and worry that going for help confirms that they are weak or "crazy." If you have any ambivalent thoughts about what it means to seek professional help, try to resolve them before talking to your teens. Otherwise, they will pick up on your mixed emotions and may become even more resistant. If you genuinely believe that seeking professional help is an act of strength, your adolescent is more likely to see it that way.

It is important for adolescents to understand a few key points about professional help. First, they need to understand that they deserve to feel good. Seeking help is an act of strength because strong people know they are capable of feeling better, deserve to feel better, and will take the steps to feel better. They also need to know that professionals don't give answers or solve problems, but instead try to find the strengths of each person and build on them. Adolescents should understand they will only be guided to become stronger by using skills they already possess and by developing new skills they can use as coping strategies.

Possible Signs of Trouble

Remember that no single sign should make parents panic. Some adolescents have some of these signs and will be just fine. But these signs are signals that you should check in with your child and consider seeking professional help.

- Slipping school performance
- Sleep problems
- Nightmares
- Irritability or outbursts
- Hopelessness
- Change in eating habits
- Self-mutilation
- Anger
- Isolation/withdrawal
- Loss of friends
- New circle of friends
- Radically new style of dress
- Physical symptoms
  - ❖ Belly pain
  - ❖ Headaches
  - ❖ Fatigue
  - ❖ Chest pain
- Missing school because of frequent symptoms
- Drug, alcohol, or cigarette use

CHAPTER TEN

Stress and Its Effects

The college admissions process is stressful for everyone concerned. For parents: "This is the first step, isn't it? Will my child prove he can make it in the real world? Can she get into a college that will put her on the right career path?" For adolescents: "Will admissions officers see me as a desirable applicant? Have I proven I'm special enough to get accepted? Am I ready to leave home? What will happen to my high school friendships when we all go to different colleges?" And for secondary schools: "Will we prove that we are doing a good job of educating our students by getting them into top colleges and universities?"

Parents and schools unwittingly transfer their anxiety onto students, reinforcing and heightening adolescents' existing worries. Precisely because it is so stressful, however, the experience of applying to college is an ideal opportunity for everyone involved to learn how to manage anxiety, keep perspective, and make the most of outcomes whether they are desired or not.

We start off on the wrong foot when we buy into the Big Lie: If you sacrifice all your free time now and study really hard for your classes and SATs, you'll get into a great college and your future will be ensured. This lie implies that the admissions process is the ultimate stressor and if a student scores well on one test, a perfect life will be delivered on a silver platter.

This Big Lie puts far too much importance on any given test or college decision. Neither the SAT nor admission to a particular college establishes an individual's life path. If adolescents believe their whole lives will be determined by the answers they fill in on a single Saturday morning or by an envelope they receive in April of senior year, the amount of pressure they are likely to feel will create so much stress that it will undermine their chances of putting their best foot forward. How can they possibly perform their best or fully concentrate that Saturday morning if the idea is spinning around in their heads that their life's direction is at stake?

The truth is that life is never delivered on a silver platter. Even people with 4.0 grade point averages, 2,400 SATs, and degrees from the college that *US News and World Report* decides is No. 1, cannot slack off and wait for the accolades and checks to flow in for the rest of their lives. Successful people need to continue to work hard. Stress will continue in one form or another throughout adulthood. If the present is consistently sacrificed on the false belief that life will begin later, reality will eventually strike, and those who've believed the Big Lie will awaken to the fact that many of the joys of life have passed by. The ability to delay gratification is a virtue at times, but the present should never be completely sacrificed for the future. People with joyful lives learn to achieve balance. They work hard, but they also live fully in the present. They learn how to relax, have fun, replenish themselves, and make the most of their human relationships.

Young people who are prepared to manage stress have one of the most essential ingredients needed to remain resilient, and resilient people are able to cope with obstacles while becoming successful and experiencing life's pleasures. It's important to focus on stress management now because adolescence is the time to prepare for a life of continued hard work and abundant pleasures. Now is the time to demonstrate that hard work always pays off, but not necessarily as expected. This is the time, as teenagers prepare to enter adulthood, for adults to model optimism and resilience during high-pressure times by managing stress and still enjoying life. This chapter is a primer on stress and its effect on health, emotions, and behavior. Chapter 18 offers parents a stress-management strategy so that they will be prepared to reinforce it and, more importantly, model it. A similar plan will be presented to adolescents in Part Four.

Stress 101

All families today feel the real presence of stress in daily life. For parents it's pressure at work, mortgage and car payments, rising prices. "How will we ever save or pay for college?" Everyone is rushed. Meals are consumed in the car on the way to ball games, drama practice, tutoring sessions. Weekends are no longer leisurely. Routine family gatherings, like Sunday dinner at Grandma's, are events of the past because family members are running in separate directions.

For young people, stress is not only a matter of having too little time. In addition to crammed academic and extracurricular schedules, they face constant social and emotional pressures. Friends dare them to take risks. Coaches demand higher performance levels. The media pound them with messages that they aren't thin enough, cool enough, sexy enough, or attractive enough. If that's not enough to worry about, every time they turn on the television, they absorb more anxiety (terrorism, school violence, hurricanes, earthquakes, nuclear threat).

Stress is all too real. We try to reduce it by reordering our priorities and trimming the less important events from the calendar, but we can't erase stress entirely. We cannot isolate or protect children from pressures at school, their friends, or the world at large. We can't make them invulnerable. How can we help them cope and become well balanced both now in these critical adolescent years and later throughout their adult lives? The first step is to help them understand the nature of stress—where it comes from, what it does to the human body, and how they can manage it in healthy ways.

The word *stress* is most often used in the midst of a complaint: "My teachers really piled it on this week. I have so much work to do, I don't know if I can survive the stress." While stress can be a worrisome problem, it is far too simplistic to see it only in a negative light. Stress actually was designed to be a lifesaver. Stress gets our adrenaline going in times of threat or peril so we can move quickly to avoid harm. A reasonable level of stress can be a positive influence that drives us toward achievement. Moderate stress, for example, pumps us up to prepare for an exam. A little stress energizes a musician to play at a recital or an athlete to train for a game. Without some occasional, moderate, well-timed stress, we might have trouble mounting the energy to focus more intensely and give the extra effort. Problems arise, however, when stress becomes chronic or when we don't manage it well enough to perform all the tasks and responsibilities before us. Then stress can become a destructive force that harms our bodies, paralyzes our efforts, or drives us toward risky behaviors.

When stress reaches that point, the human body gets confused. Why? Our bodies were not designed to survive 21st-century lifestyles. They were designed long ago to survive in the jungle when a tiger might leap out of the brush at any moment. Imagine the scene: Our ancestor feasts on berries and basks in the warmth of the sun, as relaxed as he could be. He suddenly sees a tiger. His brain registers terror before he can even bring the grave danger to consciousness. His nervous system immediately begins firing, which causes hormones to surge throughout his body. Some of those hormones, such as adrenaline, give him the needed initial burst of energy to get up and run, while others spark a cascade to mobilize his body's immediate needs (increased blood pressure and a release of sugar for energy) and prepare for some of its longer-term needs (replenishing water and sugar).

Our ancestor—let's call him Sam—first experiences a sensation that we're familiar with: butterflies in the stomach. This is because the blood that has been circulating in his gut to digest food now rushes to his legs so he can run. In times of rest, muscles use only about 20% of the blood that the heart pumps every minute, while the kidneys and gut each use another 20%. Within an instant of a stressful event, the strenuously working muscles use up to 90% of the blood that the energized heart is able to pump. Because the heart pumps much more vigorously than it did at rest, the muscles are actually bathed in 18 times more blood than during calm times. In the meantime, the kidneys and gut are only receiving about 1% of the blood during these stressful times. No wonder we don't want to eat during times of extreme stress.

When Sam leaps to his feet, he notices his heart beating fast to pump blood quickly. As he runs from the tiger, he breathes rapidly to oxygenate his blood. The sweat dripping down Sam's body and brow cools him as he runs. His pupils dilate fully so he can see any obstacles in his path. He thinks only about running because he is not supposed to stop, turn around, and suggest to the tiger that they negotiate their differences amicably.

Without the stress reaction, our ancestors would not have survived. But stress has helped us do more than run from tigers. It keeps us alert and prepared. You can be sure that the next time Sam sat down to munch berries, he was attuned to the sounds of brush rustling. Heightened vigilance caused by lower levels of stress can help us today. It is what pushes us to meet deadlines and helps our children study when anticipation of a test generates just the right amount of stress.

We don't need to race from tigers today. Most events that cause stress are not immediately life-threatening—a fight with a spouse or ex-spouse, pressure at work, the challenge of juggling many roles, and for our kids, getting into college. Yet our bodies weren't designed to meet those ongoing needs day after day. Imagine if they were: Your boss warns you that she might downsize. Immediately that part of your brain that stored her favorite joke becomes energized and you retell the joke to lighten her mood. Or your emotional centers help you come up with the perfect flattering comment. You'd need no sleep because your survival at work requires you to clock those 92-hour workweeks. Eating no longer feels necessary because your body has learned to run on last Tuesday's dinner.

Back to reality: When your boss warns you that she might let you go, your first sensation is to vomit because you just ate a big lunch. Suddenly there is not a drop of blood in your gut. All your blood has rushed to your legs, and you just want to escape her threatening words. But you don't. You stand still because you remember that it would be unprofessional to race out the door.

Your heart beats as fast as it would if you were running, however. Your breathing intensifies. You sweat and feel flushed because the adrenaline coursing through your veins is confused about why you aren't listening to it: Why are you standing still when the tiger (your boss) is ready to devour you?

Wouldn't it be great if we had multiple sets of hormones to help us deal most efficiently with each crisis (hormones that turn us into study machines with no biological needs—no sleep, no food, no bathroom needs…and certainly no sex—when we have to prepare for exams)? But we only have the hormones that prepare us to escape from the tiger and other, subtler jungle-based problems.

If stress is a survival tool, you're wondering, why does it eat us alive? In his sprint for survival, Sam used up every hormone, reveled in his success, and in time his body was able to return to normal. But in the modern world, those same stress hormones remain in our bodies because, unlike Sam, we don't react as fully to our hormonal bursts. We don't sprint away. Instead, our stress hormones continue to circulate through our bodies, unused and confused: Why did my body remain seated when that tiger attacked?

We do have more subtle varieties of hormones than those generated during a carnivorous attack. The body's intricate wiring allows us to meet a broad variety of needs. Blood pressure, for example, ranges widely during the day. During sleep it can be quite low. At times of crisis or maximum exertion, it can become quite high. When we're functioning in the midst of a hectic day, blood pressure is somewhere in the middle range. Factors that control blood pressure—heart rate, how constricted the blood vessels are, salt load and water load—are in a constant dance to meet the body's needs. That dance is carried out through the movements and fluctuations of nerves and hormones, all brilliantly choreographed by the brain.

The brain is not an objective choreographer, however. It is heavily influenced by emotion and passion. Sometimes blood pressure goes up because of a real need, such as the need to run or even to stand up after lying down. At other times, blood pressure goes up because of an intense emotion or stays up in a state of vigilance for a coming crisis. And the world is always ready to offer us another crisis.

The body's reaction to stress is mediated through a complex interplay of sensory input—sights and sounds—as well as the brain and nervous system, hormones, and the body's cells and organs. Emotions play an important role in how we experience stress because the brain conducts this system. This means that the way we think about stress and what we choose to do about it can affect the impact of stress.

Stress, Emotions, and Behavior

Everyone has different ways of dealing with ongoing stress (exercise, meditation, long walks, painkillers, smoking). Depending on their age and temperament, some kids withdraw, sulk, or zone out. Others act out or talk back. Adolescents may turn to the coping mechanisms that they see their peers using (smoking, drinking, drugs, fighting, sexual activity, eating disorders, self-mutilation, or delinquency). Adults usually view these activities only as "behavior problems" because they underestimate the amount of stress on young people that drives these unwise choices. In actuality, these negative behaviors are often attempts to counter stress, push it under, chill out, and make it all go away.

When young people are stressed, their impulse is to relieve the discomfort. They find relief by acting impulsively or by following paths most readily available to them, the ones they see other kids taking. Most adolescents simply don't know more healthy and effective alternatives. Unless we guide them toward positive ways to relieve and reduce stress, they often choose the negative behaviors of their peers or the culture they absorb from the media. They will become caught up in a cycle of negative coping methods and risky behaviors. We need to help them break that cycle, especially before they leave home for college.

An example of how a teenager can get caught up in the cycle: He has worked hard all week to finish his essays and study for tests. He's gone to every hockey practice, met with his tutor, and rehearsed his lines for the play. By Saturday night when friends invite him to a party, he's ready to kick back. Instead, peer pressure kicks in. Someone brings a keg to the party. He doesn't want to drink but experiences internal pressure because he doesn't want to feel like an outcast. The dilemma of whether to drink increases his stress. He has seen how alcohol relaxes his parents after a difficult day at work, so he decides to drink to relieve his stress.

Behaviors like this are actually effective at relieving stress—in the short term. A teenager who is anxious about living up to expectations of parents or teachers may turn to drinking or drugs for relief. His feelings of inadequacy or fear of failure are diminished when he uses drugs or alcohol. The feelings resurface after the high wears off, so he is likely to drink or use drugs more frequently to keep his stress at bay. Negative strategies are easy, quick fixes that do relieve stress, but we know that the consequences are harmful to teens, families, and society.

"I Just Don't Care"

Many behaviors that frustrate parents are really teenagers' attempts to fend off stress. Procrastination, feigned laziness, and boredom are often ways of dealing with school-related pressure. While it is not cool to say that they are struggling to keep up with all the demands, it is cool to say they just don't care. It is not acceptable for them to admit that their perfectionist tendencies make it too difficult to consider producing anything less than a flawless product, so they just put off getting started. They push it out of sight and mind for a while. Sometimes when they are just too overwhelmed to keep up with their schedules, they suddenly become "bored" with their activities and stop participating. They have too much trouble admitting they can't keep up with expectations, so they say they have lost interest. Finally, exhaustion is another tool to manage being overloaded ("I'm too tired; I have to take a nap.").

Stress and Physical Symptoms

Stress also creates some of those nagging, prolonged physical symptoms that we worry about in teenagers. Their bodies accumulate stress, just as our adult bodies do. Frequent patterns of headaches, belly pain, chest pain, dizziness, and/or fatigue point to the possibility that stress is driving those uncomfortable feelings. But most adolescents don't understand how their underlying stress, moodiness, or irritability can cause their physical symptoms. Therefore, they not only have to deal with the stressors that drive the symptoms, but they also have to worry that they are seriously ill. Parents working with health professionals can be helpful in guiding teenagers to awareness that the body and the mind are intimately connected.

Teenagers often feel embarrassed when they realize that their physical symptoms are related to stress. They believe that other people will think they are faking or crazy. Parents can play a particularly important role in removing shame from the equation. Parents need to assure young people that everyone has physical symptoms with stress. It doesn't mean they are making it up or losing it. Parents also need to help teenagers identify the source of their stress and agree to come up with a plan to manage it. A mental health professional can be helpful in distinguishing whether physical symptoms can be adequately reduced by addressing the stressor and implementing a stress-management plan or whether the adolescent may need more intensive treatment for anxiety or depression.

Stress and Control

Virtually all the behaviors we fear in children and teenagers are misguided attempts to diminish their stress. Two behaviors that are becoming increasingly common in highly scheduled kids are eating disorders and self-mutilation. These very worrisome behaviors are both disorders of control. When young people feel overwhelmed and out of control, they sometimes go to extreme measures to feel that they are in control. The classic prototype of a patient with an eating disorder is an overcommitted perfectionist who thinks she can't live up to the expectations that she perceives others have imposed and that she certainly has put on herself. She can't be good at everything, so she picks one thing she can fully control—what she eats.

Other young people have so much frustration or pain in their lives that they feel emotionally out of control. The thought of feeling that pain is overwhelming. Instead, they substitute a controlled pain. They self-mutilate or cut themselves so that they are fully in charge of when and how deeply they feel their pain.

Adolescents may choose other worrisome behaviors to deaden or numb their emotions. They use substances to take away pain or even just to relax. Alcohol, cigarettes, and drugs offer almost instant vacations from their rational minds that have to face problems.

Attempts to control stress take other directions as well. Sex fulfills a need to be loved and valued. Young girls who hope to become mothers are often filling a need to experience love fully. Gang members are trying to find protection and security in an unsafe world. Teenagers who engage in violence or bullying often are releasing pent up anger and trying to experience a sense of control to compensate for those times they felt powerless.

The antidote to these behaviors is learning how to manage their problems and be comfortable with their emotions. If we could eliminate stress, all of these problems would not simply go away, of course. We need to heal society in ways that will diminish some of the sense of powerlessness and lack of support many of our youth feel. Some of these behaviors serve as more than stress-reduction strategies; they are also fun or feel good. Even kids who are ideally parented may choose to try out some of these behaviors. But the kids who get stuck in these behaviors are those who use them as coping strategies.

Stress, College Admissions, and the Parent's Role

Parents have a critical role in supporting kids' use of healthy, productive coping strategies. Parents of young children may have their greatest influence on preventing worrisome adolescent behaviors by teaching youngsters a wide repertoire of positive coping strategies. Children equipped with healthy ways to manage stress will choose those strategies rather than dangerous quick fixes. In late adolescence, parents can most effectively reinforce positive coping strategies by consistently modeling them.

Parents always need to be open to talking with children about stress so there's never any shame in admitting that they feel stressed. Parents also can have a pivotal role in helping adolescents sort out what's a real crisis and what's not. During the high school years, when teenagers are preparing to leave home, so many potential stressors arise that it's easy to blow something out of proportion, to have trouble telling the difference between a bump in the road and a catastrophe. A tiger running at us is an authentic crisis. An oncoming car suddenly veering into our lane instantly energizes us to steer out of its path. But is a C+ on a chemistry quiz a major crisis? If a young person blows a mild stressor (such as studying for tomorrow's test) way out of proportion, he will undermine his chance for success. Instead of being alert, he will be scattered, unfocused, and too nervous to study at all. He'll be running from the test-tiger and incapable of concentrating on anything but escape. In situations like these, parents' subtle and not so subtle messages determine how children define crisis and how their stress hormones mobilize.

To high school juniors and seniors, the college admissions process often seems a major crisis worth every ounce of reserve. But it is not. Our job is to make sure they realistically assess just how important it is in the context of their lives. The difference between a college acceptance at their first versus fifth choice is rarely a make or break situation, and is never life-threatening.

Certainly parents' words can be reassuring, but remember how closely children—even adolescents—watch their parents. Young people recognize when body language and anxiety belie a parent's reassuring words. For this reason, it really matters that parents first put the admissions process in perspective themselves. If they see the end result as reflective of whether they have succeeded as parents, their adolescent will grasp their heightened anxiety, and this will put an inordinate amount of pressure on the outcome. The more parents reinforce that the trophy at the end is more important than how the game is played, the more likely it is their teenager will feel like a failure when the goal is inaccessible. The stress caused by this fear of failure is precisely what may limit success.

But if we help teenagers keep perspective and manage stress, they will be prepared to mount their best effort to meet challenges and remain flexible enough to make the most of whatever good fortune comes their way.

CHAPTER ELEVEN

Fostering Resilience

One of the most potent antidotes to stress is resilience: the ability and strength to face challenges and bounce back from adversity. Every child is born with natural resilience. Some children seem graced with a natural ability to recover from adversity, while others need extra support. But every young person can become *more* resilient—particularly during adolescence when challenges increase to excel in school, get into college, and stay out of trouble. In considering how resilient your teenager is and how you can help foster greater resilience, keep in mind this important factor: your influential role as parent. Keep these 3 critical facts in mind.

■ Kids live up to or down to their parents' expectations. If parents expect the best, children tend to live up to those standards. High standards are not the same as achievements. I don't mean straight-A report cards or 3 varsity letters. I mean being a good human being: considerate, respectful, honest, fair, generous, and responsible. You know, the qualities you hope your children have. On the other hand, if parents have low standards, or simply don't make clear that they have high expectations, kids are likely to have low expectations for themselves.

■ The second key point that affects their resilience is whether an adult believes in them unconditionally. Hopefully that adult will always be a parent, but a grandparent, uncle, aunt, or teacher can fill that role. The more strong, supportive adults, the better. As children grow up and away from you, push your buttons, and try your patience, be sure to show them your unconditional love and belief in them. Don't assume they know it or take it for granted.

■ As children's most powerful models, parents are in the best position to
teach them about stress and resilience. All children observe parents closely.
If we show them negative ways of coping with our own stress, they will
follow our example. If we binge on junk food whenever we're anxious,
they are likely to do the same. If we drink heavily after work each evening,
we're sending the message that alcohol is an acceptable stress reliever. On
the other hand, if we talk about our anger or discuss work-related tensions,
we demonstrate that talking about frustration and stress is a healthy way
to vent. Or we can model constructive coping methods by going for a walk
or a jog after a bad day at work, taking time for ourselves to relax before
rushing to make dinner, or practicing deep breathing or yoga.

As we demonstrate beneficial ways to deal with stress, we are not only
offering them good role models, but we also are treating ourselves well. We
may not think that children always pay attention to what we are doing, but
they do. We probably won't be perfect models every time we're stressed, but
each time we attempt to offer a constructive model, we reduce the potential
that our kids will turn to negative ways of coping with stress.

Roots of Resilience

It's vital to remember that all young people come equipped with assets and
abilities that can become sources of pride and springboards to ongoing accomplishments. Our job is to help them develop confidence by recognizing their
own abilities, inner resources, and competencies so they can become more
competent and resilient. Just as we develop and strengthen our muscles by
exercising them, we can develop resilience by paying attention to those
strengths and building on them.

Resilience isn't a simple, single-part entity. It has 7 integral, interrelated
components—competence, confidence, connection, character, contribution,
coping, and control. A brief description of these components follows, with a
few questions about each. Let these questions rattle around in your mind for a
while. They are designed to help you reflect about your own teen's resilience
and how you affect it. The 7 components, as they relate to the college admissions process, will be expanded on in subsequent chapters. A fuller discussion
of their role in building children's resilience is available in the book, *A Parent's
Guide to Building Resilience in Children and Teens: Giving Your Child Roots and
Wings* (Ginsburg KR, Jablow MM. American Academy of Pediatrics, Elk Grove
Village, IL; 2006).

Competence—Competence is the ability to handle situations effectively.
It is not a vague feeling or hunch that "I can do this." Competence is acquired
through actual experience. Young people cannot become competent without

first developing a set of skills that allows them to trust their own judgments, make responsible choices, and face difficult situations.

In thinking about your children's competence and how to foster it, ask yourself

- Do I help them focus on their strengths and build on them?

- Do I notice what they do right or well? Or do I focus on their mistakes?

- When I need to point out a mistake, am I clear and focused, or do I communicate that I believe they always mess up?

- Do I help them recognize what they have going for themselves?

- Am I helping to build the skills necessary to make them competent in the real world? (These include educational skills, social skills, and stress-reduction skills.)

- Do I communicate in a way that empowers them to make their own decisions? Or do I undermine their sense of competence by lecturing them or giving them information in ways they cannot grasp?

- Do I let them make safe mistakes so they have the opportunity to right themselves? Or do I try to protect them from every misstep?

- As I try to protect them, does my interference mistakenly send the message: "I don't think you can handle this?"

- If I have more than one child, do I recognize the competencies of each without comparing them to their siblings?

Confidence—True confidence, the solid belief in one's abilities, is rooted in competence. Children and teenagers gain increasing confidence when they demonstrate competence in real situations. Confidence is not warm and fuzzy self-esteem that supposedly results from telling kids they're special or precious. Young people who experience their own competence, and who also know they are safe and protected, develop a deep-seated security that promotes the confidence to face and cope with life's challenges. When parents support them in finding their areas of competence and building on them, kids gain enough confidence to try new ventures and trust their own ability to make sound choices.

In thinking about your children's degree of confidence, consider the following questions:

- Do I see the best in my children so that they can see the best in themselves?

- Do I help them recognize what they have done right or well?

- Do I treat them as incapable children or as young people who are learning to navigate their world?

- Do I praise them enough? Do I praise them honestly about specific achievements, or do I give such diffuse praise that it doesn't seem authentic?

- Do I catch them "being good" when they are generous, helpful, or kind, or when they do something without being asked or cajoled?

- Do I encourage them to strive just a little bit further because I believe they can succeed? Do I hold realistically high expectations?

- Do I unintentionally push them to take on more than they can realistically handle, causing them to stumble and lose confidence?

- When I need to criticize them, do I focus only on what they're doing wrong, or do I remind them they are capable of doing well?

- Do I avoid instilling shame in them?

Connection—Adolescents with close ties to family, friends, school, and community are more likely to have a solid sense of security that produces strong values and prevents them from seeking destructive alternatives to love and attention. Family and friends are the central forces in any teenager's life, but connections to civic, educational, religious, and athletic groups can also increase a sense of belonging to a wider world and being safe within it. Some questions to ponder include

- Do we build a sense of physical safety and emotional security within our home?

- Do I allow my children to express all types of emotions, or do I suppress unpleasant feelings? Are they learning that going to other people for emotional support during difficult times is productive or shameful?

- Do my kids know that I am absolutely crazy in love with them?

- Do we do everything to address conflict within our family and work to resolve problems rather than let them fester?

- Do we have a television and entertainment center in every room, or do we create a common space where our family shares time together?

- Do I jealously guard my teenagers from developing close relationships with others, or do I foster other healthy relationships that I know will reinforce my positive messages?

Character—Young people need a fundamental sense of right and wrong to ensure that they are prepared to make wise choices, contribute to the world, and become stable adults. Adolescents with character enjoy a strong sense of self-worth and confidence. They are more comfortable sticking to their own values and demonstrating a caring attitude toward others. Some basic questions include

- Do I help my children understand how their behaviors affect other people, both in good and bad ways?

- Am I helping my teens recognize themselves as caring people?

- Do I allow them to clarify their own values?

- Do I allow them to consider right versus wrong and look beyond immediate satisfaction or selfish needs?

- Do I value them so clearly that I model for them the importance of caring for others, and do I demonstrate the importance of community?

- Do I clearly express that I expect the best qualities (not achievements, but personal qualities such as fairness, integrity, persistence, and kindness) in them?

Contribution—It is a powerful lesson when a young person realizes that the world is a better place *because he or she is in it*. Adolescents who understand the importance of personal contribution gain a sense of purpose that can motivate them. They will not only take actions and make choices that have a positive impact on the world, but they will also enhance their own competence, character, and sense of connection.

Before we can foster this sense of contribution, we must consider these questions.

- Do I teach the important value of serving others? Do I model generosity with my time and money?

- Do I make clear to my children that I believe they can improve the world?

- Do I create opportunities for each child to contribute in some specific way?

- Do I search my teen's circle for other adults who might serve as role models who contribute to their community and the world? Do I use these adults as examples to encourage my kids to be the best they can be?

Coping—Adolescents who learn to cope effectively with stress are better prepared to overcome challenges. The best protection against unsafe, worrisome behaviors may be a wide repertoire of positive, adaptive coping strategies. Before we begin teaching this repertoire of coping and stress-reduction skills, we should ask ourselves some general questions.

- Do I model positive coping strategies myself on a consistent basis?

- Do I guide my children to develop positive, effective coping strategies?

- Do I recognize that, for many young people, risk behaviors are attempts to alleviate the stress and pain in their lives?

- If my children participate in negative behaviors, do I condemn them for it? In doing so, do I recognize that I may only increase their sense of shame and therefore drive them toward more negativity?

- Do I model the importance of caring for our bodies through exercise, good nutrition, and adequate sleep? Do I model relaxation techniques?

- Do I encourage creative expression?

- As I struggle to compose myself so I can make fair, wise decisions under pressure, do I model how I take control rather than respond impulsively or rashly to stressful situations?

- Do I create a family environment where talking, listening, and sharing are safe, comfortable, and productive?

Control—When young people realize that *they* can control the outcomes of their decisions and actions, they're more likely to know that they have the ability to do what it takes to move ahead or bounce back. On the other hand, if parents make all the decisions, young people are denied opportunities to learn control. An adolescent who feels "everything always happens to me" tends to become passive, pessimistic, and depressed. He sees control as external: Whatever he does really doesn't matter because he has no control of the outcome. But a resilient teen knows that he has control. By his choices and actions, he determines the results. He knows that he can make a difference, which further promotes his competence and confidence.

Some questions about control include

- Do I help my children understand that life's events are not purely random, that most things happen as a direct result of someone's actions and choices?

- On the other hand, do I help them understand that they aren't responsible for many of the bad circumstances in their lives (such as parents' separation or divorce)?

- Do I help them think about the future, but take it one step at a time?

- Do I help them recognize even their small successes so they can experience the knowledge that they can succeed?

- Do I help them understand that no one can control all circumstances, but everyone can shift the odds by choosing positive or protective behaviors?

As you think about the building blocks of resilience for your own children, do not be surprised when you notice that they are already strong in one of these categories and that you may need to focus your energies on supporting them in another area or two.

CHAPTER TWELVE

Building Competence

You may wonder, "Why bring competence into this discussion?" Your teenager is probably quite competent. She gets good grades, studies hard, and seems mature for her age. She can drive, take care of herself, spend her allowance wisely, perhaps hold a part-time job, buy her own clothes, do her own laundry, and fix dinner if you're going to be late from work. She's almost an adult.

Yes, most kids are undoubtedly competent by the time they reach mid-adolescence. Most parents and teachers have been encouraging independence and self-reliance for years. But we can't take competence for granted as children prepare to apply for college and leave home because this is a time when their competence is most needed and most challenged.

Competence builds throughout childhood. The more kids master life experiences, the more they realize, "I handled that; now I can handle this," and they develop genuine confidence in themselves. With a strong sense of competence comes tenacity, an ability to stick with tough tasks like handling a heavy load of schoolwork while managing other activities. Competence derives from a wide range of achievements—from small steps to major leaps. A teenager experiences competence when he reads the assigned books, takes good notes, constructs a logical outline, and writes a coherent paper. The A-he earns is only a letter, but the sense of plugging through a rigorous assignment represents his real competence. Teens enjoy a rich, satisfying competence in many ways. For example, when they are able to stand for their convictions and choose not to cheat on a test, shoplift, or try drugs when their friends are doing so.

As competent as we believe our children already are, what more can parents do to support their competence at this point in their lives? The answers lie in 4 basic areas.

- We can get out of their way—stay behind Dean Jones' sideline.

- We can encourage and praise them effectively, but criticize and lecture less.

- We can make sure they have more downtime, more free time to decompress, relax, daydream, and explore their real interests.

- We can help them to think clearly, to decatastrophize and stop thinking in a self-destructive manner.

Let's consider each area.

Getting Out of the Way

When children are very young, it's normal to protect them from falling down, warn them of impending danger, and praise them abundantly. Involvement is good—certainly better than ignoring them. Yet while involved parents are more likely to produce motivated kids, we have to find some balance, especially during adolescence. Overly involved parents can unintentionally get in the way of their children's acquiring confidence and drive to achieve new competencies. If we push them too hard to master the next step, we may push them into feeling incompetent.

Getting out of the way is a tough challenge, isn't it? We naturally want to help ("Do you want me to read your report before your turn it in? Maybe if you read 2 extra books, you'd get bonus points on your history project."). We want to fix ("I noticed you spelled that wrong. Those algebra problems aren't correct."). We want to guide our kids ("I think you should look at Ivy Wall U and apply to 5 other colleges, just in case you don't get in there.").

If we hover over them as they do their homework, if we constantly harp about taking the "right" courses to get into a competitive college, if we hound them to participate in impressive extracurricular activities so they'll stand out in the applicant pool, we aren't allowing them to use their own strengths. We undercut their growing sense of competence and therefore actually inhibit their natural resilience.

If we solve all their problems for them, they will remain dependent on us. We have to remind ourselves often that our job as parents is to create capable individuals. To do so, we must let them figure things out for themselves. If we get out of their way or offer only gentle guidance when necessary, we foster their growing sense of self-reliance and independence. If we let them handle things, we are communicating a powerful belief, "I think you are competent. I think you are wise." When we allow them to finish their projects without our intervention, we are saying, "I think you are clever and innovative." And when we let them select colleges to visit and apply to, we're telling them, "I think you have good judgment."

Why do so many parents have difficulty trusting in their children's competence to face challenges? It's the "parent alarm"—our instinctual rapid response to steer children away from potential trouble. The parent alarm is beneficial, of course, when a situation involves danger. When your child was 3 years old and reached toward a pot of boiling water, you yelled "No!" and pulled him away from the stove. If a teenager is drunk and getting in a car, you step in to prevent tragedy at all costs. These are lessons that we cannot afford to let children learn on their own. But the parent alarm can be counterproductive when it prevents young people from learning valuable lessons on their own.

When parents jump in with solutions, their intervention also can stifle conversation: "Mom, I haven't finished my essay for State U yet." "What! You'd better get moving. I'll help you write it. Give me what you have so far." This is a lost opportunity to learn what the teenager wanted to say. Maybe he wanted to talk about how overwhelmed or nervous he's feeling. Perhaps he wanted to talk about why he doesn't think State U is the right match for him. Either way, he will walk away unheard, swallow his emotion, and resent his parent's over-involvement. He will also, of course, hear that he is incapable.

Less Lecturing and Criticizing, More Listening

Many parents believe that they know exactly how to get children to figure out what's wrong or to make a wiser choice. They tell them. They lecture about every possible dire consequence of the "wrong" choice or action. Why do we jump in as soon as our parent alarm rings and try to fix their problems or correct their mistakes?

We worry that they will not be successful. We think that they aren't trying their hardest. We think that they'll embarrass us or reflect poorly on us. We see them as reflections of ourselves; they become the "product" we have produced, and we want our work to seem perfect. We're uncomfortable when we make mistakes and assume our children share that insecurity. We wish to spare them the same discomfort. We have strong standards of right and wrong, and we don't want our children to stray too close to the boundaries of what we believe is wrong.

The problem with lecturing is simple: It doesn't work. When we launch into a lecture, young people tune out before our second sentence is complete. We can list solid reasons why they should finish their homework and get to bed by 11:00 pm ("You were up late last night talking on the phone. You'll be too tired to pay attention in class. You need to bring up your grades. Why don't you listen to me—I know what's best for you."), but all they hear is "Waaa…waaa…waaa."

We need to shorten our speeches, be direct, and get them involved by asking them to make a choice: "Do you plan to finish your homework before your favorite show or skip the program?" Short, sweet, and simple enough. The teenager hears your parameters and has a choice, which gives her control of the outcome. If she chooses to make a poor choice, say by not finishing her assignment on time, the consequence is dealing with her teacher. She owns that problem; we don't.

Lecturing doesn't work for several other reasons. As soon as their "parent alarm" goes off, many parents jump in and start lecturing. But the teen rarely has a chance to express her concern, so she feels cut off, unheard, disrespected, or even shamed. When lectured, adolescents often are made to feel stupid. No wonder they tune out or become hostile or defensive. Lecturing certainly does nothing to enhance their sense of competence.

Another significant reason to stop lecturing is that it may backfire. Teenagers try desperately to prove to parents, and more to themselves, that they control their destiny. When they think parents believe their decisions are wrong or dangerous, or that they are naïve or stupid, kids have a lot more invested in proving parents wrong. If a parent's lectures make them feel incompetent, they need to prove they are competent. Unless parents guide them to come to different conclusions by giving them some choice and control, they will go to great lengths to follow through on their original plan just to show parents that their dire predictions were wrong.

How can we break the lecture cycle? Let's look at a traditional lecture and see how ineffective it is. Michael got a D on a biology test and is in danger of failing unless he buckles down to study. He finds it easier to refuse to study and to say, "Biology is boring," than to face his fear of failing the class. His father launches into a typical lecture: "Why do you refuse to study? Are you crazy?! You think I work this hard so you can be lazy? You won't be able to get into a decent college. You'll only be able to find a menial job, live paycheck to paycheck! Then what happens? Your job gets moved overseas. You'll be on the street. You'll turn to drink. No son of mine will be a failure!"

Does Michael accept the message? Hardly. He's not studying because it's an easy way out—in the present, right now. He doesn't even follow what his father is thinking. How does not studying for tomorrow's test make him a bum later? He says to himself, "I know a lot of people my age who have jobs and own their own cars. My father is lame. I'll prove it and he'll tell me he's sorry in 10 years." Michael thinks his dad considers him foolish and incapable. He feels stupid and frustrated. He knows his father usually trusts his judgment, but has lost faith in him. He thinks his father is making a huge deal of nothing. In other words, he is thinking of everything but what his father wants him to focus on: studying biology tonight so he can bring up the D.

Instead of listing a string of abstract possibilities, we need to speak in ways that young people understand. Then—and this is critical—we listen to their response before moving to the next step. This approach builds their competence because we're asking them to go through possible consequences step by step with their own ideas rather than those we dictate. Michael's father, for example, might have focused on Michael's past successes in biology, or asked him what's on his mind ("Is tonight's assignment harder than usual? Could a classmate go over his notes and study with you? Do you have too much to do in your other subjects this week?"). By asking helpful, leading questions instead of launching into an obtuse doomsday lecture, his father could have guided Michael toward discovering his own solution.

The Downside of Criticism

Lecturing and criticism frequently go hand in hand. Both focus on what kids do "wrong" or on their shortcomings, so we tend to overlook their strengths and abilities. Instead of noticing, appreciating, and praising their assets, we pay more attention to their faults because we want to "improve" them. We usually criticize them with good intentions. After all, we have the mature wisdom they lack. But pointing out what's wrong usually puts them on the defensive. Instead of thinking objectively about what we've said, they want to defend themselves. Criticism also shames them, which can breed anger and resentment. Criticism can make adolescents feel inept—just the opposite of competent.

But we must not be reluctant to point out how they could do better. If criticism is offered in a constructive manner that doesn't denigrate a child in a personal way, it can be helpful. Two basic points: The most important guideline is that criticism must be specific. And when we want to help adolescents get past a shortcoming, it's more effective if our constructive criticism also recognizes their strengths. Specific criticism points out errors that a teen should avoid in the future. But no matter how angry or upset you are, be careful to target the specific behavior and avoid making generalizations about your child. Two examples:

When a teenager ignores her mother's plea to help with housework, it's appropriate to say, "I really need your help now. I feel you're acting selfishly— as if going out with your friends matters more than my being able to relax after working a 10-hour day." It's not appropriate to say, "You are a thought-less, selfish girl." If she fails to make the tennis team, it's OK to point out, "You only started playing tennis last summer. Maybe if you practice and take more lessons, you will make the team next year." But it's demeaning to say, "Well, I'm not surprised. You never practice." Such a comment will hardly motivate or encourage her.

When we need to point out children's errors or shortcomings, it's far more effective to build from their strengths. This is particularly true when they are stuck and don't know how to accomplish or finish a task. Point out what they've done well in the past, ask what they've learned from that experience, and invite their suggestions about how they might use past experience to handle the current problem.

If we want to help teenagers build competence, we have to help them develop their own strengths. We need to capitalize on real experiences in which they have learned appropriate skills and allow them to practice those skills and apply them to new settings. And when they fall into difficulties, we can help them draw on those experiences as opportunities to learn to avoid or prevent similar difficulties in the future. When we're about to open our mouths and utter a critical comment, we should stop and ask ourselves, "How can I use this experience to help my child learn from this mistake without destroying his confidence or instilling shame?"

Our criticism needn't be blatant or intentional to be harmful. Children sometimes simply don't understand where our criticism is directed. An example of how this misunderstanding occurs: Mr Smith was congratulating his neighbor, whose daughter was just accepted at University of Michigan: "I'm not surprised Beth got in. Her grades were terrific and she had so many honors and activities. You really raised a superstar." When Mr Smith's daughter overheard him, she thought her father must think she could never be a superstar because her grades weren't as good and she didn't have the arm-long list of activities that Beth had. Mr Smith never meant to be critical of his daughter, but we have to be aware that children are super-sensitive to comparison with others and may interpret comparison as criticism of themselves.

Not all criticism is verbalized either. Sometimes a parent's actions can be critical without saying anything. Calling a college admissions office to make an appointment or ask for a view book and application without consulting your child is one example. It's critical of your child because it implies that you don't think he is capable of making the request himself. Calling high school teachers or the guidance office to discuss applications is a similar kind of nonverbal, indirect criticism. It's fine to remind your teenager to make these calls, but don't do it yourself.

Now that we've discussed lecturing and criticizing, let's look at some positive things that parents can do to enhance an adolescent's competence.

Noticing and Praising

When our children were very small, we probably ooohed and ahhhed at their accomplishments much more often than we do now that they're teenagers. We praised our son for being a "big boy" when he climbed into the dentist's chair and lauded our daughter for being "such a good girl" when she put her toys away neatly. Somewhere along the line, we fell out of that habit.

As busy as we are, we shouldn't become too distracted to notice or take our teenagers' achievements for granted. If we have the attitude, "Isn't that what you are supposed to do, after all?" we will miss opportunities to reinforce their competence. Without the gooey praise we used when they were toddlers, we can help our teenagers recognize their own competence in reaching various achievements.

We usually do praise them for something outstanding, like winning a chess trophy or scoring the winning goal. But if we want to reinforce their competence in many areas, we need to pay attention and point out the minor, routine accomplishments as well. For example: "That was a difficult assignment. I struggled with the *Iliad* in college, and you've read it in 10th grade. You really stuck with it. You can be proud of yourself." Or, "I heard your friends trying to talk you into signing up for the track team. I think you made a smart decision not to because you have enough other stuff on your plate. That's using your head."

A few brief words about praise: Don't lather it on too thickly. If we hype ordinary accomplishments to sound like Olympic gold medals, kids see right through it and don't believe us. Or when they do something extraordinary, it won't stand out because all our praise has come to sound the same. The most effective kind of praise is specific. For example, "You used a lot of contrast in that painting, and the line is sharp." is more authentic than saying "You're a great artist." The first comment shows that we're really looking at the work and appreciating it. The second comment sounds vague and canned. On the other hand, no praise or attention at all takes the luster out of achievement and stifles motivation. Remember, the point of praise is to encourage kids and strengthen their competence. We don't want to overuse praise in ways that may make them strive for perfection. Think of praise as a seasoning that you use in small amounts and at appropriate times to bring out the flavor—and in this analogy the flavor is your child's innate competence.

The Value of Truly Listening

Listening to children attentively is more important than any words parents can say. This is true in routine situations as well as times of crisis. Young people often say, "My parents never listen to me." More than anything else, kids want parents to listen to them and respect them. They crave our attention, even though they don't tell us openly. The best way to show them we're paying attention is to listen closely and with empathy. Some parents say they just don't know what to say to their kids. They worry that they'll give the wrong advice or say something that will backfire. My response is always the same: "Don't worry, just listen. If you can be a sounding board, you will help her figure things out."

We may think we're listening to our children when we are only hearing their chatter. Hearing the noise and listening to the meaning in their words are entirely different. Just listen. Let them finish speaking. Give yourself the gift of losing the fantasy that you're supposed to have all the answers. It's a myth that good parents always have ready solutions. If you believe that myth, you'll never feel adequate as a parent because no one has all the answers. But if you listen well, your children will always have someone on their side to help them unload their worries and develop their own solutions.

If you want to become a better listener, remember to turn off the parent alarm. You don't have to jump in with a solution before your child finishes a sentence. Don't do what this mother did as soon as her son uttered 6 words: "Mom, Brian was caught cheating in…" "I told you that kid was a bad influence. I never liked him. I don't want you hanging around with him. You should switch out of his study group." This is a lost opportunity to talk about honesty, the value of hard work, and the satisfaction of accomplishing something yourself. Perhaps it's even a lost opportunity for her son to say that he considered cheating and feels bad about it. She'll never know.

Most adults find silence awkward, so when children are groping for the right words, struggling to tell us something, or simply thinking about what to say next, we tend to fill those silent gaps with our own words of wisdom. It's better to allow some silence and give them time to put their thoughts into words. But if they seem to be struggling, you can use some brief prompts like, "Hmmm…this must be difficult."

Most parents are uncomfortable when children make mistakes. Instead of letting them think things through, we wish to correct or redirect their ideas before they get out of hand. So we start talking, telling them how to prevent or correct mistakes instead of listening to them as they try to figure out their own solutions.

How Do We Know When They Want to Talk?

If only kids held office hours. How about Wednesday night from 8:00 to 9:00? If only they would start conversations with, "I'd like to talk. Do you have some time?" Adolescents are rarely direct when they want to talk to parents. They don't arrive with a well-organized agenda of concerns. Instead, they approach us in many different ways, often depending on their mood at the moment. Sometimes they come to us in silence, perhaps with a furrowed brow that says they're upset. At other times they feign indifference, casually signaling something with that "What, me care?" look to see if it sparks our interest. Or they may open with the classic "I have a friend who…" story so they can seek advice without making a confession.

There's also the one-step-at-a-time approach: They reveal a tiny piece of the story, not just to whet our appetites but also to test us and see how we'll react. If we leap in, judge, criticize, condemn, or give "lame advice," we fail the test. Then, of course, there's the bombshell: "Take this, Mom, Dad, what are you going to do with it?" If we jump in with harsh criticism or a lecture, we have lost an opportunity to understand what the bombshell meant, and again we fail the test.

Rage is the most difficult approach of all, and common in adolescence: red-hot anger that blames parents for problems. Why us? Because we are the only safe people to blame, the only ones who will receive their rage and still love them. Let them let it out. Tell them if they have been inappropriate, but stay calm, don't punish. Say something like, "Wow, you really needed to get that off your chest. I'm here to listen."

If your parent antennae are tuned to the wide range of their clues, you will have taken a giant step toward becoming an effective listener. The next step is availability. The timing of their needs usually doesn't meet our schedules. Flexibility is key here. No matter what you planned, listening becomes the most important thing you can do. Of course, children have to respect your schedule. You don't need to allow them to interrupt your phone calls, for example. It's not always possible to be flexible at every moment. When your sensors are raised, but the world gets in the way, explain to them that you know they need your time and attention. Then tell them precisely when you can give it to them. If you know they have something on their minds that you've put off discussing, then call them after school, before you get home, to let them know you're thinking of them.

Busy parents often talk of making quality time for their children. Only a few moments, when parents are truly present and undistracted, can be most meaningful whether a child is 5 or 15. But *quantity* of time does matter. Yes, families are stretched for time to fulfill their obligations, but parents need to make as much time as possible available for children. To some extent, the quality of our time with them is influenced by the quantity of that time. We don't have to quit our day jobs, but there will be more opportunities to listen if we spend more time with our children. We won't always be there for the crises, the triumphs, or the heart-to-heart moments. But the more time we can find to be with them, the more likely we will be available to listen during a significant moment. And the more we schedule them for "enrichment" activities, or the more their time is taken up with extracurricular activities, the less time we have with them.

Keep the Ball Rolling: Encouraging Them to Talk

The key to getting an adolescent to open up is to say very little. Just try to be a sounding board. Utter only short phrases to reassure and prompt more conversation. This is particularly important at the beginning of a conversation because we want kids to reach a point where they're comfortable enough to express whatever is on their minds. To reach this point, they must know that we are present, paying attention, and have only their agenda in mind.

Remember the power of silence. Saying nothing, while being in the present moment, sends a loud message that you are accepting of the person talking. This doesn't mean that you approve of everything he says; it means only that you are glad he's saying it. As your child warms up and gets comfortable talking about an uncomfortable subject, listen attentively and silently. But when you feel you will burst if you don't say something, just nod and say, "hmmm" and "I see." These brief statements let your child know you are eager to hear more. Other examples include: "Tell me more." "Keep talking, I'm really interested." "It sounds like you have a lot on your mind, so I'm glad you're talking." "It means a lot to me that you feel comfortable talking to me." "You are doing a great job of describing what happened." "Could you just repeat that? I want to be sure I understand what you're going through."

You'll know when your teen has unloaded. She finishes what she wants to say and feels an emotional release. The pace of her conversation may slow. Her body language may soften. She may even blow you out of the water with, "What do you think?" When that happens, be certain you are completely clear that you have gotten the story straight. If you aren't quite sure, you might say, "This is what I heard.... Did I understand you correctly?" Or check her emotions: "It seems that you are feeling.... Is that right?" When 12 people hear the same story or witness the same event, the result is often 13 different interpretations. It is important that we understand our child's interpretation because that is what matters here. She will greatly appreciate that you want to understand her correctly and that you've listened so carefully that you can recount her story.

Sometimes there may be absolutely nothing more parents can do but be fully present to listen without giving advice. At other times, though, teenagers may seek guidance without outwardly asking for it. When you think this may be the case but you're unsure, the best way to proceed is to ask this simple question, "How can I be most helpful to you?" Or you can take a first step by starting with "Hmmmm…How are you thinking of handling this?"

Occasionally teenagers will ask for your advice directly. When that happens, go ahead and give it, but always try to avoid lecturing and critical judgment. Break your wisdom into separate digestible servings. If you offer 10 brilliant pieces of advice in one broad swoop, you may overwhelm or confuse your child, and he'll miss much of what you are saying. This is especially true of children younger than 13 or 14. But even for older adolescents or adults, it's difficult to absorb too much information at once during a stressful time.

Parents can master all these effective listening skills and still blow it if their body language projects a different attitude. A frown, rigid posture, furrowed brow, and clenched teeth don't indicate an open, accepting willingness to listen without judging. Defensive postures (tightly crossed legs, folded arms, finger tapping on the table, or leg shaking) say you are uncomfortable, anxious, bored, or annoyed. When young people talk about a worrisome situation, it is difficult to listen without tensing up. You're concentrating on their words, not on your own body language. But try to avoid off-putting body language because it can stop a conversation cold. An adolescent who feels that a parent is angry or upset will clam up. Some other basic points to keep in mind:

- If you are saying you have time to listen, show it. Sit down. Eliminate distractions. Turn off the television and cell phone. Just be there.

- When you feel yourself becoming angry or overly worried, take deep soothing breaths to turn off those surges of adrenaline that make you turn red, perspire, or make your legs tremble with anxiety. This will fool your body into thinking you are relaxed. It will help you think more clearly and prevent outbursts that could stop the conversation.

- Remember that just because your teenager rolls her eyes when you show her warmth in public, hugs are still healing in private.

Nothing is more important to becoming an effective parent than making adolescents know they are truly heard. This doesn't mean we have to agree with everything or condone certain behaviors, but before we can impart any useful guidance, we have to send the clear signal that we're really listening to the words and the emotions beneath those words. If young people feel that they cannot trust us to listen and accept them, they are likely to shut down, tell us nothing, or lie to defend themselves or get us off their backs. Whether they come to us with serious troubles or trivial everyday matters, we can create a safe zone by listening patiently and nonjudgmentally, without interrogating them or interrupting with a solution or advice.

CHAPTER THIRTEEN

The Value of Free Time

Free time is a rarity for too many young people today. Despite the well-known developmental benefits of unstructured play, childhood is packed with "enrichment" activities for every moment when kids aren't in school or asleep. Like little CEOs with day planners, youngsters slot their waking hours into tight segments for after-school, weekend, and summer programs: soccer, drama, community service, homework, music lessons, tutoring, ballet, home-work, hockey, gymnastics, and more homework. For many, this pattern starts when they're toddlers and continues through the teen years. It's not surprising that they aren't getting adequate sleep to rejuvenate. Even during 2-week school vacations, younger kids are signed up for something to keep them occupied and older ones are piling up extracurricular activities for their college applications.

Many are so highly scheduled that they have no time to think, daydream and, heaven forbid, do absolutely nothing. "Time to reflect" isn't penciled into their calendars. Downtime is important to healthy development, but many families see it as wasted time. Although many young people are thriving, some are reacting with anxiety and other signs of increased stress. Free time offers benefits that may be protective against the harmful effects of stress. As long as people continually rush from activity to activity, their bodies do not have the time to experience relaxation. This has serious health implications because it is essential to good health that children and adults take time for themselves to return their bodies to a relaxed state at least once every day. (The stress-management plan for teenagers in Part Four offers many options to de-stress, including instant vacations, reading, warm baths, yoga, and meditation.)

Free time also gives young people the critical opportunity to discover their own competencies, interests, and talents because they can move at their own pace and reflect. Ultimately, they will engage fully in the passions they wish to pursue. When they pursue something with passion, they can experience flow, the phenomenon of losing oneself in a pleasurable, rewarding experience, described in Chapter 9.

Free time has other unheralded benefits, whether it is filled with relaxing activities, time for reflection, or even sleep. More adolescents, even middle school students, are consuming caffeinated drinks because they just aren't getting enough sleep and need to stay charged to keep up with their hectic schedules. We know that new knowledge does not get consolidated—stored permanently in our memory—without adequate sleep. Even with sleep, a hectic lifestyle may prevent kids from benefiting fully from their experiences and education because they lack the downtime for reflection and appreciation. Think about those days that move so quickly you don't have time to eat or go to the bathroom, let alone think. How much of the data thrown at you become your own? How many of the nuances of daily living are you able to absorb?

How will adolescents' appreciation of downtime translate into how they manage their time in adulthood? In adolescence, downtime is used to think, reflect, or just "veg" or "chill," often with their friends. We all know adult workaholics who never leave a moment to themselves; they allow no time in their lives for reflection and rejuvenation. Many of them have shortened professional longevity because they burn out. What about their home lives? The adult equivalent of hanging out with friends is the high-quality, low-intensity time we spend with spouses and children. It is the glue that holds families together. We must not raise children who are unprepared to prioritize this unscheduled but critical time.

To drive home this point, think of the multitasking that many adults do to navigate hectic lives. People who are most able to maintain healthy home lives learn not to multitask—some of the time, at least. When spouses have something important to say, they don't pay the bills while listening. When a child shows them a piece of artwork she proudly designed, they treat that moment as privileged—so they don't make phone calls, plunge toilets, or finish their work for a few minutes.

Yet we are raising a new generation of multitaskers who are listening to music, surfing the Internet, doing homework, and chatting with friends simultaneously. They are so into multitasking that many of them feel lazy or guilty for just taking a moment to appreciate the beauty around them or a half hour to cherish the company of others. This generation has become this way because we've modeled it for them. Might we be hurting their future abilities to participate fully in family life or to take a moment to appreciate nature?

If we want our children to enjoy the many benefits derived from downtime, we have to make a determined effort to limit the over-scheduled, over-stretched atmosphere present in so many communities today. Unfortunately, we may feel like we're swimming upstream because we receive carefully marketed messages that "good parents" expose their children to every opportunity to excel, and ensure that their children participate in a wide variety of activities.

It is not clear whether this highly scheduled, rushed routine is offering a developmental benefit or producing young adults who are genuinely better prepared for the future, but it is clear that this fast-paced, jam-packed lifestyle has serious repercussions. It has fed on itself and produced a new set of expectations. No sooner do college admissions committees produce more spaces to fit all of those activities on the application forms, than parents and guidance counselors push kids to fill those spaces. ("Blank spaces are bad!") Now normal kids—those with an intense interest and maybe a couple of other lesser interests—suddenly look boring or underachieving. Kids who go to school all day and hold a part-time job seem lazy compared to the kids who can fill up all of the lines. The cycle is endless and dangerous. We must stand up to it.

Many parents see the damage that this pressure is creating and want to protect children from it, but they fear slowing their pace in case it allows their kids to fall behind. We need to take a deep breath and help young people find an appropriate balance between preparing for the future and living fully in the present. That balance will be different for each child, based on individual academic needs, temperament, environment, and family situation.

Because there is so much pressure to prepare kids for the future, it is important to talk with guidance counselors and teachers about turning down the pressure, trimming some activities from children's schedules, and allowing them more time to exist in an unstructured, relaxed way. We urge you to talk with other parents in your community so you can reassure yourself that you are not alone.

Young people aren't the only victims of over-scheduling and today's hurried lifestyle. Our families are suffering as well. Parents who are burdened by work and household responsibilities find themselves sacrificing their own downtime because they need to arrange activities and drive children from appointment to appointment. They feel pressure to meet every single need they perceive (or are told) their children require to excel, which makes them feel inadequate, anxious, and guilty when they cannot meet each demand ("I'm such an awful parent because I can't drive Savannah to practice tonight."). Ultimately these parents have less personal satisfaction in parenting.

Most importantly, they lose opportunities for some of the highest quality time with their children. Some of the best interactions occur during downtime—just talking, preparing meals together, working on a hobby or art project, or hiking or playing sports together. To the extent that over-scheduling interferes with that high-quality, low-intensity essential parent-child time, it has far-reaching implications.

We recognize that parents are reading this book at different times in their children's development. If your adolescent is a high school senior, we know it will be challenging to change your lifestyle significantly at this point. But if your teenager is over-scheduled, don't give up. It is still important, perhaps more important than ever, to suggest they carve out free, unstructured time. It can have short-term benefits to help a junior or senior get through a grueling year, but it will also help set your teen in the right direction for college life and adulthood.

For readers with younger adolescents, we implore you to help them achieve balance in their lives starting today. Let them be exposed to a variety of activities, but allow them to find a personal interest rather than craft a resumé designed to impress someone else. We believe that if they follow the stress-management plan in Part Four, they will learn to maintain balance and thrive, and will coincidentally produce a resumé that will be impressive to colleges.

For readers who have even younger children, a gentle warning: A hurried lifestyle often begins in infancy with all the enrichment activities that marketers tell parents they must have to get their kids off to the best start in life. We remind you that free, child-driven play remains the tried and true way to help children learn and develop and forge strong connections to you. One of the best ways to do

B. Smaller

this with young children is to play along side them without directing the activity. Just ask them what you can do, what role they want you to play; don't take over and instruct or orchestrate. (This is also good practice for parents to learn to stay behind the white line when their children play sports, as well as later when they start applying to college.)

We aren't suggesting that busy parents must spend hours playing alongside young children, of course. Give them plenty of free time to play by themselves too, without any adults directing them. Unstructured play (child-only, adults stay away, thank you) allows youngsters to use their creativity while developing imagination, dexterity, and physical and emotional strength. Spontaneous, creative play is a terrific opportunity for children to become more competent on their own and thus more confident. Studies have shown that when adults drive or direct their play, children acquiesce to adult roles and lose much of the benefit of play—creativity, learning, negotiation, and a sense of control.

If we regulate children's time and activities to the exclusion of free, leisurely play, we deny them the opportunity to figure out what they're good at and what they enjoy doing. Unstructured play allows them to learn how to work in groups—to share, negotiate, and learn to advocate for themselves. In contrast to passive entertainment (like watching television), play builds active, healthy bodies. Above all, play is a simple joy that is a cherished part of childhood.

CHAPTER FOURTEEN

Changing Thinking Patterns

From their earliest years, children develop patterns of thinking about and interpreting events. Even the most insightful teenagers are not usually aware of those patterns. Consider how your son or daughter thinks about experiences, particularly uncomfortable or negative ones. Does he tend to blame others for problems? Does he understand his role in determining outcomes? Does he blow things out of proportion by seeing minor setbacks as major defeats? Does he tend to think of himself as a victim?

Every child has his own lens through which he sees the world, depending on individual temperament and life experience. Even within the same family, siblings can share an identical experience but interpret it in totally opposite ways. The patterns adolescents use to interpret events are important to understand because they strongly affect each child's competence and resilience.

How is this relevant to the college admissions process? As teenagers grapple with all the demands in their lives, they can become more resilient if they think in positive patterns that don't undermine their confidence or hold them back from exploring the present and future. If they don't find healthy ways to think about their problems, they can easily become overwhelmed with pessimism, anxiety, and even depression. If we show young people how to use their thought process to address issues realistically and resolve them wisely, we can help them enhance their growing sense of competence and increasing resilience.

A Little Background

Some of the best studies of thinking patterns began with the Penn Resilience Project headed by Martin E. P. Seligman, PhD, of the University of Pennsylvania. He studied what makes people resilient in the face of difficulties and mentored several experts in resilience research, including Karen Reivich, PhD. Working with hundreds of children and families, they demonstrated that people can become more resilient, more optimistic, and better able to cope with life by changing the way they think about problems. They don't have to remain stuck with their first impulsive, negative thoughts when they become frustrated, disappointed, anxious, or sad. They don't have to be self-defeating thinkers. Instead, they can use their cognitive ability to rethink the situation, decatastrophize it, and find workable solutions. Instead of feeling defeated or depressed, they can find a path that leads to optimism and greater resilience. They can reduce their stress levels and become more effective problem-solvers. Ultimately they grow more confident about facing the next obstacle. If you believe that your child's way of thinking is negative or creates unnecessary anxiety or sadness, you may want to read *The Optimistic Child: A Proven Program to Safeguard Children Against Depression and Build Lifelong Resilience* (Seligman MEP, Reivich K, Jaycox L, Gillham J. New York, NY: Houghton Mifflin Co.; 1995) and/or *The Resilience Factor: 7 Essential Skills for Overcoming Life's Inevitable Obstacles* (Reivich K, Shatté A. New York, NY: Broadway Books; 2002).

We learn several relevant points from the work of Seligman et al: Young people come up with their own explanations of why they succeed or fail. This is called their "explanatory style." In response to a problem or setback, they ask why and a story unfolds that makes a difference in how they respond to failure. They may generalize it and become paralyzed from further action, or they may use it as a springboard to try again or find a new solution. Part of their answer to why lies in who's to blame. Is it the teen's "fault" or was it someone else's? People who always blame themselves for problems tend to see themselves in a negative light.

Another part of the answer lies in how long it will last. If they believe their problems are going to last forever and are outside their control, they are more likely to give up. Adolescents then explain how much this failure has affected them—is it a small bump in the road or a catastrophe? Kids who catastrophize are much more likely to become anxious and feel incapable of coping with the situation. If they judge a lost homework paper as a catastrophe and spin into an end-of-the-world-I'll-flunk disaster, they're unlikely to find a calm solution, take control, and call a classmate to ask for the assignment so they can do it over. Or if they see a missed application deadline as a slammed door on their entire future, they're unlikely to look for another open door.

Parents, teachers, counselors, and coaches can help adolescents correctly assess their successes and failures. The first step is an accurate rather than a catastrophic story line. What's really happening? Resilient people can realistically distinguish when they have control over a situation and when they do not. They gather their resources for situations in which they do have control and conserve their resources when they do not. They can assess when something will pass easily and quickly; they're able to talk themselves down when they start to magnify events in their story lines to catastrophic proportions.

We can teach young people to rein in and rethink the impulsive thoughts that fly through their minds and influence their responses. Four steps that can help them take control are

- Learn to recognize negative thoughts. Seligman and colleagues call this "thought catching."

- Evaluate these thoughts for accuracy. ("Is that the only college in the world?")

- Develop more accurate explanations, or story lines, when bad things happen. ("I have an acceptance from one college and haven't heard from 3, so I'll be able to go somewhere, even if it's not my first choice.")

- Decatastrophize to let go of harmful, anxious thoughts that the event at hand will inevitably lead to disaster. ("OK, so maybe it's not the end of the universe if Stanford turns me down. Steven Spielberg wasn't accepted at 2 of the best film schools in the country, and he's no loser." Spielberg attended Cal State Long Beach, dropped out 2 years' short of graduation because he was offered a movie contract at age 21, and went back and earned his degree 30 years later.)

Seligman and Reivich draw on a cognitive technique originated by Albert Ellis, a leader in cognitive behavioral theory, called the ABC technique. The A refers to the problem or adversity itself; C, the consequences that flow from the adversity; and B, the connector. B is critical because it represents beliefs about the adversity, determines how someone reacts to that adversity, and therefore produces the consequences.

Cognitive behavioral therapy works primarily by identifying inaccurate beliefs. In most conversations with young people, we focus on the A ("What happened?") and jump to the C ("How do you feel now?" or "What are you going to do?") while ignoring the B connectors—their beliefs and interpretations. Instead, we can help our children hear that silent voice in their heads (sometimes called self-talk) that explains their beliefs, forms their interpretations of events, and guides what will happen next. We can help them get in touch with their beliefs by talking about the connections.

A good time to help them listen to and catch their self-talk is when you notice a sudden shift in their mood. This may be a clue that they have experienced something stressful and that their beliefs about it are in process. At this time, you could simply ask, "What are you thinking about?" Whether we're trying to help teens hear their self-talk or we're listening to our own, consider these points:

- Identify the adversities that consistently push your buttons, and notice which negative emotions and behaviors they trigger.

- Watch your patterns of reacting. Do you usually blame things on yourself or others? Do you tend to see problems or their causes as permanent or temporary? When you observe your reaction patterns, you'll probably notice a theme. Perhaps you fall into certain traps ("Why do I always do that? I'm so dumb. It always happens to me.") or ways of instinctively reacting in negative ways.

- Once you recognize habitual reactions, you can begin to pull them apart and think of alternatives. If you always magnify the probable outcomes of a situation and expect a disaster, you can begin to train yourself to look for other ways to balance that negative tendency. Rather than blame yourself as usual, you might ask yourself, "What did I do well in that situation? What good things came out of it? How much of the difficulty was caused by me or by someone or something else?" You may not have all the answers or solutions, but you can begin to break your pattern and stop reacting reflexively.

If we help kids think differently, they will be able to break self-defeating thought patterns and negative emotional reactions. This can go a long way in preventing anxiety, depression, and other harmful consequences. If you sense that you need a supportive step-by-step approach to help your child do this, I suggest that you speak to your pediatrician about a referral to a cognitive behavioral therapist.

■ ❖ ■ ❖ ■ ❖ ■ ❖ ■

Remember that the brain controls the body's stress reactions and the brain is deeply affected by emotions. Adolescents who catastrophize or paint gloomy scenarios will turn on their stress hormones, and their bodies will prepare for a life-saving run. This is not motivating; it's immobilizing. No one can fill out college applications or write a polished, authentic essay while preparing to sprint from a crisis. A little heightened anxiety—caused by knowing something is important—is energizing. But if students believe that the words they write on a paper or the ovals they fill in on an SAT will be life-altering, they will perform below their potential. Parents need to support their adolescents—enough to mobilize them—in understanding that tests and essays matter but are not life-determining factors.

CHAPTER FIFTEEN

Strengthening Confidence

By the time kids reach high school, parents hope they have developed a fair
share of self-confidence. But even the most confident adolescents are challenged by social pressures from peers, demanding academic work and, of
course, the big scary question mark—the future: Where will I go to college?
Will I make new friends? What about leaving my high school friends? What
will I do with my life? The combination of those present pressures and
unknown futures are enough to rattle anyone's confidence. So it's critical
for parents to be aware of these assaults on adolescents' confidence and
bolster it without taking over or clipping the wings of independence.

Let's consider the nature of confidence. People can't have genuine confidence without experiencing their own competence. They develop confidence
over time by facing and managing challenges. They know in their bones
"I can do this" because they've done something similar previously.

Adolescents need confidence to take the risks necessary to grow up and
become independent young adults. Authentic confidence, which they earn
by demonstrating competence, assures them that they have some power over
their environment. They are more likely to persevere and have an optimistic
outlook instead of feeling passive or powerless. Confidence earned during
childhood and adolescence will be a springboard toward success in adult
life. Genuine confidence isn't the same thing as the overused, feel-good term
self-esteem. For years, a self-esteem "movement" has urged parents and
teachers to build a child's self-esteem as if this quality can be bestowed by
piling brick upon brick. That external approach presumes that adults can
give self-esteem to children by telling them 3 times a day that they're terrific,
or beautiful, or brilliant. Children should have a high degree of self-esteem,

but to be deep-seated, authentic, and permanent, it must be grounded in their own competence.

Another problem lies in the way self-esteem is often reinforced. When parents are so concerned that children "feel good," they often emphasize kids' moods over their experience. But that attitude implies that feeling bad is a disaster, which can be a setup for problems later because every sad, uncomfortable, or anxious feeling can take on a disastrous meaning: "I'm supposed to feel happy, so what's wrong with me because I don't feel happy?"

Rather than trying to cheer up a child every time she experiences failure or disappointment, we should focus on resilience. We all have failures and shortcomings. Resilient people learn a bit from each one. They learn how to do better the next time. They are persistent. They use those bad feelings to motivate themselves a little more. So when a teenager doesn't make the team, gets a C+ on a test, falls 100 points short of the SAT score she expected, or doesn't get into her first-choice college, wise supportive parents will listen and acknowledge "how bad you must feel." They won't denigrate or deny her emotions with "It's nothing. You worry too much." But they will help her focus instead on her strengths and how she can build on those strengths for the next challenge.

Emotions like sadness and dismay are beneficial when based on an authentic event. They exist for a reason. If we paint over those emotions with a feel-better approach, we do not support resilience. We want children to feel good as a result of what they have done, not to believe naively that they will do good things because they feel good about themselves. Real confidence, not self-esteem or "confidence lite," fosters resilience because it results from demonstrated competence. A young person knows he has mastered a task, so he believes in his ability and is truly confident. We adults can nurture kids' confidence by recognizing their assets and helping them use those strengths to overcome difficulty and bounce back.

Catch Them Being Good

Adults do this all the time with very young children. We make a big deal of every developmental milestone and minor accomplishment: "Oooooh, you ate all your cereal. You're such a big girl to get dressed all by yourself!" Fast-forward to the teenage years: "Why can't you ever pick up your things? Why do I have to remind you every morning not to forget your homework? Are you EVER going to finish your chores?"

What has happened in the intervening few years? We stopped being thrilled by their good behaviors and achievements. Why do we become so concerned and focused on what's wrong with them? We should still try to catch them being good by noticing their efforts, perseverance, and unprompted acts of kindness and by offering a few words of appreciation and praise. It's just as important to older children as it was when they were toddlers. They still crave our attention and approval, despite their occasional efforts to deny this.

During the tumultuous teen years, we parents need to remind ourselves to give kids our attention; offer genuine, specific praise (as discussed earlier); and express our appreciation not only for the little things they do but also for who they are. ("I'm glad you were honest with the guidance counselor about your real interests. You are sensible to cut back on those activities that were exhausting you. I appreciate your thoughtfulness when you help me out around the house.") Look for one or two things every day that your teenager has done that is worthy of a verbal pat on the back.

Occasionally parents get so caught up in their love for their kids that they heap enormous amounts of praise on them and tell them how perfect they are. On some level parents may do this in hopes of creating a self-fulfilling prophecy. ("If I keep telling him how wonderful he is, he will become that terrific person.") On another level, parents may do this to build a teen-ager's self-image and, they hope, self-confidence. ("You are the kindest, most generous kid in the world. You don't have a mean bone in your body. You're the perfect child I'd always dreamed of.") Well, no one is perfect, even your child. And if anyone knows your child isn't perfect, it's your child himself.

Living on a pedestal is difficult. As we saw in the discussion of perfection-ism (Chapter 8), an adolescent can become too hard on himself. If he is told he doesn't have a mean bone in his body, for example, how will he feel when he's justifiably angry with someone? It's a setup for denying emotions or for anxiety when upsetting emotions surface. Taking it a step further, a young person may decide to jump off that pedestal to show the world he isn't perfect. It can also be much harder to bounce back after a failure because perfect people aren't supposed to fail. So the next time, why take any risk at all? It's OK to tell your child something like, "You are the perfect kid for me" as long as it's combined with clear messages that no one is truly perfect and that you love every bit of him, including his imperfections.

Setting Reasonable Expectations

We know that children live up to or down to parents' expectations. As kids' competence and confidence grow, we should hold up high expectations (completing homework, giving their best effort, organizing their time) to keep them moving in the right direction. But high expectations are not the same as unrealistic expectations. Not every high school senior can get into an elite college. We cannot expect teenagers to be perfect, but we can expect them to be honest, caring, and responsible, and to try their best within reasonable limits. We can hitch our expectations not to their achievements but to their human qualities.

You may be thinking, "OK, I get it. Hold them to high expectations for their human qualities, but what about the day-to-day accomplishments—don't I have to keep holding the bar just above their reach?" I have no simple answer because it has to be individualized for your teen's temperament. Adolescents gain confidence through their successes, and that gives them the push to test whether they can master other, perhaps more challenging, tasks. But if the next task is far more difficult than they can handle, they will undoubtedly fail and probably lose confidence. They may tie that failure to your high expectations and turn their disappointment with themselves into anger toward you. When they are struggling to please you, their failure is magnified. When this is the case, they may experience shame, which can prevent them from reaching for achievements they certainly are able to master.

Our challenge as parents is to monitor their responses to achievement and failure and to have a handle on their capabilities. Some questions to consider include: Does a particular achievement seem like just a stepping stone to the next one? Are they energized by a failure to try again, or do they become paralyzed? After a success, do they like to stay on that level for a long time until they feel comfortable enough to move forward, or are they eager to proceed quickly to the next level?

When they are ready to try the next challenge, try to see where they would like the bar to be set. Support them to determine what they can handle. If you set the bar too high, they will fail you—emphasis on *you*. This has to be about them, not you. If you set it too low, they will think you haven't been watching them closely enough to know their abilities. Most importantly, react supportively when they do fail. It's essential for young people to know that adults fail and recover, and those who are successful are the ones who keep trying. Many opportunities will arise to support your kids to try again. And there are numerous opportunities for parents to model that we don't always succeed, but we make another attempt without shame and with good humor.

Smothering Confidence

One of the greatest ways to destroy confidence is by emphasizing incompetence and by shaming young people. As discussed previously, we know we undermine their sense of competence and their growing confidence if we let ourselves fall back into the old pattern of lecturing and criticizing. We don't want to disempower kids during these few years when they're preparing to leave home for college or make them feel small, inept, stupid, unheard, and shamed. But sometimes they make us so angry or worried that all we can focus on is what they are doing wrong. We want to shout repeatedly, "Stop that, you fool!" in the vain hope that they will come to their senses.

Adults often blindly assume that kids will change when they become aware of all their dangerous behaviors or human frailties. I see a lot of adults, both parents and professionals with the best intentions, point out everything young people are doing wrong as if to rattle some sense into them. Then as these adults get frustrated with kids' inability to change, they begin pointing out every character fault. I call this "mud slinging." It usually sounds something like this: "Maybe you're not ready for college because you have no motivation. You're so lazy. You're too disorganized to get your application together, so how will you handle a college load? How can I trust you if you don't tell me the truth about your grades? You're such a liar. You're really an embarrassment to us." Mud slinging creates a series of blots on young people's self-image and robs them of the confidence they could have used to rise above a challenge. They will never have the confidence to change if they feel denigrated or become hyper-aware of their faults.

A student who procrastinates about homework will not respond to "You are so lazy!" or "You can't go out with your friends until you finish your homework." She may be immobilized by anxiety or feel as if the task is insurmountable. Being called lazy only shames her and certainly doesn't convince her that she can handle the homework. Prohibiting her from going out won't help if her roadblock is anxiety. But if her problem lies with her organizational skills, a suggestion to stay home and develop a strategy for approaching her work may help. Remind her that she will have a better time when she does go out if she knows she has started on a plan to complete her work. It's also likely to be effective if she is reminded how overwhelmed she was last week when she couldn't organize her biology report. But once she got started, she felt much better because she divided the large assignment into small sections and tackled them one at a time without worrying about the others.

Building on Strengths

When adolescents are reminded that they have already done better in the past, they know they can change or improve. They have more than enough strengths and capabilities to overcome the "bad stuff" they've done. The best way to promote positive attributes and behavior is by accentuating their strengths. If we want them to get past negative behaviors, especially those they do by habit, their chances of success will be much greater if they have developed confidence. It takes confidence for anyone to change direction or alter patterns, stop harmful but comfortable habits, and move toward something more positive but less familiar.

Confidence comes from knowing that success is possible. This strength-based approach allows us to build on something. Simply being highly aware of problems and faults can lead to paralysis, but a ripple of positive energy can flow from each strength, each island of competence. When we allow that to happen, problems begin to disappear amid a sea of success. When your adolescent is having difficulty or is worried about the future, recall past experiences when she overcame a challenge or dealt with a problem effectively. Help her go back and draw on that successful experience and use it for the difficulty now facing her. This approach to challenges will carry into adulthood as she learns to recognize and build on her own strengths whenever she's faced with adversity or seemingly overwhelming tasks.

CHAPTER SIXTEEN

Connection, Character, and Contribution

When parents think about preparing young people to leave home, they are concerned about far more than whether they will be academically or professionally successful. They want to know that their children will have the kind of values and strengths to maintain healthy human relationships and contribute to society. Three components of resilience—connection, character, and contribution—are particularly important in preparing adolescents for what really matters in life. Let's look at each.

Connection

If young people are to become resilient, self-sufficient, and independent, we have to encourage them to be *inter*dependent with other people. We don't want them to believe that their newfound independence equals isolation or disconnection. We want them to desire interdependence with family, friends, and community. We don't want them to think that these relationships conflict with their growing independence.

Maintaining connections with other people is crucial for teenagers who are straddling the gap between the security of childhood and the uncertainty of adulthood. It allows them the luxury of being vulnerable at times, of letting others care for them while they reenergize. When they know that they're connected to other people who care about them, they gain a strong sense of security that is essential to resilience. Without a firm social foundation that ensures their base will remain stable no matter what, young people are reluctant to test themselves and try new ventures. And if they won't take such risks, they may remain isolated and timid. They won't move forward to develop new competencies, ongoing confidence, and the meaningful connections to other people that will lead to a joyful life.

Some young people may not understand how secure interdependence makes us because they have only weak or limited connections to others. *Weak* because families are so busy and have so little time together. *Limited* because families move frequently, which requires children to leave friends behind. Extended families are spread around the country. Many children see grandparents only a few times a year, if at all. Other adults pass in and out of their lives on an irregular basis. Many young people are increasingly isolated and disconnected. Even in their own homes, family members may pass each other like ships in the night. Each person has a separate thing to do or place to be. Teenagers often try to fill this gap by creating a "second family" from a group of friends.

In a hurried world that de-emphasizes the centrality of family, parents should maintain the importance of shared downtime. As soon as we no longer need each other's company to avert boredom or recharge, the connection to family begins to erode. The reality is that more and more children are alone in their rooms with computers, DVDs, and video-game players. Young people walk around the house with personal listening devices that allow them to avoid engaging with us at all. A record number (68%) of American youth have televisions in their bedrooms.

I strongly recommend keeping televisions out of bedrooms. Instead, have a central room where the family is entertained together. The "ban the television from the bedroom" battle may not be one you want to start waging with older adolescents because it's hard to change the rules this late in the game. But if you have younger children, it's well worth restructuring your home in ways that promote family togetherness.

In our increasingly complicated world, we recognize that youth are in some ways more connected than ever through instant messaging, chat lines, and cell phones. Most of these technologies do not support family togetherness while children are at home with us, but they do make it easier to maintain contact when we are apart. It is important, though, to prevent these electronic connections from becoming virtual leashes that keep the connections so tight that young people feel forever monitored. Will these technologies offer a wonderful new kind of support, or will they further dissolve the need for the authentic kind of human interactions that can only occur when we are together? Time will tell.

There are 2 ways to ensure that your children feel comfortable remaining interdependent with you and others, even while they march down the road to independence. First, young adults must never believe that their growing independence is being challenged. If they think that they run the risk of losing independence, they will be driven to break connections that they perceive are overly restrictive and will therefore prevent authentic autonomy. Second, young adults must believe at their core that all feelings are safe to share with you.

Parents need to recognize that their responses to a teen's emotions, particularly his unsettling emotions, are critical. When his emotions run real and deep—let's say his best friend has embarrassed or humiliated him—and parents lack empathy, ignore him, or denigrate his feelings by saying, "Oh, it'll be OK" or "It's nothing. You're making a mountain out of molehill," he may not let himself feel those emotions again. He may not trust his own feelings. At the least, he may not turn to his parents the next time he's upset. He may learn to deny his emotions or decline connecting with others to process them.

If we cause young people to disconnect from their emotions and not share them with another person, we deprive them of a profoundly important tool they'll need later to recover from difficulties. We know that people who have experienced tragic events recover best when they are deeply connected to other people. A simple, "Tell me how you feel" or "I really want to understand how you're feeling. Please tell me so I can try to understand." can go a long way toward preparing teenagers to use other people as a support system throughout their lives.

Adults can also help adolescents understand that even unpleasant emotions are useful because they inform us when we should be cautious. Anxiety tells us that we have stepped outside our comfort zone and may be approaching danger. Fear tells us to be vigilant. Anger tells us that someone has stepped over our boundary zone, and we may need to defend ourselves. Sadness reminds us how much we care when we experience a loss and teaches us that we need to appreciate what we have. Above all, emotions signal us to turn to others for support.

It may seem odd to discuss how to help adolescents understand their emotions at this stage. Ideally parents have been doing this since early childhood. But the emotional ups and downs of adolescence—particularly as students find their way through the college application process and look ahead to life after high school—make it necessary to pay extra attention to their emotional challenges and the importance of ongoing, supportive connections to other people.

Creating Family Rituals

An effective way to enhance family connection is to establish rituals, such as eating at least one meal together every week. "Oh," you're laughing, "Whose family has time for that? Everyone has to be in a separate place, at a different activity, every night." But you can change your family schedule if you believe this is important. Your children won't be living at home much longer. Do it now, or you never will. On weekends, choose an evening in the coming week when your whole family will sit down and eat together. No matter how busy everyone is, set the date. Be respectful of your teenager's social schedule by being flexible about the day and time, but plan in advance and stick to it. Attendance is required; dress optional. Take no excuses (no last-minute "but I have to go to my friend's house" or "I forgot..."). If you are especially busy, prepare something in advance or bring home take-out food, but make the weekly sit-down dinner a routine. Turn off the phone and television or light candles on the table, but make it an event.

Other valuable family traditions include sharing hobbies and spending regular time with your children, both as a family group and one-to-one. You can designate 10 or 15 minutes each evening or alternate evenings to spend with each child alone. This may sound counter to family connection or togetherness, but the point is to devote individual attention to each child. Many parents find that when life gets chaotic, their children blend together— bad for children, bad for parents, and a setup for sibling rivalry.

And always, *always,* say goodnight to your children or have them come to you and say goodnight before they go to bed. We do this with younger children, but it is no less important when they are teenagers. In fact its potential to make a real difference is even greater with teens. I have been promoting the nightly check-in rule for years with my preteen and teenaged patients and their families. It is not meant to be punitive, but it does work to ensure a safe return home when they have been out.

Here's how it works: You expect them to come in and tell you when they get home. Make sure they understand this clearly. Even if you are asleep, they are to wake you and tell you they're home safely. Ask them to talk with you for a few moments. Don't ask them details about their evening—they will see this as interrogation—but remain open if they want to share details. Tell them you're happy to listen to them no matter how tired you are.

Be firm and don't permit any exceptions or excuses like "I didn't want to wake you because I knew you were tired and it was late" or "I forgot 'cause I was so sleepy." If you establish this family rule early and hold your children to it, they will understand that there will be a predetermined consequence or loss of privilege if they break the check-in rule. The rule has several benefits. It is an effective way to monitor adolescents. It reduces your worry that they're drinking or using drugs because you will be able to determine their coherence as soon as they get home. It also gives them a great refusal skill to use with friends. "I can't smoke weed with you because I have to check in with my parents as soon as I get home. They smell my hair and clothes!" Their friends will sympathize and reduce the peer pressure because of your "stupid" check-in rule.

If you use the nightly check-in in a loving spirit—as in "I'm glad you're home safe. I need to know you're OK. I love you."—your teenagers will see this ritual as caring, not punitive or authoritarian. They will see your concern as positive attention, not interrogation or distrust. This in turn helps them feel even more connected to you.

One caution: As important as connection is to building resilience, parents have to be careful not to allow connection to become control. Some parents forge an overly tight connection with their children that subtly transforms into unhealthy control. These parents don't intend to be overly controlling. They certainly aren't harsh disciplinarians or dictators. But they may control their kids through taut emotional ties—particularly when they try to be their "best friend." I grow concerned when parents tell me that they don't worry about their child "because she tells me everything—we're like best friends."

Remember that a teenager's job is to become an individual, separate and distinct from parents. Until adolescence, most of children's values and perspectives are formed by observing their parents' words and actions. Young people cannot become independent, autonomous adults until they confront their parents' values, decide to reject some of them (they tell you how uncool and ridiculous you are), and form their own values. When adolescents are going through this normal process, they need parents to be a stable rock that they can keep referring to by saying, "That's not me. I'm not at all like Mom or Dad."

If parents try to be their teenager's best friend, how will this developing young adult figure out how far she has to go to come up with her own standards? I worry that well-intentioned parents may drive their children off track as they move closer to outrageous choices just to differentiate themselves from their parents. They need loving, connected, even fun and friendly parents, but they don't need parents to be best friends.

Adolescents' Connections Outside the Family

Connections with adults outside the family are particularly useful during adolescence because many preteens and teenagers go through periods of "hating" their parents. This is an upsetting but normal part of their growing independence. It is helpful to remember that much of their reaction stems from how much they actually *love* their parents. To figure out who they are and who they want to become, they need to reject almost every idea their parents have and try out new ideas of their own. If parents wisely support their adolescents in forging other positive connections, teens will turn to other trusted people for guidance during that 2- to 3-year period of mid-adolescence when everything parents say is ridiculous and during that last year at home when every parent is seen as more controlling than a prison warden.

Here's a hint: Be subtle about fostering other connections. If they seem too forced or directed by a parent, teens may think these other people are parents' stooges and their views will also be seen as ridiculous. So don't be obvious and suggest, "Why don't you hang out with that mature college kid down the street?" Instead, set up situations where someone like this model neighbor can interact spontaneously with your teenager (maybe drive him to the mall or watch a movie), and let the relationship develop from there. Or if your child has a favorite older cousin, aunt, or uncle, make it possible for your teen to spend more time with them.

By belonging to sports, civic, and religious organizations, young people learn that they are part of a larger, supportive community that values them. Children who participate in such organizations learn that parents aren't the only ones who expect them to play fair, be honest and loyal, and show responsibility. In our disjointed, harried, and often chaotic world, it is more important than ever for young people to have as many adult connections as possible. But we must add the caveat: Belonging to worthwhile organizations is beneficial, but belonging to too many can overburden young people with excessive demands on their time and energy.

Character

Every family has its own standards for what constitutes good character. We may prioritize these character traits differently. Some families may value humility, while others believe it is more important that their kids know how to promote themselves. Some parents' top priority is that their children are generous, polite, and respectful. Other families value individuality most highly. We're not here to tell you which traits to develop in your child, of course. We can probably agree about traits that we *don't* want in our children: hatred, bigotry, self-righteousness, deception, and insensitivity.

Throughout childhood and adolescence, character development responds to feedback and direction. Parents need to make certain that direction comes from them and from people they believe will help their children build strong character. And they must reinforce it with feedback. In short, we cannot leave character development to chance because many forces—from media to peers—consider integrity, sincerity, and other forms of character as merely incidental compared to the shallow trappings of success: the right clothes, flashiest cars and, yes, the "best" college.

When teenagers are preparing for college, parents need to focus on 2 particularly relevant objectives: We must be aware that, as an initiation rite, the college application process is a critical opportunity to test character, and we must model good character for them now more than ever. Because this is an initiation rite, it is an ideal opportunity to build character and reinforce traits like authenticity and fairness. It's an opportunity for adolescents to reflect on what they stand for, how they desire to contribute to the world, and how they choose to portray themselves.

No teenager sails through high school without a scratch. Even the best and brightest are unprepared for a pop quiz, fail an occasional test, don't get the lead in the school play, or are turned down by their first-choice college. For most high school students, these shortcomings and disappointments are common. And that's exactly why adolescence is an ideal time to build character—because teens may not get exactly what they want. These experiences not only offer great lessons in learning how to make lemonade out of lemons, but they also prove to kids that they can bounce back and remain optimistic.

In applying to college—whether in the application essay or face-to-face interview, if there is one—teenagers have to portray themselves. They can choose to do so with truthfulness, sincerity, and authenticity. Or they can choose to portray someone they wish they were in hopes of boosting their chance of admission. As part of the initiation process, this is a test of character. Is the prize worth any cost—even denying who you are? If it feels OK to portray yourself in an exaggerated manner, how great a leap is it to feel OK about plagiarism, lying, and getting around rules of early decision? How can we clearly convey that playing the game fairly is such an important demonstration of character? Teenagers have to answer such questions for themselves, but parents also model these character traits by their behavior. If a parent writes the essay or looks the other way when he knows his son is inflating his list of extracurricular activities, what does that model for character development?

In our fast-paced society, we face many challenges when we try to raise young people with character. Our culture values personal success, so how do we make sure that children are hard workers but still value kindness, cooperation, sharing, and caring for other people? In a society that fosters winning the prize, how do we reinforce that it is how we play the game that defines us as humans? In a world in which independence is a hallmark of success, how do we convey that the finest people are those who can admit they need others to achieve contentment?

I wish I had brilliant answers for those rhetorical questions, but I do know this: Character development does not come in a bottle, nor will it come through a lecture. Children learn character by the values you teach, by your words of praise, or by the way you correct them. They'll learn character by observing your values and behavior in daily interactions outside your home, and they'll learn it by watching how adults treat each other in your home.

This process may be your best opportunity to make clear to your teenager how you view success. That is why it is so very important that you are careful about your behavior. If success is defined only by test scores and class rank, or by the college that admits your child, he will very narrowly determine whether he is a success or failure. And he might do anything to ensure "success," including making choices that are counter to positive character development. This initiation rite is the time to share what really makes you proud—his concern for others, tenacity, honesty, kindness, reliability, generosity, and sense of fairness.

We need to focus on character now, during the college admissions/initiation period, not only to pass on strong values to the next generation, but also to ensure that individual members of that generation will thrive. When children develop strong character, they gain the lifelong ability to return to a set of core values during times of crisis, which makes them more resilient in the most trying of times.

Contribution

Adults used to criticize young people for being so idealistic: "Don't they know how complicated the world is? Why don't they just get a job? They can't cure all of society's ills." When was the last time you heard anyone criticize young people for being too idealistic? Now youth are more likely to be seen as the problem: Teenagers are careless, selfish, irresponsible, and dangerous.

This shift in the perception of youth is unwarranted and unfair, even harmful. It's unfair because, if children are spoiled or rude and teens are dangerous, that is a reflection on us, not them, because young people live up to or down to our expectations. The perception is also harmful because we need them to be idealistic contributors to society. Who else will improve the world? When they work to improve their communities, they develop a meaningful sense of purpose. The appreciation they earn will protect them from some of the negative, destructive messages about youth. They will hear from numerous people besides their parents, "I think you are wonderful" and absorb the important belief, "I have high expectations for you."

Young people need to feel important, to know that they can contribute to our families, communities, and the world. Volunteering to serve people in need is one way kids can understand that they matter. But they shouldn't have to leave home to know that they are contributing. Adolescents should have a clear sense that their household is a better place because they are in it. Their ideas about how the family could work together better should be heard and valued. When a family member is in need, a grandfather is sick, or a younger sibling needs help with homework, for example, the adolescent who helps out should be as appreciated and respected as one who goes across town to serve others.

Contemporary culture is so focused on material things: video equipment, expensive shoes and clothes, cosmetics, and cars. Children naturally get swept up in this tide because they see it all around them. To counter this influence or put it in perspective, parents can support opportunities for young people to give rather than receive. Children will learn that the universe doesn't revolve around them or owe them everything they desire. When they raise money for hurricane relief or tutor younger children, they gain a more realistic perspective of the world and their place in it. They begin to see beyond their isolated, self-oriented circle. They will recognize themselves as part of a larger community where they can make a difference no matter how small.

Teenagers can contribute to society in a multitude of ways, but they also need to balance their generous impulses with schoolwork and other demands. In the context of preparing for college, teenagers should pick an activity that really interests them, not something that they think will look good on their application or increase their chance of a scholarship. One activity that really captivates their interest is better than 3 activities that they care little about.

Contribution is about more than listing a do-good activity on an application. Contribution can directly foster resilience because it helps young people gain a sense of purpose in life—something positive to strive toward and achieve. By contributing to efforts greater than themselves, they increase their life experiences and thus become more competent—"I can do this!" They gain a solid sense of their own ability and worth.

They will also learn that giving and receiving, sharing during times of plenty, and asking for help during difficult times are normal, healthy things for humans to do. We want young people to know that just as they give, they will receive if misfortune hits. If they are to be resilient in the face of an unforeseen tragedy, this is a vital lesson. The positive feedback they receive for their efforts and their own sense of accomplishment also enhance character. The more their generosity and caring are acknowledged, the more generous and caring they are likely to be.

CHAPTER SEVENTEEN

Assuming More Control

Adolescents need to take increasing control of their choices and actions as they prepare for college and increased independence. To build resilience, they need to grasp the clear connection between their actions and consequences. Young people who understand that they have control over their lives take responsibility rather than blame others for problems and failures. They understand that things don't just happen to them. They can be decision-makers and problem-solvers who determine the results.

The development of resilience depends on parents' relinquishing tight control in favor of guidance, attention, and support so that young people have opportunities to test their inner control. That is not to say that parents take a completely hands-off approach, of course. Parents can enhance adolescents' growing sense of self-control by observing, offering a steadying hand, and guiding them rather than controlling their every action.

Before discussing various ways to help your teen develop control, I ask you to consider your own parenting style. Of the 4 general styles of parenting—authoritarian, permissive, disengaged, and authoritative—which best describes you?

Authoritarian: This parent's attitude is "Do as I say. Why? Because I said so. Don't question my authority. Until you're out of this house, I'm the boss!"

Permissive: This parent may teach sterling values and give terrific support and love but ultimately says "I trust you" instead of setting appropriate boundaries. Permissive parents often treat a child like a pal and fear their child won't like or love them if they clash.

Disengaged: This parent is too busy or otherwise occupied to monitor a child's activities and behaviors closely or set limits unless he is in trouble or imminent danger. This parent either says nothing or says, "Do what you want." When major problems erupt, the disengaged parent may come down hard on a child, leading to inconsistency and mixed messages.

Authoritative: This parent sets the tone and reasonable limits, expects good behavior, offers a lot of love, and encourages kids to make choices and be independent, but when it comes to the Big Issues, it's "Do as I say."

If you find your parenting style leans toward the authoritarian, permissive, or disengaged models, I would suggest you consider how to become more authoritative. Ample evidence suggests that children raised with authoritative parents are less likely to engage in worrisome behaviors and are more likely to be resilient. Authoritative parents give a lot of love, attention, and opportunities to gain increasing independence, with close supervision and clear boundaries.

The word discipline means *teach* or *guide*. It doesn't mean punish or control. Parents who discipline successfully see discipline as an ongoing responsibility to teach. The best disciplinarians (or teachers) hold high expectations for young people and give appropriate consequences, or allow them to occur naturally, rather than dole out arbitrary punishments when kids fall short of those expectations.

Children crave parents' attention even when they reach adolescence. When they don't get enough of it, they find ways to make us pay attention by doing something we cannot ignore: talk back, whine, slam doors, pick a fight...or worse. Then our attention is usually paid in negative ways: lecturing, threatening, and punishing. These negative ways of paying attention are ineffective and instill powerlessness rather than a sense of control. But the cycle continues because kids begin to see that type of attention as what they expect, and learn to need, from parents.

As we list a litany of reasons why kids should or shouldn't do something, they don't think about how correct we are. In fact, our efforts tend to backfire because we make them feel inadequate and incompetent. They want to prove our dire predictions or assessment of their actions or decisions wrong. If we want to diminish negative behaviors, we can short-circuit them by giving kids more frequent doses of positive attention. But unfortunately we tend to focus primarily on their undesirable behaviors and fall into a pattern of responding only to those.

If this has been your experience, here's a simple way to break the pattern: Keep notes of all your interactions with your children for a week. When they want your attention, how do they get it each time? Begin to recognize that many of their annoying or undesirable behaviors may be attention-seeking ploys. How do you respond? Once you become more aware of your pattern, you'll be better able to replace negative attention with positive attention. I've already mentioned some ways to pay positive attention: Catch kids being good. Praise them with words that show you've really noticed and appreciated something they have done, and let them know *why* ("You really showed enthusiasm in that game," or "I think you're terrific to help your friend review for that test; you didn't have to do that, but it showed real generosity.").

Another way to help adolescents develop greater inner control is to encourage them to negotiate when you're discussing problems and solutions. Remember that you are the ultimate limit-setter, and certain misbehaviors are nonnegotiable, such as verbal abuse, cheating, stealing, ignoring curfews, or whatever you deem unacceptable. But most issues that you will consider with them will probably be negotiable, such as ways to meet deadlines, how much time to spend on the phone, when to study, and when to take on new activities or give up others. By actively negotiating with you, young people reap several benefits: They exert some control of events. They will be more likely to follow through on compromises that they've had a role in reaching. Through these negotiations, teenagers learn give-and-take skills that will come in handy when they must negotiate with peers, teachers, or bosses.

Not all their decisions and actions will be smart, of course, and they'll have to face unpleasant consequences. When they do mess up, let your essential message be "Yes, you've done something wrong, but I still love you." Statements like this help ensure that your child feels secure enough to come to you with problems. If you don't communicate unconditional love, even in the face of your disappointment, they may turn away from you the next time they do something wrong or find themselves in trouble.

As children grow, parents often feel that they're holding 2 reins. One is gripped tightly to keep kids safe, while the other is looser as we gradually give them a little more slack to move away from us and explore the world with increasing freedom. We're constantly jiggling these reins, pulling one a bit tighter, letting one out an inch or two. We don't want to overprotect or con-trol them too strictly, yet we don't dare let them have too much freedom or they may make big-time mistakes. It requires a delicate balance, but the trick is to increase their freedom gradually throughout adolescence while at the same time minimize chances that they'll make unsafe or unwise choices.

Delaying Gratification and Trusting Their Decisions

So many things that feel good for a moment can get in the way of success. Especially when we're stressed, we may look for easy answers, quick fixes, and feel-good solutions that end up creating more stress in the long run. Adults know they're more likely to succeed when they postpone immediate gratification and deal with a temporary stressor because the delay helps us keep an eye on the ball. Those who maintain control while striving toward a larger goal are more likely to move beyond obstacles and adversity. Adults who build a foundation slowly, painstakingly, and brick by brick are able to create a solid base from which success can be launched.

But delayed gratification is often difficult for teenagers to grasp. For example, if they face a big test on Monday morning, they may prefer to party all weekend than to study. And having fun takes their mind off the scary (though overblown) prospect that the test could make or break their chances of getting into the college of their choice.

Yet control and delayed gratification are cornerstones for preparing children to have self-discipline for life. Parents need to teach kids the need for delaying gratification throughout childhood. Small delays of gratification will prepare them to put in the necessary, sometimes boring, effort and time that will reap success later. They learn, for example, that a lot of research and homework can create a science project that they can show with pride. And the knowledge that an investment of time and effort produces desirable results is also key to choosing positive coping strategies instead of easier, quick-acting but dangerous ones that perpetuate stress.

Trusting Their Decision-Making Skills

Adolescents who are able to make wise decisions learn to trust their ability to control their own lives. They are less afraid of taking the appropriate risks that resilient people must take to meet and rise above obstacles and adversity. They don't fear failure. They don't assume they are powerless because they have seen the fruits of good decisions. They learn from mistakes and don't repeat the pattern of decisions that led to those mistakes.

Parents can help young people learn that they control their destiny through their choices. Parents can support positive, independent decisions and thwart the less wise ones in many ways.

- To learn the consequences of their decisions and actions, kids occasionally have to experience some emotional bruises. They need to recognize and feel their emotions; parents shouldn't ignore, diminish, or denigrate those genuine emotions or try to "fix" them for their children.

- Young people who are lectured about what they should do never have the opportunity to figure out on their own how to handle challenging situations. Lectures backfire by making them want to prove to parents that they can handle everything by themselves in their own way. They need guidance delivered in a way that puts them in the driver's seat so they can learn through experience which decisions are wise and which are foolhardy.

- Parents who listen effectively give children just enough security, safety, and support to allow them to trust their own judgment. When a child's plan goes astray, parents can engage more active listening skills and help decatastrophize negative thinking patterns.

- Teens need confidence to be able to make a decision and stick to it. They may need even more confidence to be able to be flexible, to shift to a new path when they have figured out that an initial strategy is unsuccessful or even harmful. We should help them understand that they are capable of sound decisions and avoid—at all costs—the shameful messages that tell them they are incompetent.

- Adolescents who learn that their actions are linked directly to consequences learn to evaluate their choices and behaviors. Parents who understand that discipline is about active, loving teaching and not about punishment will nurture young people who are prepared to adjust their decisions.

One Step at a Time

When teenagers try to look into their futures, many become anxious or even overwhelmed. "So many important decisions to make. What if I make the wrong one?" Sometimes a decision seems so huge or a goal so difficult to reach that young people feel they can't even think about trying. They feel powerless and scared. They may think they have no choices, or they sense that they're controlled by outside forces that just push them along.

One way to help a teenager get "unstuck" is to explain that you sometimes get overwhelmed yourself. Tell your child that you don't have all the answers, but you do know there are a couple of different possibilities. You can take out a pencil and piece of paper to sketch the problem into smaller, more achievable parts. The first step is to think about where you are in the present moment, and write that down near one edge of the paper. Scribble the far-off goal at the other edge. You'll then begin to draw a ladder that leads, one rung at a time, from the starting point to the ultimate goal.

Let's say that the end goal is to read 6 books by the end of the semester or to fill out 6 application forms by a certain deadline. Begin by posing open-ended, leading questions like, "What about this? What would happen if you did this first? What would follow after that?" Don't supply answers or fill in the blanks for your child. Ask your child to suggest what steps will lead to the desirable end.

As you write down the steps he suggests, explain that you find it easier when you divide difficult tasks into many small steps. You keep an eye on the future goal to keep yourself motivated. But you focus on only one step at a time so you don't become weighed down and have a better chance of success.

By breaking challenges into small segments, young people develop a greater sense of their own control of a situation. It helps them overcome a sense of powerlessness, lack of control, or belief that only fate will determine their future. They will experience success in each small step and learn that they can manage not only the outcomes but also how they make the journey. Once they feel the initial success, the expectation of failure that first paralyzed their ability to act will disappear.

When teenagers become responsible for their own decisions and actions, they learn to face the joyful *and* disappointing results. They learn to accept that mistakes happen, but the next time they will be more prepared for them. If they are given many chances to exercise control, they are far less likely to see themselves as passive victims and to blame others. This is the core of resilience: Young people who have a true center of control will be able to bounce back. Ultimately they will be happier, more optimistic, and better equipped to face the next challenge.

Not Everything Is Within Our Control

As much as we want teenagers to take increased control and responsibility, both parents and kids need to recognize that there are times when we simply don't have control. If we don't recognize that, we will bang our heads against the walls and waste vital resources and energy needed to handle those things we can control. The key is to assess realistically what can be controlled and what cannot.

To overcome any adversity, young people must be able to distinguish when they have the power to change something and when they should reserve their energy. Think about anxiety. At some level, it results from the confusion about what we can control and what we can't. Like all emotions, anxiety can be helpful, but when it's out of control it can be paralyzing. Isn't it better to know what we can handle, realize that our confidence is well earned, and have the good sense to recognize what not to worry about? Parents can teach the lesson about conserving energy in no-control situations by modeling. If we do a little self-talk aloud when our children are present, we can demonstrate how we decide to let something go and free our energy to approach other problems.

When kids reach an impasse and can't control a particular event or outcome (such as a rejection letter), that's the moment to put an arm around them, support them, give them a hug, and remind them of your unconditional love. Help them understand that some things are simply beyond our control—

for adults and kids alike—and the only thing we can really control is how we choose to react. Often the best thing we can do in these situations is to conserve our energy and move ahead without tearing ourselves apart.

CHAPTER EIGHTEEN

Coping With Stress

To this point, we've discussed various components of resilience. But no matter how competent and confident kids are—no matter how secure their connections, how sterling their characters, or how much control they develop—teenagers still require a repertoire of skills to cope with pressures and challenges at this critical time in their lives. The bottom line is simple: Life is stressful so we need to prepare them to handle it effectively. In other words, they need to become competent at coping with stress if they are to be resilient now and in the future.

Throughout this book, we've discussed how parents can support their children, with the focus on adolescents. In this chapter, we switch pronoun gears to talk about coping strategies "you" and "we" (adults) can use to deal with stress, as well as those teenagers can use. The high school years—and the college application segment in particular—are stressful times for parents as well as teenagers. We want you to have positive strategies to manage stress not only for your personal benefit but also to model for your adolescents. How you choose to demonstrate effective coping skills is more meaningful than any spoken plan you might give them. Stress is a lifelong struggle. The stressors may change from early childhood through old age, but everyone needs to manage stress. We hope you will use the advice in this chapter for your teen and yourself. Take care of yourself. You would be amazed by how important it is to teenagers that their parents take care of their own problems, bodies, and emotions.

■ ❖ ■ ❖ ■ ❖ ■ ❖ ■

Although we sometimes imagine that childhood is idyllic, even young children are not shielded from stress. Teenagers especially feel stress as they worry about school, their peers, and their appearance. They want to please us and sometimes worry about us. They are concerned about war, violence, even the economy because the media brings the universe into their homes. Adolescents experience the unique pressure of finding an identity while preparing for independence.

Young people don't have the benefit of having lived through cycles of stress, so they haven't adopted the "this too shall pass" protective attitude that adults use to move on. Therefore we need to teach them, from an early age whenever possible, how to cope with the stress. The first step in this process is to understand what stress does to our bodies and emotions and to evaluate the harm it may be doing.

Stress makes us uncomfortable. We feel nervous, unsafe, insecure, and ungrounded. We can't think clearly. We become restless, lose sleep, become tired, and maybe get headaches. Our muscles ache, our bellies feel bloated, our hearts throb. We grow irritable, less patient, and much less understanding of others.

Many of the stress-reduction strategies in this section and in the following section for teens can be useful in helping to manage existing stress. But remember that this repertoire of strategies is also designed to be preventive. We hope that young people who are well equipped to deal with stress will experience less of it in the first place.

Dealing With Stress

Children, adolescents, and adults all hate discomfort whether it is emotional or physical. To avoid it, we figure out some way to cope, some way to make ourselves feel comfortable again. Anything that will banish those disquieting feelings will make us feel more settled, at least for the moment.

We have many ways of coping: some are positive and others are negative. I don't mean that the positive ways always work and the negative ways always fail. On the contrary, some negative ways offer immediate relief. The difference is that positive coping strategies enhance well-being and ultimately lead to relief. Negative strategies might feel great and offer a quick fix, but they end up causing harm to the individual or community and ultimately perpetuate and intensify the cycle of stress.

Virtually all of the behaviors we fear in teenagers are misguided attempts to diminish their stress. Procrastination, feigned laziness, and boredom are ways of dealing with school-related stress. They just want to push it out of sight, hide it under the bed like dirty socks. Bullying, smoking, drugs, gangs, sex, disordered eating, and self-mutilation are all efforts to deal with stress.

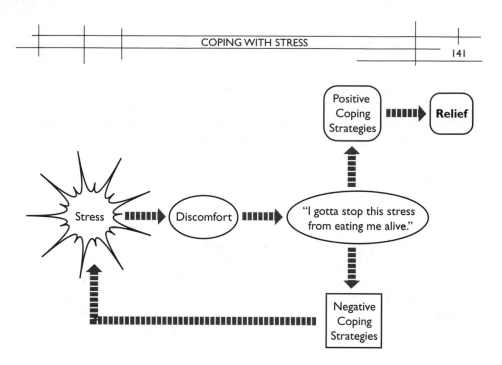

Our challenge is to raise children who have a variety of positive coping strategies that will enhance their strengths.

I can't guarantee that your teenagers will never try a worrisome behavior—even if they are emotionally intelligent and equipped with good coping strategies—because some of those feared behaviors are fun or feel good. A teen may try drugs to test his limits, rebel, or have fun with friends. We hope he will move beyond this phase quickly. But a young person who seeks solace through drugs, who uses an altered state of consciousness to mask his feelings, may be destined for addiction. Kids with better, safer, and healthier means of coping with stress don't need to blur their consciousness with drugs.

Coping Styles

People tend to use repetitive patterns when they respond to challenges. Experts have identified key differences in coping styles. Some people cope by tackling a problem head-on and trying to fix it as best they can. Others focus more on the emotions that those problems create; they tend to do what makes them feel better to decrease their discomfort. Both styles—problem-focused and emotion-focused—are active styles that attempt to engage the problem. But other people choose to avoid the problem by choosing full-blown denial or its close cousin, withdrawal. People who choose to engage a problem actively either try to change the stressor to make themselves feel more comfortable, or they change themselves just enough to adapt to the stressor.

Young people have the same styles, though they may not be aware of them. Ruby feels overwhelmed by all the homework in her 20-pound backpack. When she decides to break her assignments into segments that she can handle one at a time, Ruby uses a problem-focused strategy. When Rohan's friends challenge him to smoke marijuana and he talks with his best friend about why he doesn't want to, Rohan addresses the problem. When Maria feels frustrated with her parents' "inflexible, old-fashioned, ridiculous rules," and chooses to sit down and negotiate compromises with them, she goes right to the source of her stress to solve the problem.

Some young people who use emotion-focused strategies want to escape stressful feelings and may choose to deny the problem exists. They may drink alcohol to cloud their awareness of the problem or bully others to feel in control because these choices make them feel better in the short term. But not all emotion-focused styles are negative. Many can be positive if they help a young person deal with feelings in ways that are healthy—like exercise or meditation—or that may release pent-up stress—like journaling, crying, or laughing. (These approaches are explained specifically for teenagers in Part Four.)

As we think about dealing with challenges, a fundamental decision must be made: How much am I willing to change? Sometimes we try to change the environment. For example, when Rohan's conversation with his friend leads to their mutual decision not to smoke marijuana, Rohan creates a safer, more problem-free environment. It will be less stressful because he can hang out with at least one friend who also doesn't smoke marijuana. Rohan changes his environment without compromising. He becomes engaged with the problem rather than denying or avoiding it.

But others use denial to convince themselves and others that no problem exists. (How many times a day do we hear, "no problem" or "whatever"?) Sometimes we are aware of a problem and not truly in denial, but we choose to ignore it, play down its significance, or withdraw from the people or circumstances that cause our discomfort. In the worst-case scenario, withdrawal can lead to isolation or depression.

A word about denial and withdrawal: It would be a mistake to believe that we *should* rise to every challenge and face the problem head on. Certainly long-term avoidance of a situation will never overcome the obstacle. But sometimes a problem is so overwhelming or frightening that it is temporarily wise to say, "I really don't care. It doesn't bother me." I have learned time and again from patients who have every reason to be furious at their life circumstances that taking the position of not caring, which sometimes runs deep, is all they can handle. I urge parents to raise children who can deal with emotions and confront problems, but I caution against pushing children to show they care just because we know they ought to care. Give them time and space and allow for the skills to be developed that will enable them to react appropriately.

No one can state with certainty how any individual *should* cope, but it is generally agreed that people who engage a problem do better than those who deny or withdraw from it. This doesn't mean we should force all children to "face it" every time they're up against a struggle or dilemma. Adolescents who use problem-focused coping strategies (that address the stressor itself rather than the feelings of discomfort it produces) are usually better adjusted. But positively oriented emotion-focused strategies are also useful. Young people can learn to address problems competently and manage the physical and emotional discomfort that stress creates.

Taking Action to Manage Stress

I've asked many remarkable young people who have thrived despite enormous stress how they've managed to survive and succeed. By listening to what works for my patients and their families, I have developed a 10-point stress-reduction plan. These 10 strategies will be addressed in detail later.

1. Identify and address the problem.
2. Avoid negativity.
3. Let some things go.
4. Contribute to the world.
5. Listen to your body.
6. Fool your body into a relaxed state.
7. Eat well.
8. Sleep well.
9. Take instant vacations.
10. Release emotional tension.

Each point includes a variety of activities and actions. My goal is to offer as wide a range of useful coping strategies as possible. While this plan is quite comprehensive, it isn't meant to be a step-by-step recipe. No one should expect to use all of the techniques. I suggest picking an item or two from each category to see which ones work best for you. As you tailor a stress-reduction plan to your needs, keep in mind that approaches can change over time. You'll notice that nothing in this 10-point plan specifically addresses childhood or adolescence.

The plan can help both adults and kids cope with a stressful world, which brings me to an essential point: Adolescents pounce on hypocrisy and use it to explain why parents shouldn't have the authority to set rules of behavior.

So if we don't want them to use negative strategies to cope with stress (such as smoking, using drugs, or hurting themselves in other self-destructive ways), we have to use healthy strategies ourselves. We can't tell kids it's good to talk about their feelings if we bottle up our own emotions. We can't teach the danger of drugs while drinking alcohol. We can't talk about the importance of balancing our lives if we haven't taken a day off in 3 weeks.

This is a prescription to take care of yourself. Don't think it's selfish to have a hobby, take time to relax, or have creative outlets. When you take care of yourself, you show your children how to be emotionally healthy. You are the model they will follow as they learn to manage stress. Role modeling is most effective when you talk aloud a bit about what you're doing. Some of these self-talk suggestions will give you a glimpse of the ideas in the stress-reduction plan.

- "This is a gigantic work assignment to finish in just one month. I'm going to break it down into smaller parts that I can handle." Then, later: "I feel so much better. I really got a lot done."

- "I'm so stressed out that I can't even think. I'm going for a run. That always makes me feel better."

- "I really need to clear my head. I'm going to take some slow, deep breaths and imagine I'm on that beautiful beach we visited last summer. Remember that sunset?"

- "I really need a few minutes to myself after the day I've had. I'm going to soak in the bathtub for a half hour."

- "I'm so angry that I can't think straight. If I make a decision now about how you need to learn your lesson, you won't like it one bit. Right now I need some time to myself to cool off. I'm going for a long walk to relax. Then we're going to deal with this problem."

- "I need to figure out how to handle this problem with the neighbor. I'm going to call Aunt Mattie. Just talking makes me calmer, and sometimes she helps me find a completely new way of thinking about things."

- "I'm exhausted. I broke my rule and fell asleep while I was still worried about work. I sleep so much better whenever I relax before bed, or at least make a list of things I have to do the next day so they don't keep spinning in my head."

At first it may seem that this set of strategies is a resumé for life. In fact, if your teenagers learn some of these techniques, they will build a balanced resumé that prepares them for college and adulthood. As you guide your children in developing these approaches, keep in mind these 3 points:

- When choosing strategies from this plan, select those you think will work for you, not those that will impress someone else. For example, if a teenager focuses on musical expression as a way to relax because he loves to play the guitar, don't encourage him to take bassoon lessons because you think it will impress a college admissions committee. Just let him strum the guitar!

- The plan cannot be imposed on a child or adult; it has to be welcomed to be effective. If you or your child doesn't take to one strategy, try another.

- Don't stress about the stress-reduction plan! Don't feel that you must be exposed to everything in the plan to manage stress successfully.

When we're learning to manage stress, we need to find that precarious balance between living in the moment and working for the future. One strategy is to enjoy the little pleasures surrounding us, but it's difficult to do if we are always thinking that everything we do is designed to manage stress. So as you consider choices among this wide array of coping strategies, take it casually. Let your individualized plan develop over time and don't worry about every detail. Enjoy your family and your life right now. By your actions and attitudes, you'll be modeling a far more effective approach than any written plan.

Here are the 10 points of the stress-management plan.

One: Identify and Address the Problem

Any effective approach to managing stress begins by identifying the cause of the stress, what it's doing to you, and what you can do to solve the problem. Without this "attack the problem first" strategy, we would be chasing our tails. We would react and feel better, react again and feel better. This cycle would continue repeatedly as we attempt to deal with persistent problems.

Problem-solving is the most effective and basic way to begin coping with stress. Some of the other building blocks of resilience prepare children to be good problem-solvers. A teenager with confidence feels comfortable taking the initiative to solve a problem or face a challenge. A teenager with a sense of competence trusts his ability to make decisions. He can use the power of his own judgment because he is able to remove the barriers (like anxiety and frustration) that get in the way of solving problems. To begin to do that, young people have to understand how to assess a situation realistically. This skill (discussed in Chapter 14) helps kids manage their emotional responses by learning to reframe their "catastrophic" thoughts. They'll be able to remind themselves that overwhelming situations can be managed by thinking about them differently. Those cognitive strategies help young people calm themselves and use their emotional and intellectual abilities to solve problems.

One of the best ways to deal with an overwhelming task is to assume control over it by breaking it into smaller, manageable parts. Once the first part is completed, you can look back and realize something is behind you, and the part ahead of you is smaller and therefore less daunting. The college admissions process, an unquestionably overwhelming task, is a perfect opportunity to guide a high school student toward attacking problems effectively. Another problem-solving technique is list making to organize a crammed schedule or set of unrelated tasks. This also serves as an emotional release valve when your head spins in so many opposing directions. (Read more about this on page 207.)

Two: Avoid Negativity

The best way to manage a problem is to avoid it all together. I am not talking about denial—quite the opposite. I am talking about having keen enough insight to understand and anticipate the kind of problems you're likely to confront so that you're prepared to sidestep them entirely. A person who struggles with gambling, for example, should avoid a business trip to Las Vegas. A teen who is bullied needs to learn not to travel alone. It is important for teenagers to leave behind their helpless thinking patterns, such as "Why does this always happen to me?" and begin to recognize the scenarios that tend to present problems. This technique involves a little analysis: What brings you down? What makes you tense or upset? What always gets to you?

I teach young people to think about which situations have gotten them in trouble in the past, then to pay attention to the subtle signals their bodies send out to warn of a similar potential problem. If they learn to pay attention to those sensations—like butterflies, anxiety, and heart racing—they can recognize what might get them into trouble before they actually find themselves in a crisis.

The answers to questions like, "What brings you down or always gets to you?" usually lie in 3 categories: people, places, and things. If we teach kids to identify the people who frustrate or bother them, the places where stress usually rises, and the things that provoke or intensify stress, then they can learn when and how to avoid those stressors. They cannot always avoid them, of course.

Let's say, for example, that your child is a good student, works hard, has a reasonable amount of extracurricular activities, and seems to know herself fairly well for a 16-year-old. But she has a couple of high-pressure friends who are very competitive about grades. They want to know her PSAT scores, where she's thinking of applying to college, which teachers are writing her recommendations, and so forth. Your daughter feels peppered by her friends, but she doesn't confront them or ask them to back off because she fears losing their friendship. Yet you can see her tension and anxiety soar whenever they're around or call her on the phone.

(This is not a purely hypothetical example, by the way. Many parents observe that their usually even-keeled teenagers morph into human tornados during the college application season when kids compete for a college slot not only against 2,000 strangers from around the country but also against their own friends and classmates. So the stakes rise from "Will I get in?" to "Ohmygod! What if I get in and my best friend doesn't? She'll hate me forever!")

If you can help her identify the problem and recognize the stress it's causing her, she can look for a solution. (Don't suggest one. Let her find it herself.) She may decide to ignore their pesky questions or turn the conversations in a different direction. She may be more direct by telling them she wants to remain friends but their constant inquiries are adding to her stress. Or she may decide to spend less time with them and more with other friends who aren't so competitive.

The strategy of avoiding negativity can be applied to avoid many worrisome adolescent behaviors. Kids are pretty smart about what kinds of situations are likely to get them in trouble. But they often choose to ignore those commonsense warning signals. Instead they comfort themselves with a "Whatever. I'll handle it if it comes up." But it is much easier to avoid problems from a distance than up close. The key to staying out of trouble is recognizing which people, places, and things have brought them down in the past, are likely to present them with uncomfortable pressure, or could probably pull them down again. It's particularly important to avoid friends with whom kids have shared bad habits. Those friends have a great deal invested in making sure that others don't rise above them.

Marc, for example, used to drink with a trio of friends, Andrew, Jorge, and Jacob, every weekend. Marc found his life seriously affected by drinking. His grades started to fall, and he had a near-death automobile accident. He realized that he had to quit drinking. Jorge, his pal since kindergarten, also wanted to stop and supported Marc's decision. But Andrew and Jacob weren't ready to quit. Every time they thought about quitting, they pushed the thought away. Facing their own stress was too overwhelming. "Everybody does it," they told themselves. But when Marc found the motivation and resolve to quit, their fallacy of "everybody does it" fell apart. They became motivated to find ways to ensure Marc's recovery failed—to pull him back down again—which allowed them to avoid their own demons.

People, places, and things. Kids who understand the negative influences in their lives are prepared to avoid major sources of stress and move beyond negative behaviors. For Marc and Jorge to continue to stop drinking, they learned that they had to stop hanging out with Andrew and Jacob.

Three: Let Some Things Go

We want to tackle problems, but we need to acknowledge that not every problem is worth attacking. Some problems may upset us but are of no real consequence. Other problems (like the weather) may bother us, but we are powerless to change them. That game we were looking forward to is simply rained out. To conserve our energy for the things we can change, we need to learn to let go of problems we cannot fix.

We may be able to teach young people to be problem-solvers, but those lessons are useless if they cannot also manage emotions and discomfort caused by stress. Clear thought and steady nerves are required to solve most problems. We can't think clearly if we're running from modern-day tigers. We cannot sit down and serenely resolve our differences with a tiger or ask for a time out to plan our escape route. Problem-solving is our escape route here, and we simply can't do it while racing away. This is where the next strategies come in: They clear our minds and offer opportunities to enjoy a rich, full, and healthful life even when we're surrounded by modern-day tigers.

Four: Contribute to the World

As an ingredient of resilience, contribution helps young people gain a sense of purpose, build character, and develop confidence. Contribution also is a great outlet for reducing stress. When we contribute to our communities or attempt to repair the world in any one of many small ways, we put aside our own troubles. Whether we volunteer on a regular basis or only occasionally, we contribute to an effort bigger than ourselves and gain some perspective on our own stressful situations.

Five: Listen to Your Body

Before learning to manage or reduce stress, we have to recognize what it does to our bodies. Whenever I talk to teenagers about coping with stress, I explain that our bodies contain many hormones that help us respond rapidly to danger and calm us at other times. Fear causes the release of adrenaline, but endorphins and other brain chemicals are calming.

A rush of adrenaline is harmless in certain situations, like taking a scary amusement park ride. It puts us on alert at other times, such as when we're walking along a dark, deserted road. Or it prepares us to run from tigers or modern dangers. Few kids today have to run from actual tigers, but they certainly have figurative tigers in their lives that provoke the same physical responses to stress. When they learn to listen to their bodies and read their stress responses, they become better able to cope. This is particularly true when those stress responses are inappropriate and actually get in the way of meeting a challenge. If a bully starts to chase them, the transformation from a calm state to one of arousal makes kids ready to run and is an appropriate response. But it's counterproductive if the tiger is a history exam because they can't study if they're only focused on fleeing.

Move It!

The most direct way to listen to your body is to exercise when you're stressed. Your body is preparing for a sprint, so it gets confused if you simply sit still. It's shouting, "Hey, brain, a tiger is gaining on me fast. Why do you want to get eaten? Get those legs moving." And when you don't move, the stress hormones keep circulating. You can't think clearly because you're not supposed to sit at a negotiating table with the tiger.

When one of my patients is cramming for a test and feels tense and nervous, I tell him to go outside and run, jump rope, play some basketball, or kick around a soccer ball. This physical activity simulates running from the tiger and relieves stress by using up that surging adrenaline. Once the body thinks it has survived the challenge, it can kick back, chill, and plan the next adventure. Oh, yeah, and it can study better. When teenagers tell me, "I can't exercise; I have no time because I've got to study," I tell them, "You have no time NOT to exercise."

How Much Exercise and What Kind?

Exercise reduces stress when there is no figurative tiger chasing us. We should exercise regularly even when all is going well because it keeps our bodies healthy. Healthy people manage stress better. If we raise our children to be active, they'll enjoy lifelong physical and emotional health benefits.

Parents sometimes tell me, "But my kids get plenty of exercise. Tonya plays soccer 4 times a week and volleyball year-round. Eriq is on the swim team and plays ice hockey." Participating in organized athletics is wonderful. But I worry that some young people are pushed too hard to become superstars, which is simply not healthy if they focus on one sport intensely and year-round.

Traditionally sports' seasons lasted 3 to 5 months. Kids trained, played hard, and then went out for another sport the following season. Each sport uses different sets of muscles, bones, and joints so the body has an opportunity to alternate movement patterns from season to season. In recent years, though, a trend has appeared to breed young athletes to focus on the same sport all year long. This causes more repetitive wear and tear on their developing muscles, bones, and joints, which leads to an increase in sports-related injuries.

Athletic pursuits offer young people a chance to be at their most competent and confident, but I urge parents to make sure that they are well managed by coaches who understand young athletic bodies. If they love a sport and enjoy playing, that's terrific. But if they are pushed to excel for the primary purpose of getting into college or winning a scholarship, that is not always healthy and can produce unnecessary pressure. A better solution is to encourage them to exercise and participate in a variety of athletics.

Needless to say, parents shouldn't select sports for children or make them sign up for certain leagues if they aren't really interested. Encourage them to play sports, but let them pick their own activities based on what they enjoy with their friends around the neighborhood or at school. Some young people shy away from competitive team sports. That's OK, as long as they remain active through play or individual sports. Whether they enjoy team sports, all kids should be exposed to individual sports like track, swimming, bicycling, or skating and some 2-player sports like tennis, golf, or racquetball because they'll be able to do these activities and reap the health benefits well into adulthood.

Most importantly, exercise should be fun. If teens feel that participating in sports is a chore or just another kind of pressure, they will give up on exercise as soon as they can opt out. But lifelong sports—walking, bicycling, hiking, swimming—can make the most difference in adult health and are great family activities. You don't have to push any of these on your children, but if you do them as healthful, fun ways for the family to connect with each other, your kids will enjoy them for a lifetime.

Releasing Anger

Stress hormones generate a fight or flight response. Fear or nervousness makes us want to flee, but raw anger drives us toward fighting—a behavior we certainly want to discourage. When teens are angry, I urge them to recognize what that rage is doing to their bodies and to release it by screaming, ripping up papers, or hitting pillows or punching bags. I call this sham fighting. These are excellent ways to release anger-induced stress. When they're irate and want to get something off their chest, I tell them literally, "then lie down on your back and lift weights—get it off your chest!" Push-ups also work for teens who don't have access to weights or to a partner who can spot them for safety.

Six: Fool Your Body Into a Relaxed State

By exercising or being physically active, young people use up all those stress hormones that tell their bodies to flee. But after they use them up, or if they are unable to exercise them away, they can still learn to fool their bodies into thinking they aren't stressed. To see how this is possible, it's necessary to understand the power of the mind over the body.

We have 2 nervous systems. The voluntary nervous system makes our muscles do what we want—stand up, walk, lift a heavy box, run, sit, and brush our teeth. The involuntary nervous system controls the functions that we never have to think about—swallowing, breathing, digestion, and heart beating. It's the system that rapidly adjusts to prepare us to sprint from a charging rhinoceros. The involuntary system actually has 2 components. One fine-tunes our body for relaxation, thinking, and digestion. The other rapidly transforms us for a sprint. We can take control of our involuntary nervous system if we use our brains to "trick" the system. The 2 parts of the involuntary nervous system cannot operate at the same time. Our bodies cannot be calm and in crisis simultaneously. That simple fact is the key to our mind's ability to relax the body. If we can learn to fool our bodies into sending out the signals to our relaxed, involuntary nervous system, our stress hormones stop firing and our relaxation, chillin' response takes over.

Because the 2 components of the involuntary nervous system cannot work together at once, we can fool our bodies by making them do the opposite of what they'd do under stress. This isn't always easy. We can't reroute our blood back to our bellies after it has shifted to our legs in preparation for running away. We can't shrink our pupils, reverse our sweating, or stop our faces from flushing. It's extremely difficult to calm our thinking and slow our heart rates. But breathing can easily be slowed. The next few paragraphs offer a brief overview of techniques to calm the body. Some people spend a lifetime learning to achieve a state of calm and use these approaches in a much more comprehensive way. I wish only to help you consider techniques to choose and explore further if you wish.

Breathe to Relax

Controlled breathing is at the core of almost every relaxation technique. Slow, deep breathing is a highly effective way to fool a stressed-out body, and breathing exercises can be done at any time. Deep, slow breathing is the simplest way to calm your racing mind. Yes, outside thoughts may intrude ("I have to remember to…"), but keep refocusing on your breath. Breathing exercises can be used whenever you feel tension rising, but it's beneficial to make it a regular routine even when you're not stressed. Try to breathe this way for about 15 minutes a day and make it as much a daily habit as brushing your teeth.

If teenagers struggle with deep, meditative breathing, I make the analogy to smoking. If they are smokers or have tried cigarettes or marijuana, they catch on right away. And if they are regular smokers, this is a way to help them quit. I explain that half the relaxation they get from smoking comes from the drag. If they try deep breathing as a regular stress-reduction strategy, they can enjoy the drag without the poison and it won't cost them 5 dollars a pack, risk a drug bust, make them smell, or pollute their lungs.

Teenagers who thankfully aren't smokers can also learn to take fuller, deeper breaths by placing a hand on their bellies and feeling it rise and fall while they repeatedly breathe in a rhythmic pattern. Swimming laps is another great way to use breathing as a stress reliever. Swimmers not only get good exercise, but swimming laps also requires rhythmic breathing that can help them relax.

Body Position

Some simple physical postures can fool a tense body and reduce stress. If someone confronts you in an aggressive way and moves in close—gets in your face, as kids say—don't stand chest to chest. That's a hostile posture and makes you want to fight back. Instead, turn slightly to the side and drop your shoulders into a more relaxed position. Tense situations can be neutralized by sitting down, angling your body, and taking deep breaths to control your thoughts—then problem-solve through negotiation.

The "study posture" is a common position that makes the body tense. How often have you seen kids hunch over a desk or table with tight, rounded shoulders, bent heads, and curved spines? Their legs and hips are bent in a position as if they're preparing to leap up from the desk and sprint. Often their legs are shaking to work out their nervous energy. Their entire posture seems to say, "Why am I doing this homework when I should be running from this tiger?"

If they want to be calmer while doing homework or taking a test, suggest that this posture and leg shaking make them even more tense. Instead, they can fool their bodies by sitting up straighter, with shoulders back and relaxed, and legs stretched out comfortably, no shaking. They can take some deep breaths to remind themselves that they are calm. They aren't about to run from a tiger. Now they are prepared to problem-solve in a testing environment.

Simply knowing these easy tricks makes kids feel more in control of their situations and thus less anxious.

Yoga

Yoga has been practiced around the world for centuries. While there are many variations, the core of yoga is breathing. By concentrating on slow deep breathing, people who practice yoga can relax while moving through poses that build bones and stretch muscles and tendons. Yoga is sometimes described as meditation through movement.

Meditation

Meditation is an ancient technique practiced throughout the world. In some cultures, it is used in a spiritual or religious context, but it need not be seen only in this light. As a stress-reduction tool, it induces deep relaxation. If practiced on a regular basis—about 15 or 20 minutes every day—it can reduce chronic stress.

The goal of meditation is to turn off mental activity and calm the wild thoughts racing through your mind. While meditating, you turn off your thinking process but remain in a clear state of awareness. This gives your mind a rest and lets your body relax. You can use meditation to concentrate on getting through a task step by step without letting it overwhelm you with anxiety.

Seven: Eat Well

Nutrition is vitally important to physical growth and development, but it must also be seen as part of an overall stress-reduction plan because a healthy body helps us manage stress. As I have repeated throughout these pages, parents' modeling is more important than any words. If parents drink cases of soda, for example, but tell kids it should be only an occasional treat, teenagers will spot the hypocrisy. Keep in mind that we parents buy the food and model eating habits.

Don't make food a battleground. Model good nutrition yourself, make sure your family has healthy foods to choose from, but don't take away the pleasure of eating. Mealtime is a great opportunity to enhance family connection and check in with your children. The atmosphere should be relaxed.

When we talk with young people about good nutrition and healthy bodies, we should be clear that this isn't about how kids *look*. So many destructive messages are out there in the media and in society at large about what we should look like. Men are supposed to have 6-pack abs, and women should be skinny. Please be careful not to add to those images. I have worked with many families whose parents want a child to lose weight but inadvertently trigger an eating disorder by implying how much cuter the child would be if she only lost 20 pounds. Some parents are confrontational: "If you can't even control what you eat, how do you think you'll ever be successful? No one wants to hire people who don't take care of themselves." Never tell young people that they don't look right. If they eat well and get regular exercise through play or sports, they will be fine.

If you think your son or daughter is overweight or obese—yet you're modeling healthy eating habits and providing good foods at home—let a health professional counsel your child. When food becomes a battleground within families, not only does it add extra stress, but serious consequences may result during adolescence and later in life.

Eight: Sleep Well

For teenagers, getting enough sleep on a consistent basis is essential for good health and for keeping stress levels manageable.

Sleep research data indicate that adolescents require 9 to 10 hours of sleep each night. But most of them aren't getting that much, which is why excessive daytime sleepiness has become a widespread problem among teenagers. Inadequate sleep and excessive sleepiness can have a profound negative effect on their health, school performance, cognitive function, and mood. Sleep is needed to solidify newly gained memories or skills, so it is not surprising that school performance declines with lack of sleep. Sleeplessness has also been associated with other serious consequences such as increased incidence of automobile crashes. And if a child is sleep-deprived, stressful situations are even more difficult to handle.

The American Academy of Pediatrics (AAP) and the National Center on Sleep Disorders Research (National Heart, Lung, and Blood Institute, National Institutes of Health) say that although sleepiness is rather common in teenagers, we should pay special attention to those who exhibit excessive sleepiness because it could indicate an underlying medical or mental health condition. According to their 2005 report, "Excessive Sleepiness in Adolescents and Young Adults: Causes, Consequences, and Treatment Strategies," most cases of excessive sleepiness result from insufficient time in bed and are associated with intrinsic changes in the sleep/wake cycle. External pressures (like studying) to go to bed later and wake up earlier are also involved.

Although these factors are the most common reasons for lack of sleep, they may not be the only reasons. Depression, obstructive sleep apnea, insomnia, narcolepsy, and other sleep disorders, medications, and stimulants, such as caffeine, can also impair sleep quality and cause daytime sleepiness.

During routine examinations, pediatricians may ask your child the following questions, or you may wish to think about them as they relate to you or your child:

1. Do you have trouble falling asleep at bedtime?
2. Do you feel sleepy a lot during the day? In school? While driving?
3. Do you wake up a lot at night?
4. What time do you usually go to bed on school nights? Weekends?
5. How much sleep do you usually get?
6. Has anyone ever told you that you snore loudly at night?

If your child often has trouble sleeping or is unusually sleepy during the day, talk with your pediatrician, who can help determine whether your child may be suffering from chronic sleep deprivation or an underlying sleep disorder.

Making the Bed Sacred

When I talk with young people about the importance of sleep, I suggest that they make their bed a special, almost sacred place. It should only be used for sleeping. Bed should not be a place to eat, read, listen to music, play games, veg out, talk on the phone, watch television, or play videos (another reason to keep televisions out of the bedroom). Teenagers who use their beds only for sleeping will get in the habit of relaxing and falling asleep more easily.

A leisurely bath an hour or so before going to bed helps relax the body and prepare it for sleep. As they are falling asleep, I urge young people to cool down from the day and put aside worrisome thoughts. It's easier to do this if they have followed one of the strategies for releasing emotions (discussed in the tenth part of this stress-reduction plan). They must release their emotions, however, somewhere other than in bed—sitting at a table or in a comfortable chair. Their bed should not be a place to worry, just to sleep. If it becomes a place to worry, it will become a figurative counselor. They will want to talk for at least 50 minutes and will wake up through the night for another "appointment." If they remain tense even after releasing their emotions, they can lie in bed and use deep breathing or visualization to help relax before sleep.

Nine: Take Instant Vacations

We don't always have to make reservations, travel for miles, or spend a lot of money to take a vacation. There are several ways to reap the benefits of a vacation and de-stress wherever we find ourselves. If we use the following techniques, we can escape stress for a while, find a safe refuge, and reenergize ourselves.

Visualization: When my daughters were 5 years old, I was able to take my family to Hawaii where I did a visiting professorship. We found an out-of-the-way beach with black sand, crashing turquoise waves, and salt spray in the air—one of the most beautiful places I have ever visited. I wanted my daughters to remember this place so that they could return there if they ever needed to get away from anything, a place of extreme calm whose memory would be bathed in love. I wanted to help them imprint the spot into a deep memory so we used each of our senses one by one. First I told the girls to close their eyes and pay attention to everything else.

> What do you feel? The warmth of the sun on one side of their bodies and a cool breeze on the other side. The wetness of the ocean spray against their skin. What do you hear? The sound of the crashing waves, the softer sounds of birds singing. What do you smell? The salt in the air. Now open your eyes, look around you, and tell me everything you see. Now close your eyes and describe it to me again.

There are many simple ways to learn to visualize. Visit a serene, beautiful place or go outside on a quiet, clear night and gaze at the stars and moon. Or suggest that your kids imagine their own special place and make it a memorable mental snapshot that they can pull out whenever needed. It doesn't have to be on a vacation or even a visually astounding place; it could also be a place of profound warmth and safety, such as a grandmother's house. The key here is to take the step beyond the visual or sensory memory and bathe the place in the security of your love for your children. Use this moment to tell them how deeply they are adored and remind them that whenever they are worried or troubled, they should remember this spot and how stable and secure your love will always be.

Think of your instant vacation spot as a screen saver on your computer—a spectacular view of sparkling blue water, a long stretch of sandy beach, a few gauzy clouds drifting across the sky. Like a screen saver, you can click on this tranquil picture in your mind's eye whenever you need to escape the stress of the moment. Simply close your eyes, picture this special tranquil location, and be in the moment: Do nothing else, be still, think of nothing else.

Hobbies: Hobbies provide another way to escape for a little while. A hobby may start with casual play and become such an interesting activity that it takes on a focus, even a fervor. It's terrific if kids develop a wide variety of interests during childhood. It gets a little more complicated when they reach adolescence because typical hobbies may be pushed aside in favor of organized group activities. But individual hobbies that they can do alone, in whatever "free" time they can muster, can offer mini-vacations. When young people develop a real love and passion for a hobby, it can be more than a good way to spend a rainy day; it can become something they turn to when they're feeling stressed or upset.

Reading: Instant vacations can come in many forms: Listening to music, watching television, or going to a movie can provide entertaining, relaxing escapes. But there's nothing quite like reading as a full-immersion experience for a true, full escape. A reader has to visualize the panorama, hear the dialogue, and smell the aromas. Unlike television where the sound and visuals are handed to you, reading requires several senses to kick in actively so you get a fuller, more engaging escape. Adolescents may think they have enough reading to do for school assignments, but they should also be encouraged to read as a way to relax and for the sheer pleasure of the experience.

Baths: Soaking in a warm bath is a great way to relax. A bath is also like a mini-vacation: a private time, a protected and safe space. Thirty minutes a day that you deserve to decompress with no disturbances allowed. You may want to light candles or scents or play soothing music.

"Is he crazy?" you're thinking. "He doesn't know my family. Thirty minutes without interruptions? Must be a fantasy." I urge you to protect this time for yourself. Think of it as a selfless act because you'll be modeling for your children the importance of a daily, private relaxation zone.

Preteens and teens crave a private space of their own. If you've modeled the soothing bath routine, they may find it's a useful tool for them too. Even if they don't use a bath, they will understand that their parents have private time to replenish themselves at the end of a long day—an important lesson that they can use to give themselves permission to refuel throughout their lives.

A bath an hour before bedtime is a particularly good way for adolescents and adults to cleanse away the day's stress and get a better night's sleep. Baths have a meditative quality. As you take deep breaths, your body gently rises and falls in the water if you allow your upper body to float. If you submerge your ears under water, leaving only your face above the surface, you can draw those deep cleansing breaths and listen to your rhythmic breathing. If you take your pulse, you will notice it slow as you "fool your body." The bath becomes an effective biofeedback machine to help achieve relaxation. One man told me that he bathes nightly to replenish himself as well as to visualize his problems and concerns disappearing. After he soaks and unwinds, he lets the water drain slowly and visualizes his concerns swirling away and, whoosh, they're gone.

Smelling Local Flowers: People who are able to take pleasure in the simple things can find instant vacations everywhere: in the scenery they drive by, the softness of a misty rainfall, or another person's smile. Even during times of extreme stress, they are able to see a little beauty and restore their energy. So many of us live hurried lives, always rushing from one activity to the next. We are so immersed in work that we don't notice what is all around us.

Children and teenagers benefit if they learn from us—forgive a twist on the cliché—to take time to smell the local flowers. When we take time to be refreshed by the beauty in our yard, a visit by dear friends, or watching a baby gurgle in delight when we make silly faces, kids notice our small pleasures and learn that it takes little to please us.

This is yet another reason to carve out free time for our children and teenagers. If they are constantly rushing from activity to activity, they'll never notice or explore their immediate environment. They don't learn to have pleasure and fun exactly where they are—without needing bells and whistles or adults to tell them how to enjoy the experience.

Ten: Release Emotional Tension

Young people often tell me that their biggest problem is anger, and they don't know where it comes from. Others tell me that they cannot sleep because their heads spin with the day's worries or excitement and their anticipation of the next day. I worry most, though, when they tell me that they feel numb and have nothing worthwhile at all in their thoughts. What these youngsters have in common are disorganized, overwhelming thoughts. In some cases, they have been exposed to emotional, even physical, traumas that overwhelm their capacity to deal with or even feel their emotions.

Many of my teenaged patients lead what would seem to be charmed lives—a wealth of material goods, good schools, intact families—but they feel numerous emotional forces coming at them from every direction. They can't figure out how to diffuse the pressure. As it builds, that pressure produces a variety of swirling emotions: anger, frustration, confusion, and a sense of being crushed by all the expectations placed on their shoulders. We visualize these overwhelming feelings as a chaotic maelstrom.

To maintain our sanity, we can build a symbolic container to enclose and control what would otherwise be chaos. People with healthy outlets have release valves attached to their containers that prevent the pressure from blowing in a dangerous way. Many of us, however, become afraid of opening our containers because the emotions within feel too painful, scary, or totally unmanageable to face. Instead, we keep squeezing our day-to-day troubles into the container for safekeeping so we can avoid dealing with them—we fantasize that we will deal with the contents...later. Over time the container becomes thicker and thicker to keep all our stresses inside. It becomes a figurative lead box—too heavy to lift, impossible to see through, and indeed toxic.

What happens when we have so many important, though painful, thoughts and emotions trapped inside our self-created lead box? Occasionally someone will push our buttons and cause the lid to pop open. Inexplicable, uncontrollable rage pours out.

The anger described by many teenagers erupts from their crammed lead boxes. Most of the adults in their lives only see the anger and problem behaviors without understanding the maelstrom of emotions and experiences that explain the rage. Some kids describe this sensation as head spinning. One young man said it feels like a tornado. Another visualizes his head squeezed like a tennis ball by a tough man intent on making it explode.

Many teenagers agree that drinking and drugs do a great job of stopping the spinning and releasing some of the pressure. They may be correct for the moment, but we know that drugs and alcohol just create bigger problems that will accelerate the spinning out of control. Hence the cycle of abuse— more spinning, more drugs, more spinning, and so on.

Just think of the many things adolescents commonly struggle with in the course of a few short years: sexuality, pressure to earn high grades, competition and social pressure from peers, perhaps parents' separation and divorce, and the inevitable college admissions process. How can they possibly savor the smell of spring flowers or recognize the unconditional love of their parents? How can they engage in polite conversation when they are working so hard to suppress their intense emotions? No wonder many of them stuff it all in their lead boxes.

That lead box can create something arguably worse than anger. It can create a sense of numbness. It can stop us from caring. It can make us lose what we value the most: our humanity. When we expend so much energy squeezing those painful, passionate, but real experiences inside our boxes, it becomes too difficult to care about the little things that make life worthwhile.

Numbness is a lost opportunity for cherishing every moment. When the present is not cherished and small things are not appreciated, it is hard to be resilient. We don't want this for our children. Though they will be exposed to challenges and pressures, we desperately want them to thrive, live life to the fullest, and have the resilience to survive regardless of the curveballs thrown at them. We have to raise children who can be exposed to stressors without locking their thoughts into emotionally toxic leaden containers. Our children need to be secure about accessing their emotions rather than fear them. But to do this, they need a strategy for feeling and for dealing with their experiences and concerns in manageable doses.

Containment is a good thing. People who feel everything fully in the moment can become dysfunctional. You probably know people who share every thought, feel every experience intensely, spout off reflexively, and send group e-mails in response to every perceived slight. While these people do not have a lead box, they are rarely happy and find it difficult to maintain relationships because they exhaust themselves and others.

Building a Better Box

I propose a different kind of container—a Tupperware-type box. In contrast to a lead box, it is made of light, flexible, nontoxic material. The container may be transparent, so the contents can be seen but don't stink. And they're safely stored in neat portions. More importantly, you can remove one portion at a time, lift the lid, burp the box, and tightly reseal it. People who know the contents of their boxes are aware of issues that challenge them and the experiences and memories that haunt them. Rather than letting tornados swirl in their heads, they can choose to release a bit of pressure by selecting one issue to deal with at a time.

When I work with young people who tell me that they have unpredictable, uncontrollable anger or frustration, I help them build a Tupperware box. We talk about how this type of container allows them to name the issues in their lives that overpower them. This is an important initial step because once they can name those troubling issues, they can begin the healing process by choosing one at a time to confront...and store the others for a while.

The parallel process of naming their *strengths* is vitally important. Not only would it be inefficient to make someone categorize all their problems before they're equipped to deal with them, it might even be dangerously frustrating. So before going through the process of identifying their stressors, it is equally important to be aware of their strengths and feel confident about having strategies to deal with feeling overwhelmed.

The Tupperware box technique can also be a preventive strategy, especially when used with young children. You don't need to discuss lead or Tupperware boxes to young kids—just help them learn to identify and name their problems. But preteens and adolescents will understand the box analogy. Parents can guide them to understand that when they feel overwhelmed or confused, they can identify a few manageable problems in their boxes and work on them one at a time. And if they are equipped with some of the techniques that follow, kids can manage the swirling emotions that numb them or paralyze them from taking action. The techniques that follow are the figurative release valves for the Tupperware box.

No part of this coping plan, including this technique, can substitute for ongoing counseling if an adolescent is heavily burdened, anxious, or depressed. If you are worried about your child's ability to cope, remember that you are so madly in love with your child that you can't always be objective. Use your child's teacher, counselor, pediatrician, or clergy to help you decide the level of support your child needs.

Using Creative Energy

Creativity is more than a component of coping; it is a facet of our inner selves that enables us to develop perspective and flexibility—both of which help us to be more resilient. Creative expression can give kids a voice to articulate their emotions as well as a way to lose themselves in the act of creation.

People with creative energies have a built-in antidote to perfectionism. It may take years to develop the skill to paint a perfect picture or sculpt a flawless statue. But the process itself is rejuvenating. Learning a new process and making many messy attempts can be more exciting than the end product. Those of us who appreciate the creation may assume that it flowed effortlessly from the artist, but most artists know that their best results usually come after many attempts, much practice, and hard work. They enjoy the process of creating and, despite frustrating fits and starts, keep trying to improve their creative work.

Take photography, for example. The viewer may see a magnificent panorama and marvel at the photographer's talent. Dozens or hundreds of rolls of film have been shot and developed, but that single photograph is the only one that satisfied the photographer fully enough to print. A perfectionist would never take the chance to "fail" so often, by shooting roll after roll, before producing the desired result. Artists strive for the perfect picture but know they can never achieve it without many attempts, learning each time how to do better. This flexibility to keep trying to do better enhances resilience. Artistic expression as a steady presence in young people's lives allows them to continue having open-ended opportunities to express themselves with less emphasis on the final product.

Creative expression also draws on our ability to look at situations from different angles and approach a problem from various perspectives. It's like the photographer who changes vantage point, lenses, and camera angles many times to capture totally different images, while most people would have just snapped a shot. People with only one perspective, who see life through a single unchanging lens, are limited in their approach to problems. But people who shift perspectives can reframe or paint an entirely new picture and make changes. They understand how to focus on a problem, attack it from different angles, as well as see other people's perspectives. These benefits of creative expression make us more flexible and resilient in confronting challenges. Young people who develop their creative selves enhance their resilience by learning to see problems from many angles and meet challenges by using varied techniques and perspectives.

Artistic ventures can be instant vacations. The processes of singing, acting, drawing, painting, sculpting, writing, dancing, and composing or playing music can be joyful releases. For some, artistic expression is a solitary event that allows time for reflection, introspection, or simply quiet private time. For many others, participating in a group effort, such as a class performance, church music project, or a group mural, offers an opportunity to express themselves while connecting with others.

Many young people use their creativity as a means of coping with problems. They use music, art, dance, poetry, or prose to express their feelings vividly and intensely. These outlets allow a degree of privacy; whether to show them is the artist's choice. Each creative work is subject to interpretation, but only the artist/creator needs to have a full understanding of what the piece means to him or her. Rather than containing emotions to fester within, artists are essentially able to say to themselves, "I know how I feel, there it is!"

I am amazed by how many poets and artists I find among adolescents who have lived tough lives. It isn't uncommon for them to rap, sing, recite poetry, or draw their feelings when words fail them or don't come easily. As I explore with them how they have survived difficulties, they frequently tell me, "I draw," or "I write music." These are powerful survival tools that soothe their souls. I am totally uninterested in whether their artistic product pleases the masses—I am not talking about training the next generation of cutting-edge artists. I simply want all young people to be able to draw on their creative side because it gives them an avenue to release their tensions and fears, develop their hopes, and express their dreams. Creative expression trains them to see other perspectives. It gives them other ways to cope and opportunities to experience the joy of creating.

Spirituality

People with strong faith or a deep sense of spirituality find comfort in prayer or meditation. While parents certainly can expose their children to religious practices and beliefs, ultimately each child will decide what role religion has in his life. He may see it as a community institution, cherished family institution or tradition, or personal means of managing his life, or he may reject it entirely. Young people can use spirituality in several ways—as a moral compass to build character, a means to reduce daily stress, solace in times of crisis, and a means to solidify a sense of purpose in their lives.

Spirituality can be a way for young people to grasp the interrelatedness of life on earth and strengthen their sense of connection and responsibility to others. I advise parents for whom spirituality is important to speak with their own spiritual leaders about how to encourage adolescents to use their religious beliefs as a personal, portable tool to manage life's stresses and disappointments and to draw inspiration.

Journaling

Journaling, or keeping a diary, can be a powerful tool for releasing emotions. It's another technique that says, "You want to know how I feel? Here it is, tucked away securely. My emotions are in a safe place where I can access them when I want to. I am in control of them. They aren't swirling around inside and taking control of me."

It can be tempting to gain insight into a teenager's secret world and innermost thoughts, but I strongly urge parents against looking at a teen's diary. I have seen this happen many times and, though parents can explain that they looked at the journal out of love and concern, adolescents never accept this argument. They see it as a serious violation of trust. I always tell parents that the journal is a place to write absolutely everything, true or untrue, real or imagined. If it's to be effective as a way to release emotional baggage, it must be a place where young people can play out their fantasies, darkest thoughts, or most romantic dreams. If parents read a journal, they might get an unnecessary scare. In other words, their yield will be low and they'll have taken away their child's release valve.

If parents become so worried about their child's behavior or emotions that they feel the need to check the journal, it is far better to open up communication instead of the journal. If the teenager shuts parents out, get professional help, starting with your school counselor or pediatrician.

As much as privacy should be respected, parents should be aware of a new type of journal: the Web log or blog. Many young people who may not take to a journal, perhaps because pen and paper are so old-fashioned, are blogging. These online journals can become very public. Anyone can check in on your child's most private thoughts, or at least those they choose to make known through the blog. Some blogs can be made more private; kids give passwords only to those friends they want to keep in the loop. If your children do blog, talk to them about the possibility that some of the things they reveal online may find their way to people who don't respect their privacy even if they do use passwords. Perhaps an old-fashioned paper journal would be more secure for their innermost thoughts and feelings. (The National Center for Missing & Exploited Children has wonderful free resources for teens and parents on Internet safety: www.ncmec.org.)

Talking With People Who Have Earned Trust

The greatest release of emotion for many people occurs when they share their thoughts, fears, and frustrations with others. It is a way of letting it go while getting needed attention. Sometimes talking is also a way to problem-solve, either because it helps the talker focus ideas and develop strategies to deal with the problem, or because the listener has a different perspective or experience with a similar challenge. Someone else's viewpoint can throw new light on a problem and shed wisdom on another set of choices.

Talking to another person also provides a chance to decompress, to let it all go. Sometimes we feel better when someone else knows all the things we're trying to handle—it somehow validates our feeling overwhelmed. But no one can resolve all his stresses at one time. Talking can be more effective in 2 phases. First, get it off your chest. Use the opportunity to talk about what's bothering you as an escape valve to prevent all your emotions from swirling inside your lead box. Then focus. Pick one issue to make it manageable. Talk about that one issue. Just talking about it may be all that's needed for you to begin bringing it under control. Or talking about that issue may be the catalyst for solving the problem. Either way, your Tupperware box is burped and less chaos will spin inside.

Young people need to be exposed to different perspectives, so it's important that they can talk to a variety of people. Parents often become frustrated when teenagers talk endlessly with their friends (in person, on the phone for hours, and by instant messaging), yet they're monosyllabic at home. When we ask them, "How was your day?" they're likely to reply, "OK." We make another attempt: "What did you do?" The answer: "You know, stuff."

They talk more with friends who, after all, do share more of their time and experiences. We hope those friends care enough about our kids and have the good sense to steer them in the right direction. Friends can be ideal sounding boards, or they can be poor influences. Other people can also offer children varying perspectives: older, mature adolescents, teachers, relatives, clergy, and coaches. Some parents feel guilty or insecure when teenagers confide in another adult, but they should know it's more beneficial for their child to talk with someone than to talk to nobody at all. During mid-adolescence in particular, when teenagers' struggle for independent thinking is at its height, it's vital for them to know people other than parents who will listen and talk.

Most parents naturally want to be their child's favorite listener. When I first meet families, parents sometimes tell me, "Oh, yes, we can talk about anything. My kids tell me everything." Sadly teenagers tell me a different story. Many say that they stop talking to their parents because their parents "just don't listen." This is partly developmental—a distorted perception that's a side effect of their need to trust their own decision-making skills. They reject out of hand their parent's potential for good advice. But their statement is frequently the truth. Parents often don't listen so kids stop talking. The good news is that parents who learn to listen well discover that their kids will talk to them more readily. Parents earn their trust when they make themselves worthy of talking to by responding less and listening more carefully.

Some young people's stress levels can become so high that they need to talk to a professional. It's an act of great strength and resilience to seek help when burdened. Never feel as if you have failed because your children need someone more objective and trained to help them through critical times. Sometimes a parent's job is just to love them unconditionally while another trusted adult helps them resolve an important struggle. As parents let this other adult do much of the talking, they should remember that the security of their love remains the bedrock of any solution.

Laughter—It's No Joke

Laughter is good for all of us, and we probably don't get enough of it. If you think about it, laughter is such a silly looking thing. We snort, we grunt, we make ridiculous sounds. There must be a biological reason that we're given this gift. Laughter releases stress. I see laughter as a refresh button. Let's say you're listening to a boring presentation at work. You can't pay attention for another minute and then a well-timed joke wakes you up. Or you're feeling down and someone tells a story that evokes a belly laugh. Afterward your mood is completely changed. You're refreshed. You feel you can start over.

Crying

Crying is another of those biological oddballs. People look so vulnerable and unattractive when they cry. Something so different from our normal way of being must have a purpose. Perhaps vulnerability is the point. Perhaps our need to get others to pay attention to our grief is the reason that crying is so entrenched in our social repertoire. Perhaps we need the attention to gain the sense of security that reminds us we remain connected to others.

Certainly crying is a powerful tool for releasing pent-up emotions. The old saying, "Have a good cry," is on target when we're sorrowful or consumed with stress. Think of how we comfort someone who's in tears: "That's OK, let it out." Letting it out is the goal. People feel lighter after they've released those pent-up feelings. Crying doesn't solve the basic problem, but it cleanses the emotions and prepares us to move toward a solution.

When teens are upset and crying, parents may say, "Oh, stop sobbing. It's not such a big deal." About half of our kids are raised to believe that crying is a sign of weakness. What do we call this half of our population? Boys. "Big boys don't cry! Take it like a man! There's no crying in baseball!" Then we expect men to be caring, sensitive, and in touch with their feelings. We must do better. If crying were reserved for girls, boys wouldn't have been given tear glands.

Discouraging young people from crying can create a disconnect between emotions and an ability to express them. It makes kids ashamed of their very authentic feelings and therefore may prevent them from seeking the support they need and reaching out in whatever way they can. When they are genuinely hurt or upset, it's more empathetic to say something like, "I see you're sad. Would you like to tell me what's bothering you?" and then listen and encourage them to talk about it. Often no words are necessary. A hug and a shoulder to cry on silently communicate, "I'm here for you; this is your secure base. Lean on me." Teenagers who have a secure place to recuperate from sadness are better prepared to move ahead.

Making Lists

Getting organized is a key problem-solving strategy, as well as a release for emotional frustration. Parents and teens know the feeling of being pulled in a hundred different directions (too many demands, too much responsibility). The stress seems overwhelming and chaotic. You can't enjoy anything because your head is spinning with thoughts about everything you must accomplish and all the work you aren't doing at the moment. You can't focus, you're inefficient, you can't fall asleep because you're making tomorrow's plans. You need an escape valve.

Like a lot of adults who feel snowed under, teenagers often make excuses and procrastinate. Sometimes it seems so impossible that they freeze and do nothing. It's quite helpful for adolescents to understand that getting organized can remove a lot of their stress. They don't have to accomplish everything at once; they simply can begin by breaking a big job into smaller, manageable steps.

Older kids and teenagers can break down jobs and to-do schedules by making lists on paper or on a computer: "What I need to do today. What I need to do tomorrow. What has to be finished by Friday." When their lists are printed or written down, there's a strategy in sight. They begin to feel they've taken some measure of control over this chaos by organizing it, and the pressure is diminished. Their mental and emotional energy can then be directed toward tackling the problems.

Two tricks make list making more effective. First, make sure something on the list is pleasurable. The second trick is meant to keep anxiety low by designing lists realistically. It's OK to have a long-term plan with goals that may not be accomplished for weeks, but it's also important for daily lists to be constructed in ways that assure teenagers that they're moving forward each day. As each segment is completed, they can check off that item on the list, see that they are making progress, and diminish their anxiety about completing the entire project.

Once again, parents can show the effectiveness of list making as a stress reducer by modeling the technique. When kids see you making your own to-do lists, they'll pick up the lesson more easily than if you simply say, "Get organized." When you do so, talk aloud about the fact that you make lists not just to organize all your responsibilities, but because it helps you reduce stress, preserve your energy, and enjoy the rest of your time.

■ ❖ ■ ❖ ■ ❖ ■ ❖ ■

Now that you have read through this comprehensive stress-reduction plan, I want to remind you that you can adapt these suggestions for your younger children, your teenagers, and yourself. No one is expected to use all of them all the time. You probably knew many of these techniques previously but may not have tried them, or you may have other techniques that I've omitted.

I hope that you expose your family to a wide selection of stress-management techniques so they are better prepared to deal with stress when they feel challenged. When I say "deal with," I have a specific point: Teenagers can be helped to cope with stress and somehow get past it, but nothing in this plan can make them immune to stress or make stressors disappear entirely. Everyone has times when we feel we simply cannot take any more stress.

I believe that the tools in this plan can equip young people to bounce back faster and stronger. But I don't want to leave you with the false sense that this plan is an answer to every problem or that your family should be able to handle everything just because you have a plan. It's OK to go through periods of anger or sadness. Don't deny your own emotions. Give your children the comfort zone to acknowledge their own feelings. We're all human. If we deny emotion, we deny the most complex, perhaps richest part of being human.

CHAPTER NINETEEN

Getting Ready to Leave…and the Year After

Parents want the college admissions process to go smoothly and successfully because it is their child's first important step toward higher education and a career. But the process carries a deeper, more emotional significance because our babies are flying out of the nest. This is the Real Show. They are actually about to leave home—leave us! We will have to learn how to manage new-found time (unless we have younger children at home). No more shuttling them between activities, worrying about their safety, and looking over their shoulders.

I can't imagine the prospect of my 10-year-old twins, Ilana and Talia, going off to college—but I know I'll weep. It will happen in a single day for me. Both girls will be gone at once. Suddenly my wife and I will be home alone. How will my babies handle it? (Oh, I know, they'll be 18, but they'll still be my babies.) How will I handle it? Some wise parents of high school seniors always assure me, "Don't worry. You'll be ready." I know they mean, "You'll be glad to have them out of the house by then." I cannot imagine that now, but I am certain that I won't be sending 10-year-olds to college. They'll be taller, wiser, and quick to prove to me that they're ready to go. They'll make extraordinary efforts to show me, even though some of that "proof" may be painful because they will be trying to convince themselves as well as me.

This time represents an overwhelming change in any parent's life after being a nurturing caregiver for almost 2 decades. Parents will have to focus again on themselves and on their relationships with other adults. Parents who imagine that the joyous years of parenting are about to end will desperately want the last year or two of high school to be spectacular, filled with love and good times. They want their teenagers to leave home with tears in their eyes while saying something like, "Thanks for all you did, Mom and Dad, for your nurturance, love, support, and wisdom. Oh yeah, and I will be calling you several times a day to tell you how much I cherish you, and I will be coming home every weekend, just to give you hugs, OK?"

Unfortunately this is an unlikely scenario. What happens in these last couple of years before college that often changes parents' and kids' connections? Let's look back to gain some perspective.

Remember how we used to snuggle our precious, vulnerable babies with their smiles and playful moments? There was no ambivalence in their gurgles of delight. No power struggles, no pushback, just squeals of pleasure. But the journey toward independence kicked in almost immediately. When they were ready to take their first steps, they wiggled their bottoms just before pulling themselves up to stand on wobbly little legs. They pushed away the arm of any adult who offered help. They wanted to say, "Gosh, thanks. I sure do appreciate your effort, but I'm struggling here to assert this new step toward independence."

Throughout childhood they became increasingly independent. The process went on through adolescence when it became painfully obvious that they didn't believe parents were needed, or so they told us. The first date? What a wonderful opportunity to have a conversation about sexuality, puberty, and morality. Time for "the talk" that parents looked forward to (with dread) since the first day of kindergarten: "Darling, I think that you are a maturing young lady and there are some things I think you are ready to learn." A noble try. Why did she respond, "You're such a dork, Dad. I don't need you to tell me anything!"? Because that's much easier for her to say than the truth: "I'm really scared. This emerging sexuality is really overwhelming. Only 3 years ago I wanted to marry you. I still think you're the most wonderful man ever. That's too weird, so I am going to ignore those feelings."

During this march toward independence, teenagers really don't need as many protective bonds with parents as they had when they were younger. But they also break those bonds to create the appearance of independence, if only to deal with the turmoil and anxiety within them as they take the next step. Teens may be excited when they reach new developmental milestones, but they are also frightened about the future. They may not tell parents clearly, but they worry about whether they will succeed. Uncertainty is scary. They worry about losing their secure relationships with parents, just as strongly as they worry that parents will stand too closely by their side.

At times like these, it's useful to think of milestones (entering high school, a first date, getting a driver's license) as a huge, gaping chasm that needs to be crossed. A young person can't simply stand on the edge and jump across.

Bending his knees and swinging his arms won't propel him across. He must go back several steps and get a running start. He has to stop thinking, suppress his fears...and leap! Is it any wonder that kids always seem to take a few steps backward just before they reach major milestones? This pattern prevails from early childhood right through adolescence.

But Can't We Help?

Why don't young people just ask for help in building a bridge across the chasm? Two reasons: First, they do—constantly—but they don't ask directly. They sometimes seek attention in ways that anger or frustrate parents. But they do get attention. Don't be fooled into believing that they need parents less during major transitions. They need parents even more. Second, if they expressed how much they needed parents or how confused or scared they are, they would become immobilized. Even the most emotionally intelligent adults have difficulty being so in touch with their feelings that they can articulate them clearly—especially in times of change or crisis. They tend to suppress emotions and come up with rationalizations that help them move forward, sometimes against their better judgment. Logic keeps warning them to stick with what is comfortable and familiar though external forces keep propelling them onward. Kids are no different. They are apprehensive, but they suppress those instincts that crave stability with a shield of indifference.

Rather than turning to parents for the security they crave, teenagers sometimes push them away. Over the years this pushback replaces so much of the joy of parenting with worries, feelings of betrayal, and occasional anger. It is critical for parents to understand the source of resistance to their nurturance if they are to figure out how to maintain a healthy connection with their children when they move toward college and adulthood.

Letting Go for College

All animals grow up and leave the nest. They go through their playful phase, practice adulthood, and then are on their own. Human children just play longer and their parents worry more. When children are ready for college, parents want that last time at home to be so special. It's the last opportunity for family togetherness. It should be a perfect time. The last family vacation before the child leaves home should be idyllic. Why then does your daughter say, "Mom, I hate you. I'd rather be with my friends. It's a good thing I'm leaving in August because I couldn't stand one more minute in this prison"? Because she is ready to cross a chasm, and it's so much easier than saying, "I love you so much that I can't even find the right words. You've done everything for me. I'm petrified. Do you think I'm ready to go off on my own? Do you think you'll miss me as much as I'm going to miss you?"

Adolescents challenge parents because they need to loosen one kind of connection—the one that involves parents' assuming full responsibility for them. When challenged this way, it's completely understandable for parents to feel hurt or even angry. If they don't understand what is happening, parents may push harder to keep control. This only breeds resentment and ill feelings. But if they recognize that their teen is struggling for independence and learn to celebrate it, everyone will be healthier and less tense.

Every time kids behave badly or speak meanly to parents doesn't neces- sarily reflect their growing independence or their conflicted emotions. Some- times they might just be acting mean. They know a parent's vulnerabilities. Whether they are justifiably or unfairly angry, they can be masters at saying hurtful things. Often it's a way of shouting, "Listen to me!" Perhaps they're testing the waters to grab attention before they can bring up something that's troubling them. If parents respond with anger and shut them down, they may feel justified for not sharing their concerns: "Remember, I was going to tell you, but then...."

When parents listen and reserve judgment, their teenagers' stories unfold. But it's OK to tell them when they hurt your feelings—not in a way that makes them feel guilty, but just a clear statement of fact that their behavior is inap- propriate and hurtful. That is an important part of a parent's job in building character. Even when kids challenge the parental connection, parents need to be consistent about one thing: Their love is unconditional and they will always be there for their children. With this clear message, parents say, "Go ahead—grow. I've got your back."

"You'd Rather Spend Time With Whom!?!"

"How come you are so sweet and faithful to your friends and so nasty to us?" Sound familiar? Most parents ask this question of teenagers at one time or another. Did your parents ask you this? Have you asked it of your teenagers, or at least thought about it? To understand the answer, it's necessary to step back in time. Until children reached adolescence, parents were the center of the universe. Mom and Dad were heroes. If kids needed answers—"Why does the tide go in and out?" "Why is there war?"—they counted on parents to supply them. They agreed with parents' political and social views. Their values were essentially the values parents instilled.

When they reach adolescence, they need to figure out who they are. They realize, in a perplexing and uncomfortable way, that much of what has defined them until now was based on what parents built. To figure out who they really are, teens need to reject parents. In this phase, almost everything a parent says is met with a subtle—or not so subtle—roll of teens' eyes. Parents are allowed to give them a ride home after the game as long as they park a block away. Parents are not allowed to talk to or about teens' friends. Parents are supposed to be silent and invisible, or at least in the deep background.

Adolescents reject parents not because they stop loving them, but because they love them so much. In figuring out who they are, they have to be clear about who they are *not*. And they definitely are not Mom or Dad.

Suddenly they need to create a new family, a group whose values they share and in whose presence they are guaranteed safety. They turn to a set of friends to begin to define themselves. Because this group doubles as their new family—one they do not have to differentiate from—friends take on a central role during adolescence. While high school friends may remain important throughout life, we adults know that some of the best relationships are yet to come. Adults also know that family remains a steadfast connection for healthy people. Teens aren't ready to come to these realizations, however. For them friends are of utmost importance, and the thought of leaving them to go away to college can be overpowering.

While parents want to cherish every moment with their kids and create new memories before they leave for college, teens want to spend every precious moment with friends. When parents push too hard or ask the ill-fated question, "Why would you rather be with your friends?" the predictably hurtful response is likely to be, "At least my friends trust me" or "I have fun with my friends. They don't always tell me what to do!"

On a subconscious level, teenagers may know that their friendships might not withstand the test of time, whereas their relationship with parents is solid and permanent. This is another reason that parents often lose out at the end: Kids know Mom and Dad will always be there, so they want to spend time now with their friends. It is hurtful but easier to manage if parents understand that their teenager feels torn in many directions.

Loosening Our Reins

Because kids are not always on their best behavior in late adolescence, for many reasons, parents are often in a quandary about how to discipline effectively. A question that parents often ask is "How do I discipline my children now that they're taller than I am, and they think they don't have to listen anymore?" or "I know they are going to be off on their own soon—so what do I do now?" These questions have no simple answer. But it is clear that parents cannot give up on discipline entirely, no matter how many times a child may imply that what parents say does not matter. A fuller discussion of discipline is offered in *A Parent's Guide to Building Resilience in Children and Teens: Giving Your Child Roots and Wings* (Ginsburg KR, Jablow MM. American Academy of Pediatrics, Elk Grove Village, IL; 2006), but we would like to offer a brief summary here. First, we want to reiterate that discipline means *teach* or *guide*. It does not mean control. This is particularly important to recognize at this stage because controlling is no longer an option, yet teaching is as important as ever. The development of resilience depends on parents' relinquishing tight control in favor of guidance, attention, and support so that young people have opportunities to test their ability to maintain self-control. That is not to say that parents take a completely hands-off approach. Parents can enhance a teenager's growing sense of self-control by observing, offering a steadying hand, and guiding rather than controlling every action. Of course, listening actively and being a sounding board for a teenager's thoughts remains the most effective means of offering guidance.

You don't want to suddenly change your parenting style just because your teenager is getting ready to leave home or is rejecting your limits. Of course, by this time he should have fewer restrictions because he should have earned more freedoms and privileges. But regardless of how convincingly or emphatically he states, "I will be on my own in 3 months!" he still needs to understand that there are always acceptable boundaries, and that safety is never to be compromised. It is not the time to become disengaged. If you do that, your teenager will interpret it painfully because she will believe you've given up on her. And while you certainly should permit more freedoms in response to your teen's increasing maturity and responsibility, it is not the time to become overly permissive.

Some parents revert to the authoritarian approach because they sense that they are losing control and want to pull the reins tight: "Listen, wise guy, you may be going to Football Champ State U in the fall, but I'm paying the bills, and while you are in my house...." The problem with this approach is that parents are conceding that they have no role once their child leaves home, turns 18, or Mom and Dad stop paying the bills. There's nothing magical about the 18th birthday. I want my children to come to me for guidance and comfort throughout their adult years, though I hope they will need a different kind of guidance as they gain greater wisdom. I want them to understand that now, always, and forever I have experience worth considering as they make decisions. At the least, I will be a loving sounding board who will always have their best interests in mind.

The Sun, Moon, and Stars

Is it possible to love our children too much? No. But it is possible to be too centered on them. While they should be the heart of our lives, children cannot be our sole focus. Many parents today are so committed to parenting that the lines become blurred between their lives and their children's. This is the "We are applying to Big-Name University" or "We are so worried about the SATs" phenomenon. Children need their own lives—lives that are interdependent with, but clearly independent from, their parents' lives. And we need our own lives, interdependent with but clearly distinct from theirs. We can take pride in their accomplishments, revel in their joys, and feel deeply when they are in pain, but we cannot live our lives through them.

When children perceive that they're the sun, moon, and stars in a parent's universe, it is too much pressure on them. They often feel the need to be perfect. Every shortcoming is magnified because they worry about their own disappointment and about letting parents down. Children who worry excessively about parents' emotions may not be willing to try new ventures. If they believe that their actions or accomplishments are the sole determinant of parents' well-being or sense of self, they may try too hard to be trophy children. They may become frustrated and ashamed when they do not excel. Or their fear of failing their parents will prevent them from succeeding—they will lack the confidence in their own strengths and resilience to take the very chances necessary to succeed. This is yet another reason why the college admissions process must be about teenagers rather than parents. It is their initiation into adulthood. When it becomes about how it reflects on you, or somehow reflects on your success as a parent, it puts added pressure on your children when that's the last thing they need.

Our Adult Connections

We certainly want kids to experience security and connection to us, but at the same time we need to maintain our adult lives—to preserve our own time, personal relationships, and connections to our community. If we maintain connections to spouses, friends, and coworkers, we will do a great deal toward keeping our families happy and together, and at the same time we'll model for our children a good example of meaningful relationships.

As an adolescent advocate who desperately wants parents to cherish their teens, I strongly urge you to take care of yourselves, savor your own pleasures and accomplishments, and nurture your adult relationships for the good of your children and yourselves. If nothing else, you will find it easier to bounce back as your teenagers inevitably grow up, lead the independent lives you've prepared them for, and go off to college.

For nearly 20 years, or longer if you have more than one child, your life has been a juggling act of childrearing, managing a career, and maintaining your adult relationships. In the last few years, much of your energy may have been focused on preparing your teenager for the next stages of life. It is imperative that as you prepare your teen to make the transition, you are also readying yourself for a life that will be much more centered on you and your adult relationships.

It is not uncommon for spouses to look at each other during this phase and wonder, silently or aloud, "What will we talk about when the kids are grown?" While some couples may have done a wonderful job of maintaining romance and mutual interests through their childrearing years, most have let that slip a bit. After all, there was only so much time in a day. But the kernel of your relationship was formed before your children entered your lives. The thing you have had most in common during the last few years may have been your children, but it was your common interests that first cemented your attraction to each other. It is time to rediscover those interests and that passion.

We are not pretending to be *Cosmopolitan* magazine here, but you really have to begin prioritizing your relationship. Renew your shared hobbies and interests. Begin fantasizing about the travel and good times you will share when your kids leave home. Make sure that you have romantic "dates" free of discussion about your children. At the same time, reconnect with your friends. Your renewed relationship with your spouse has a better chance of thriving if you have other rich adult relationships. For single parents, this is the time to focus on both platonic and romantic relationships. For parents with new part-ners, this is never the time to tell them that they couldn't understand your feelings as your baby grows up, it's the time to draw closer and seek support.

If you have become so child focused that you're resistant to investing time in adult relationships while your kids are still at home, then here's one more reason to do so: Your teenagers will only be able to leave home with confi-dence and security if they know you're OK. If they believe you are reliant on them for your well-being or sense of purpose, they will enter adult life with guilt and ambivalence.

No matter how firm a foundation your adult relationships have, you should still expect a rocky transition as teenagers prepare to pack their gear for a college dorm. Many parents say there is a readjustment period the first year or two after their last child leaves home. But they say that after this short time, their life blossoms with personal fulfillment and they go on to share the best years yet with their partners and friends.

It's Not Really Over

Letting go is hard. Part of what makes it so difficult is the fantasy that our role as parents comes to an end the day we send our last (or only) child to college. The good news is that parent-child relationships last a lifetime. When children are clear that they can stand fully on their own 2 feet, they will be ready to come back and show affection to the people who were there when they first discovered their toes. They will return to you without the ambivalent, confusing feelings that generated so much anger earlier in adolescence. Then they will be ready to understand that you are human and always tried your best. Then they will no longer push back and will be ready to demonstrate the caring that they always relied on receiving from you and that they secretly felt deeply toward you.

Many parents who had the same fear you may have now—of losing this wonderful role—learn that the best years come when they can sit back, live their own lives to the fullest, and celebrate the young adults that their children have become.

The Year After

The first year your baby heads off to college is likely to be the most difficult, both for parents and for new freshmen who will have completed the initiation ritual of moving from high school to college. Parents need to remember that moving into a dorm room does not really signify entrance into full independence. For that reason, it's important for parents to play their cards right during freshman year, to figure out how to balance parental involvement with distance, and to match this balancing act with the individual child's needs.

All parents want some reassurance that their freshmen children still love—even remember—them despite geographic separation. I can reassure parents that a time will come, in the not-too-distant future, when you will get all the love you deserve, but it may not be during the first year away from home. Until they are clearly standing on their own feet, they are likely to be quite ambivalent about contact with parents. They will be happy, of course, to keep in touch and let parents know how they're doing—though this may not be often enough for parents' tastes.

Seventeen and 18-year-olds, living away from home for the first time, usually want to maintain just enough distance so they can remind themselves that they're on their own. But some go to the other extreme. It's not uncommon to see students walking around campus with cell phones to their ears and checking in with parents several times a day. Everything in moderation. Don't hang up on them, but don't allow cell phones to become satellite-controlled umbilical cords either. Let them know you're thrilled to hear from them, and certainly always leave communications open, but try to limit calls to one a day or fewer.

Many parents express sadness when they first visit campus. They have difficulty understanding why their children seem rude or embarrassed by their presence. They notice how friendly a roommate is toward them, but feel empty because their own pride and joy greets them unenthusiastically. (Of course, they never saw how chilly the roommate was to her parents.) Rather than feeling hurt, parents need to understand the ambivalence many college freshmen feel by seeing parents on their own new turf. They love their parents, but that love makes them question whether they're really ready to be independent. These conflicting emotions create confusion and anxiety that comes out as rudeness. When they become confident that they can stand on their own, they will be more comfortable about giving parents the embracing welcome they deserve.

Always Leaving the Door Open

Independence is always the ideal goal, but freshman year can be a tumultuous time: new friends, new relationships, harder work, and new social opportunities. Formerly academic stars in high school, college freshmen find themselves on a new playing field with other stars. They often struggle with feelings of ordinariness or inadequacy. Trying to balance studying with partying in an unfamiliar environment with new peer norms and without parental guidance, most freshmen make this transition well and thrive. Some, however, do go through a difficult adjustment period.

I urge parents to check in with their freshmen and make sure they feel comfortable telling you if the transition is difficult. Most students know how much parents want this experience to go perfectly. They know how proud you are of them, and they know what a big investment is riding on their college education. So it's important that they not feel that they're disappointing you if they hit some bumps in the freshman road. Continue to lend an ear, offer your understanding from a distance, and let them know that they can always rely on your support as they make their own way in the college world and beyond.

PART THREE

The Dean of Admissions

Talks to Students

I am me, for that I came.

Gerard Manly Hopkins

The secret to being admitted to the college of your choice is to pick the right college for you in the first place. It isn't rocket science, but it does take some time, thoughtfulness, self-examination, courage, and a sense of adventure. This section is designed just for you, and it is a two-for: We'll offer sound advice to maximize your chances of admission and help you reframe your approach to applying to college. This should help keep your anxiety under control because sometimes things look different, less frightening, when they are reframed.

Applying to college is a process that yields the best results when the preparation is the most thorough. Let's start by looking at the college admissions process in another way, by seeing it for what it really is.

It is hard to be allowed to grow up these days. We adults say that we want you to be an adult, but subconsciously we often do not. There are reasons for this. Some of us love your company and want to keep you around us for as long as possible. Some of us fear getting old and see your departure to college as a signpost along the road to aging. Some of us fear an empty nest. But now is your time to move into the next important phase of life, and the process is initiated by applying to college.

An Initiation Into Adulthood, a Rite of Passage

Rather than view the college application process with terror because of the gossip you've heard from your friends, I urge you to see it as the closest thing to an initiation into adulthood that we have in this secular society. An initiation is the process through which a human moves from one level in society to another—in this case, when a teenager becomes an adult in the eyes of the culture around him or her. An initiation is a process, not an event. It happens over time. It always carries an element of anxiety and fear, or else it isn't an initiation. It calls on all skills previously learned and, most importantly, it can only be done by the initiate and no one else. In other words, it is a process through which young people are granted permission to show adults what they can do, how they can manage anxiety and still function successfully—that they are indeed ready for adulthood.

An initiation like applying to college can be a very lonely venture. It calls for courage and consistency and a certain faith that everything will work out for the best. Most 11th- and 12th-grade students feel panicky about applying to college because they fear they may not be admitted anywhere, or at least anywhere acceptable to friends and family. Many students do not feel ready to apply or ready to leave their homes. That's OK because, just as you did not go to kindergarten wearing a diaper, you will be ready when the time is right.

Applying to college happens in several steps. Don't skip any of them because each is important to the entire experience.

Step 1: The Importance of Self-Reflection

Remember, college admissions is all about the "match," the compatibility between student and school. Not all schools are alike, just as not all students are alike. The challenge—and the excitement—comes from the search for that compatibility.

There are colleges out there that will love and honor you because you are the right match for them. But to find them, you first have to know who you are. To prepare for your initiation, you need some self-examination, some time to wonder who you are (not who you "should" be), under what circumstances you learn the best (not how you "should" learn), and what makes you happy (not what "should" make you happy).

In other words, self-examination means seeing and valuing yourself as you are, separate from your family members and friends, because your DNA is unique from everyone else's, and you have a certain destiny that is yours alone. It means that you do not need to be anyone else. You don't need to be better looking or smarter or richer or more athletic or more anything. You just need to be and therefore see who you are.

Becoming Your Own Mick Jagger

I have loved the Rolling Stones since I saw them on their first US tour in 1966, and I've seen them on most of their tours since then. I realized recently, however, that the Stones' Mick Jagger is the poster boy for the concept of creating your own reality. After all, he can't really sing very well. He certainly has his own style and a unique and instantly recognizable voice, but it is not what you would call "melodic." He can't really dance well either, though he is athletic and limber and is a joy to watch as he runs the entire length of the stage many times throughout the show. And he is not the world's handsomest man. In fact, it's safe to say that he would never attract beautiful women if he wasn't, well, Mick Jagger. So how is it that he is a true superstar, an internationally known symbol of rock and roll well into his 60s when many of his peers are just old? I think it's because Mick Jagger has always believed that he is a rock star, and so he is, because his millions of fans worldwide have bought into his own inner vision of himself. He's a master at creating his own reality.

So what if you became your own Mick Jagger? What would that mean? Who do you yearn to be way deep down? Who is it that you know you are, but others have yet to see? The key to creating your reality is quite simple: If you can identify and acknowledge that true identity, you will bring it into being. And chances are, you will become the person you were meant to be, different from everyone else, with an important role in a world that badly needs you.

First Things First: Who Are You?

My favorite teacher Sharon Turner says, "How is anyone going to know who you are if you don't know who you are?" So let's start there. Can you sum yourself up in one sentence? As in, "I am a...." For example, you could say, "I am a happy, smart, loving friend," or "I am a talented, creative, persevering, resilient star athlete." The goal here is to describe the person you really know you are but never get the chance to acknowledge out loud, to be your own Mick Jagger. Try it. Put it into one sentence and then repeat it to yourself every day for at least 30 days. You will soon internalize that self-image and then, as you read college brochures, visit colleges, or write your essays, you will automatically be running that school through your own filter (Does it fill my needs? Will it be a good choice for me? Will I be happy there?) instead of just wondering, "Will I get in?" You will feel more in control and will analyze the information differently.

How Do You Learn Best?

Now that you know who you are, start thinking about the circumstances in which you learn the best. Do you learn best through reading books? Through the "see one, do one, teach one" method? By listening to the material? Through a combination of all of these? Do you thrive within structure? Do you hate structure and need freedom of choice? Do you need a relationship with your teachers, or do you prefer anonymity? Do you like to be lost in the crowd or be the center of attention? Do you prefer to work with a group or work alone? Are you a multitasker, or do you need to do things one at a time? Do you need privacy and quiet when you work, or do you like activity and noise around you? Are you more contemplative, or do you like to learn by doing? Are you the generalist or the highly focused individualist?

Answering these questions will help you to determine whether you need a larger or smaller college, a more structured curriculum or more freedom, an interactive experience or a more solitary one. There are more than 3,000 colleges and universities in the United States, each unique in its own way. There are large public universities, large private universities, small private colleges, 2-year community colleges, 4-year colleges, and professional schools. When you decide how you learn the best, many possible schools will surface as good choices for you, and others, maybe even some you thought would be perfect, will fall away because you'll see that they are not compatible with your learning style. This is the beginning of finding the right match.

Step 2: How to Find the Match

Now that you have a sense of who you are (Remember your 1-sentence description?) and how you learn the best, you need to do one more thing: Stop listening to your friends about colleges. I know, I know, that's hard, but there are good reasons to do it anyway. First, they don't know anything about college admissions or about the schools themselves even if they have siblings studying there. Second, a little competitiveness is always running through those conversations, and you do not want to insert competition into your friendships. Third, a good match for them may be a disaster for you. One size does not fit all when it comes to college. So vow to yourself right now that you will not talk about colleges or your choices of colleges with your peer group. Hold your privacy. You will be glad you did.

"My first choice college should have lots of closet space."

If your high school has a guidance office, visit it regularly when you start your junior year. Look through the catalogs and talk with the staff about possible choices. Many guidebooks offer comparison charts of college offerings that might be helpful in your narrowing process; however, avoid any book or magazine that rates colleges. Rankings are subjective and steeped in the bias of the publisher, and they offer no real information to help you decide what college is best for you. Remember—there is no one "best" college. There are only colleges that are best for you.

You'll need to understand the culture of the various colleges to decide if they would be good choices for you. The culture is defined by the values of the community, how the community members act, and why they act that way. Every college has its own culture, just as every high school, every company, and every family has. For example, some schools have very free and open cultures where the individual is prized. Others put the emphasis on the group and what is best for the group. Some college cultures are steeped in tradition while others reject tradition. Some college cultures are rule-based while others have no rules. Some are designed for students who do not yet know what they want to major in, or even do in life, while others are designed for students who are completely self-directed.

You will fit in well with some cultures and will not gel at all in others, so it is crucial that you identify the cultures this early in your application process. Look at the schools' literature and Web sites. What impressions do you get about their cultures? Trust your impressions. Some schools will present a traditional feel, others a more contemporary one, still others will seem nontraditional. See what resonates with you. How do you physically and emotionally feel when you look at their materials? If your stomach starts hurting, for example, that particular school may be making you nervous and therefore is not a good choice. On the other hand, if you find yourself grinning from ear to ear as you scan their material, put that school in your "yes" pile.

When you visit those colleges, always ask everyone you meet there to describe the school's culture. Many people will be puzzled by that question, but you will find a few common themes in their answers. For example, here are a few responses to that question I heard while visiting colleges with my daughter this past year.

"We believe that every student at our school—regardless of major—should have a shared experience of the great books of literature, so everyone studies the same 5 books. That way, the books can be discussed in every one of our students' classes, regardless of their major." (The culture values a shared experience for everyone.)

"We expect our students to hold a certain morality of behavior, one based in the teachings of Jesus Christ." (The culture is based in a particular religious tradition.)

"Our college is perfectly designed for students who do not want to be told what to do. No one will hold your hand here or tell you what to study.

There is drinking here, and it is up to the student to decide to drink or not."
(The culture values the individual and free choice.)

"At our college, we expect students to complete at least 30 hours of
community service per semester." (The culture values service to others.)

You can see how you might fit into some and not others. So when you
look at colleges, ignore the rankings from the magazines or books and ask
about the culture. It will give you a clearer idea whether that school is for
you and should be pursued as a possible choice.

The Myth of Rankings

Many students and families look at college rankings and use them as a
guide for deciding where to apply. They do not stop to evaluate what the
rankings are actually judging or their overall relevance. Accepting another's
point of view about the quality of a school defeats the purpose of education—
to think critically about what you are hearing or reading. Many ranking systems are constructed in ways that are similar to fans voting for members of
an all-star team. They are built on reputation and popularity, not so much
based on relevant fact.

If you are tempted to read an article that ranks colleges, make sure you
understand how the authors came to those conclusions. What were they
judging and how did they do that? Is that relevant to your assessment of
the quality of education you would receive there? For example, some ranking
systems include faculty salaries and "percent of endowment dedicated to
students" in their algorithm. While these facts in themselves are important
to someone at that school, there probably is no direct correlation between
them and quality of education. Do not trust others' opinions like this until
you understand what is being judged and why.

Campus Visits

It is a good idea to tour the campus of a college that interests you. You will
have an information session about the school, usually led by an admissions
officer, and then a tour led by a student tour guide. Walking around the
campus, watching the students around you interact, sitting in on classes,
eating in the dining hall, listening to hallway conversations, and reading
the bulletin boards and dorm room doors all give you the experience of
being a student at that college. Most high school students find that they
have a gut reaction to a college when they are there—they know whether
they like the place. You don't need a lot of information to make that decision
because most often it is just a feeling based on the experience itself. You'll

know if the students at that college are like you and whether you'd fit in. Trust your intuition.

It is important for you to be engaged on a campus visit. Prepare a few questions in advance and make sure to ask them yourself—do not let your parents take over. When I was touring schools with my daughter, the parents were asking all the questions. Parents so dominated the tour that they literally pushed students out of the way to squeeze into the sample dorm room. You would have thought that the parents were the ones going to college. But what was most disturbing was that the students hung back and let their parents do it all. They did not push back and engage, which was a huge opportunity lost. Remember that this is *your* initiation, and one of the colleges you visit may be your home for the next 4 years.

Before you visit a college, it's a good idea to discuss the ground rules with your parents. For example, my daughter told me that it would embarrass her if I asked any questions, so I agreed to have her preapprove my questions before I asked them. She did not want to walk next to me on the tour, but preferred to walk in the front with the tour guide while I walked at the back of the group. This gave her some privacy. We had a wonderful time on the campus visits because we established the rules ahead of time, instead of working them out when we were actually on campus and under some stress.

Some students find that it works best to have their parents go on an earlier tour and then meet up later to compare notes. That way, students can get their questions answered by the student tour guide without judgment from the parents and vice versa.

Remember that this is your initiation. Step up and ask the tour guide and the admissions staff for answers that will help you know whether that school is a match for you. Trust your instincts. If you don't like the feel of the school, it's OK to leave before the tour is finished. Move on to the next college.

One more important point: Don't let a tour guide alone turn you off to a school. Everyone has a bad day once in awhile. Check out your impressions about the school with others around campus before dismissing the school altogether.

How Many Applications?

This may come as a shock, but it turns out that there is more than one soul mate in the world for everyone. Yes, we have many soul mates in our lives and that goes for college, too. Many people believe that there is only one perfect college for everyone, but in fact there are many good colleges for you. Because there are so many students applying to college these days, however, it is more difficult to be admitted to many schools, so make sure to develop a list of good choices for yourself. Many guidance counselors recommend the following: at least 2 likely schools (also known as safety schools, where you have a good chance of admission), at least 2 possible schools (maybe you'll get in, maybe not), and at least one or two reach schools (those schools that are a long shot for you). Just make sure that you cover enough of the whole range so that you'll have at least one admission. This means 6 to 8 applications if you are willing, although some students apply to fewer and some to many more. Make sure that every one of your choices is your number one choice—meaning that if you are admitted only to your safety school, you will happily go. Do not apply to schools you would not attend if admitted.

If you cannot afford the application fees, most private colleges and universities will waive the fee if you ask them.

The "Early" Dilemma: Should You Apply Early Decision or Early Action or Not at All Early?

Many colleges offer freshman admission in different stages. The regular action stage or time usually has a December, January, or even February deadline for a September enrollment. Most students apply at the regular admission time. Many colleges, however, also offer an early admission stage, usually with a November deadline. Early admissions policies can be very confusing because so many versions are available now. Here are the standard versions.

■ Early Decision (ED): An applicant applies by the early deadline, gets a decision in December or January, and commits to enroll if admitted. Early decision is what we call "binding" for both the college and the applicant, meaning that this is a contract. Depending on the college's rules, an ED applicant can also apply to an early action school, but must withdraw all other applications if admitted to the ED college.

■ Early Action (EA): The applicant applies by the early deadline, gets a decision in December or January, and if admitted does not have to enroll. In traditional EA, applicants can apply to other schools early if they wish.

■ Single-choice Early Action: The applicant applies EA to that school, and only that school, early but does not have to enroll if admitted. No other early applications are allowed.

Students often feel pressure to apply early to a college to get the process over with by January. You should understand that early programs are designed to accommodate those students who know exactly where they want to go to college, and they should not be used strategically to increase one's chances of admission. While the urge to get the college application process over with is natural, you should only apply early to a college if you really, really want to enroll at that college. You will change a lot between September and April of your senior year, so it's OK not to apply early and to keep your options open. Do not apply ED to a college just to get in somewhere early and then plan to change your mind later about the choice. While the ED contract is not legal, it is unethical to violate the ED rules this way unless you need more financial aid than the ED college can offer you and simply cannot afford to enroll.

Step 3: Applying

The Interview

Always take up the school's offer for an interview if one exists. Applying to college through the written word only is very daunting. When admissions officers meet you in person, they always get a better picture of the match and, best of all, you'll get more information about whether the school is a good fit for you. Here are a few steps to follow when you interview.

- Do your research before you interview. Read the school's materials, be familiar with its programs and offerings, and talk with people who went there. Then identify a few questions you'd like answered by your interviewer. Make sure to write them down because no matter how excellent your memory is, you might forget things if you are anxious.

- Set up the interview yourself. Don't let your parents do it for you. This is your initiation. You must do all the work yourself.

- Dress nicely. You do not need to dress up too much, but remember that you are showing yourself off, so always look good (hair brushed, teeth clean, clothes ironed).

- Never take your parents with you into your interview. Send them off for some coffee or to conduct campus reconnaissance.

- Start the interview with small talk (about the weather or something you have in common with the interviewer) and then at the right moment, pull out your questions and get them answered. This will do 2 things. First, it will send the signal to your interviewer that you are taking the interview seriously and can hold your own in conversation. Second, and most important, you will learn much more about the school than you otherwise would have. And you will have done it all yourself—a necessary step in your initiation.

- Be prepared for the "Why do you want to go to this school?" question. Make sure you know why. Practice in advance.

- Do not ask for any information that you could have read on the college's Web site. That will make you look unprepared. When my daughter and I toured a university well known for its performing arts, one of the students asked, "Do you have music here?" The admissions staffer leading the information session groaned because that student had not done his homework. I've had students ask me in interviews if MIT had any science they could major in! Yikes! It's a big turn-off.

- Keep the conversation moving, but don't do all the talking. Some students talk too much when they get nervous.

- Make sure to talk. Some students get completely quiet when they are nervous. Don't make the interviewer do all the work. (That's why you wrote down those questions before you came.)

- Smile and thank your interviewer at the end. Be gracious and as charming as you can. Everyone likes to be treated kindly and with respect.

The Art of the Application

To maximize your chances of admission to the college of your choice, you must approach its application with care and with complete integrity. Do not just fill out the questions. Understand that the admissions officers who evaluate the applications are looking for the right match of student for their school's culture and community. Because you have already learned about the school's culture, and you feel it would be compatible with you, you can write the application with that fact in mind. For example, if a college is looking for students who will make great researchers and you know that you would be one, you will want to write your application accordingly. Make the effort to show that aspect of yourself by highlighting your past research experience.

If you know that a college values independence and you have that in excess, lace the application with examples of your independence. By showing the admissions staff what you have in common, you will make it easier for them to see the match. This is not the same as making up information to present yourself as something you are not. You must always be completely honest about who you are. You are simply making it easier for the match to be recognized.

The Essay

Students most fear this part of the application because they don't know how it will be judged or on what criteria it is based. Be assured that one essay does not lead the application to be rejected. It might give the admissions staff some pause, but there are several other documents in your application that have serious weight in the decision and can offer ballast. What are admissions officers looking for in the essay?

We are looking for a few things. Your ability to write your thoughts in a clear, coherent way because we assume that if you can write like that, you can think like that. We are also looking for cues about how you view your life and yourself, so it's another, subtler way in the application process that we get to know you and look for the match. That means that your essay must be authentically yours. It must have an authentic voice.

What Is an Authentic Voice?
Always hard to answer, this question falls under the category, "We know it when we read it." A directness, a ring of truth, bubbles up within an authentic essay and reverberates with the reader. Your essay will work if you just tell the truth as you see it, regardless of the topic. If you let others write it for you, they will dilute your own voice and it will lose that truthful tone. While it might be better written by a parent or teacher, the truthful essence of the piece will be gone and an opportunity for you to come through in the application will have been lost. It's OK to discuss essay topics with your parents, teachers, and friends—that can be helpful in fleshing out the spark of an idea you might have—but it is not OK to have anyone write or rewrite your work. Your words must be your own. Trust yourself and your words, and remember that for colleges to see the match between them and you, they must see the real you. They must hear your authentic voice. Don't be afraid.

By the way, there are Web sites that search for essays available on the Web, so many admissions officers check online to see if an essay has been lifted (or purchased) from someplace in cyberspace. This is plagiarism and it is considered to be a serious integrity violation in the academic world. If you are caught plagiarizing your essay, you will not be admitted, and your name may be shared with other college admissions offices that will follow suit. You may be tempted to do this, but please don't. It will be bad for you and besides, in your initiation, you must hold integrity.

What Are the Limits?
Writing your truth in an authentic essay means putting your best foot forward, as if you're inviting someone you admire into your home. In that case, you would make an effort to ensure that your home and room were clean and that you were showing off your best side. It's the same with the essay. Remember that the reader will make many observations about you, so "dress up," so to speak. Make sure it's neatly done and sends the right impressions about you. Don't submit a sloppy essay, one with misspellings or something written in pencil or with cross outs. Don't try to be cute if you aren't naturally cute.

Don't try to be funny unless that is your natural self. Be honest, but just dress up when you do it.

Remember that the essay is the only place in your college application where you truly speak for yourself.

Standardized Tests—You Are Not Your SATs

Although they are very helpful to admissions officers as indicators of a student's ability to perform well under stress and to code and decode, SAT scores do not define your intelligence, your talent, or your worth as a person. This culture is obsessed with numbers and quantifying performance and, as a result, many people believe that SAT scores actually mean much more than they really do. Admissions officers use SATs because they are often the only thing that is common to all applicants from different high schools with different grading systems. Some schools use them to decide placement in classes once you are enrolled in college.

Many students know the material well but simply do not score well. Some excellent studies about this phenomenon have shown that

"My parents never talk to me about S-E-X—all they talk about is S-A-Ts."

when some students think an exam will not count, they relax and do fine. But when they believe that the test score will have major repercussions on their lives, or in the case of "stereotype threat" when they've been told that they aren't as smart as others, the same students freeze up and don't do well. Clearly they know the work, but can't quite prove that on standardized tests.

The exams have been changed over time as well. I know, for example, that some MIT faculty members had SAT scores in their youth that are considered low by today's standards. Yet they are among the most brilliant and successful humans on the planet. When the topic of "success in life" is studied, it turns out that standardized test scores do not correlate with anything once the student graduates from college. Character traits such as resilience, optimism, and enthusiasm seem to guarantee success no matter what the person's SAT scores were.

You must struggle to keep standardized tests in perspective. The ability to score high does seem to correlate with good performance at most colleges, but lower scores can correlate with good performance too. So if you are one of those students who feels ashamed by your SAT or ACT results, you must not let them define your self-worth. I recommend that every time you get pinged by shame or feel "less than," you must think an opposite thought, something like, "I am perfect just the way I am. I am in the right place at the right time doing the right thing." It will help you to right any negative thoughts you have about yourself. And remember that there are many colleges that will accept you exactly as you are, no matter what scores you have.

Extracurricular Activities

So many students think that they must have a lot of extracurricular activities to get into college, but this isn't quite true. Colleges are looking for students who are happily pursuing their own interests. It is best to spend your out-of-classroom time doing things you really enjoy, not doing what others tell you that you must do to be admitted to college. If you are doing an activity that you do not love, give yourself permission to drop it. That specific activity will not be the one thing that causes you to be rejected by colleges, and dropping it will open up some valuable free time that you can use any way you wish.

For example, my daughter decided to drop varsity soccer in the fall of her senior year. It had become so competitive that she lost her love of the game and she decided to sing in the chorus instead. I think it was very brave of her to reclaim her life. She has had a much more satisfying senior year as a result, with better grades because she is so much happier.

It is very important that you have some downtime every day to access your imagination because in your imagination is found the blueprint of anything you want to bring into the 3-dimensional world. As a human being, you are a creator, and you'll need imagination time to do that effectively.

The number of extracurricular activities is up to you. Just make sure they make you happy and energize you. Try to seek balance in everything you do. You don't have to be perfect. You don't have to cure cancer to be admitted to college.

Extras

Sometimes students want to send in additional information to support their applications. Make sure to read the application material carefully because some colleges do not want extra material to read. Most schools, however, will welcome additional materials if they really do illustrate another aspect of you and your life. Letters of recommendation from people who know you well are always good. Recommendations from people who do not know you, no matter how well known or influential they are (congressmen, actors, famous alumni), are not good and won't help you. Videos, compact discs, and portfolios are good as long as the school will accept them and as long as they show something special about you. Think carefully before sending them in. Ask yourself if they really show off a side of you not already covered in the application.

The trick is to round out the picture of you without drawing too much attention to yourself. Often the thickest applications (with the most extra stuff) are the ones with something wrong (eg, bad grades, lower scores), sent by a student with a need to compensate. That doesn't always work out well.

Step 4: You're In...Now What?

What if everything works out for you, you've picked colleges that are a good match for you, and you end up with several offers of admission? How do you decide? The obvious strategy is to attend the colleges' admitted student events. Visiting the campus after having been admitted will feel very different—more real—than before you were admitted. So there is real value in another visit, or a first visit if you haven't toured the campus earlier. Once there, you can try the place on for size, and you should be able to work out any financial aid problems if you have them.

Pick the college that makes your heart sing, no matter what your parents or teachers might say. If they pressure you to choose a college other than the one you want, respectfully tell them that you are the one who has to enroll there and therefore you want to make the final decision. Tell them that this is your initiation and you are mature enough to make the right choice. And besides, you can always transfer to another school if you are unhappy. Show them this book. Speak up for yourself and your choice.

Financial Aid

College is expensive whether it is private or public, but there is money to be had if you are willing to get involved with the financial aid process. Many students feel shy about money. They do not want to accept loans because they feel that they do not want to carry that kind of debt. As a result, they may not choose to go to college at all. I believe that this is very shortsighted because dollar for dollar, college is the best investment you can make regarding your future earning power. With a college degree (regardless of where it is from), you'll make more money over time than you would without one. You will be able to pay off your loans, just as millions of people before you have done.

It should not cost you money to apply for financial aid. Make sure, though, that you meet all of the deadlines and submit your forms on time. If you find it overwhelming, follow Dr Ginsburg's advice about breaking work down into manageable chunks. (See page 206.)

Marching to the Beat of a Different Drummer

More and more students are taking a year off before enrolling in college. Most admissions offices applaud and sometimes encourage this because they know that one year usually changes the student's life forever and for the good. Students do many things during their gap year: travel, teach, work, sleep, practice skills, perform, or volunteer. But mainly they mature. And when they finally enroll, they are usually better students because of their time away from school.

If you feel burned out by high school, or want to get off the treadmill of having to be perfect to keep the adults in your life happy, you might consider taking a year off after high school. Many of us admissions officers admire students who do this because it takes someone special to do the unconventional. In terms of logistics, most students who plan to take this time for themselves apply to college during their senior year in high school and then, when admitted, ask for a one-year deferral. Colleges almost always offer one and will hold the student's spot until the following year. You do not have to apply while you are still in high school, but it is the most effective time to apply because the teachers you need to write letters are right there and it is just easier to do logistically.

Some students enroll at community colleges first and then transfer to 4-year colleges later. This is a great option if, for some reason, you do not get admitted to any college out of high school. I ran the transfer program at MIT for years, and we admitted many students like this: people who did not do very well in high school, but later caught fire in community college and did well enough to transfer later to MIT. Many students are just late bloomers, and I honestly believe that it doesn't matter when you settle down and decide to become a student as long as you do. Sometimes there are especially challenging situations at home that sap students' energy while they are in high school. Sometimes students are just not physically organized enough to do well at that age. If you are in this situation, don't despair. Just know that opportunity will open for you from time to time. You just have to recognize it and grab it when it comes.

Step 5: Managing Others

Managing Your Parents

It is hard for many of us parents to step back and let you handle this important moment in your life. It is very important for parents to take their proper role in your initiation, and often that means that they must step back. I tell them that their role now is similar to the one they have when they watch you play a sport. I remind them that when they watch you play soccer, for example, they stand behind the sidelines and cheer for you—they never run onto the field and kick the ball into the net because they can, because they've always wanted to and never could, or because they want to help your team win.

As part of your initiation, you may need to manage your parents' behavior. You may need to tell them what would be helpful to you and what makes you feel worse. I recommend that as a family you develop ground rules for certain events. Tell them how you want them to act and ask them not to take this personally because it is your initiation, and you need to do this yourself.

For example, if you hear your parent tell someone, "We'll be applying to XYZ University," when the time is right, remind them—respectfully—that they are not applying to college, you are. If your parent says, "I'd like to help you with your college essay," be respectful and say, "No, thank you. I have it under control. Thanks, anyway."

Managing Your Friends

In some ways, this is even more important than managing your parents. If your friends are also applying to college, they are probably as anxious as you are and sometimes might become competitive. To keep yourself as calm as possible during the admissions process, resolve not to discuss college with your friends. Don't listen to their gossip about different schools (They know nothing about it.), don't share your SAT or ACT scores or talk about other people's scores, and don't discuss your application essays. Sometimes anxious friends say insensitive or hurtful things. They may sometimes feel intimidated by you or might become defensive if they are wor-

"Hey, there's Sara, padding her college-entrance résumé!"

ried they won't get into a certain school and you will. It's best for everyone if you just do not discuss it.

Some Thoughts to Live By

This initiation into adulthood is hard and will demand a lot from you, but the rules you need to get through this successfully now are the rules you will live by your entire life.

Rules of the Game for Students

- **Do all the work yourself.** To believe that you have earned your admission, you must do all of the work yourself. That means making the necessary phone calls, asking the right questions, staying on top of your deadlines, and submitting your own work. It feels like a lot of work at first, but you will feel better about yourself when you take charge and exercise competencies you never realized you had.

- **Hold privacy.** It is no one's business where you apply to college or if you are admitted or not. Get into the habit of keeping some things private because they will not only mean more to you in the end, but privacy also helps you save face in case you are not admitted to the college you've been bragging about to all of your friends.

- **Hold integrity.** Your physical body and emotional self will be more relaxed and peaceful if you live with integrity and always do the right thing. Holding integrity is sometimes very hard to do because the temptation may be to cheat or cut corners. Maybe your friends cheat sometimes. But just remember that "what goes around comes around," meaning that life has a funny way of giving back what you put out. If you live with integrity, you'll be happier and will attract good friends who know they can trust you. If you do not live honestly, you will draw suffering into your life because you will always be afraid of getting caught.

- **Never speak against yourself.** My teacher Sharon Turner used to say, "It's a mortal sin to speak against yourself," and she would allow no self-deprecating comments in her presence. At first it was hard to stop the habit of saying negative things about myself and my talents because that is such a part of our culture, and I thought others would think I was bragging if I talked any differently. But she said, "Just speak the truth about who you are. That's not bragging. It's the truth." She was right. It makes you feel better about yourself when you speak good things instead of bad, and it will help you prepare for the college application process.

■ **Be kind to yourself.** Your brain is always listening, so always talk kindly to yourself. No human is perfect, no matter how old and experienced, so don't hold yourself to that standard. If you are wrong about something, or if you hurt someone's feelings, apologize, forgive yourself, and move on.

The Need to Try New Things: The Art of Failing Well

We admissions officers know that how you handle your disappointments and setbacks is more important than how you handle your successes. And how well you handle adversity is the key to success in college and in life. All humans fail at times. Failing has gotten such a bad rap. It is seen as something to be avoided at all costs rather than a helpful friend whose job it is to help you learn and grow. In an odd way, failing is at the base of all science. When we want to understand how something works in the natural world, we make a hypothesis (a guess) about it and then set out to disprove the hypothesis by systematically ruling out one guess after another. This means that, in a funny way, when the experiment "fails" to explain the hypothesis, it actually advances the line of thought, just as the true nature of failing does.

We urge you to develop the art of failing well. It is an art. No one wants you to fail catastrophically, so to avoid that you must get used to disappointment in the small things. I was always a perfectionist until I learned the skill of failing, and I developed the skill by allowing myself to screw up something small, to be wrong about something every day. Very quickly I saw that the sky did not fall and nothing bad happened. That taught me a big lesson, and I pass that on to you now. Try something new—develop a new skill, take a chance—and get used to the experience of not doing things right the first or even fifth time around. When that happens, laugh at the situation and just keep trying it until you get it right.

As you move through this initiation into adulthood—this process of applying to college—think of it as an adventure, but not a make-or-break contest that will determine your fate. Be courageous and be yourself, but don't feel you have to do everything "just right" or be perfect at everything. You'll hit some potholes and bumps in the road. You may not be admitted to your first-choice colleges. You'll feel a lot of pressure. And to help you handle the inevitable stress in your life, now and for the future, I hope you will use the stress-management guide that follows in Part Four. But remember that this is an initiation, a fire walk, and you will come out on the other side with yourself whole, happy, and resilient because you have tested yourself and discovered your strengths.

Just for Teens:

A Guide to Managing Stress

What Is Stress?

Stress is the uncomfortable feeling you get when you're worried, scared, angry, frustrated, or overwhelmed. Many adults think that kids don't have stress because they don't have to work and support a family. They are so wrong!

Stress is caused by emotions, but it affects both your mood and your body. It can cause many physical sensations like belly pain, muscle aches, headaches, dizziness, exhaustion, and even chest pain. Some people have trouble sorting out whether physical symptoms are related to stress or have other causes. A doctor can help you sort this out.

What Causes Stress?

Stress comes from many different places.

From your parents: "Hurry up, finish this, do your homework, go out for the team, practice your music, try out for the school play, do your best, stay out of trouble, make more friends, don't ever do drugs…." And, of course, "If you don't do this or that, how will you ever get into college!"

From your friends: "Be cool, try this; prove you don't need your parents; what were your SAT scores? Tell me where you're going to apply to school."

And even from yourself: "I need to get in better shape, wear the right clothes, get better grades, score more goals, show my parents I'm ready to be on my own…."

And from a lot of other sources…

- Watching parents argue
- Figuring out how to be independent
- Thinking about the future
- Worrying about whether you will get into the school of your choice

- Worrying about whether a test will determine your entire life (By the way, it will not!)
- Being pressured to do something, like smoking and drinking
- Not being good enough at sports
- Dealing with raging, and sometimes uncomfortable, sexual feelings
- Dealing with boyfriends and girlfriends
- Worrying about neighborhood or world problems
- Feeling guilty

How Does the Body Handle Stress?

The body is a finely tuned machine that can change quickly to do what we need it to do—like react to stress. The body actually has 2 different nerve pathways. One works while we're relaxed, and the other works when there's an emergency. These 2 systems cannot work together at the same time. It's important to know this because we can shut off the emergency system by turning on the relaxed system. That helps us feel better!

Is Stress Always Bad?

Even though stress makes us feel uncomfortable, it's not always a bad thing. Sometimes stress can really help us deal with tough situations. A lot of stress changes our bodies quickly and helps us react to an emergency. A little stress keeps us alert and helps us work harder.

Ages ago when people had to survive in the jungle—where a tiger might leap out at any moment—the "emergency" nervous system was a great thing to have. Imagine your great, great, great ancestors, Sam and Zelda, eating some berries and soaking up the sun in the jungle. Suddenly they saw a tiger and they knew they had to *RUN!!!* Hormones gave them the huge burst of energy that they needed to escape.

How did their bodies react? First Sam and Zelda got that sinking feeling in their stomachs as the blood in their guts quickly went to their legs so they could run fast. Then when they jumped to their feet, their hearts beat faster to pump more blood. As they ran from the tiger, they breathed faster to get more air. Their sweat cooled them as they ran. Their pupils became bigger so they could see in the dark, in case they needed to jump over a log while running away. They didn't think about anything but running because they weren't supposed to stop and negotiate with the tiger.

Sam and Zelda would never have survived without the stress reaction. But stress helps us do more than run from tigers. It keeps us alert and prepared. (You can be sure that the next time Sam and Zelda sat down to munch on berries, they listened for the sounds of a lurking tiger.)

Few of us need to outrun tigers today, but we all have problems and worries that turn on some of those same stress responses—like that panicky feeling you sometimes get when you're taking a big test. Your heart beats almost as fast as it would if you were running from a tiger. Your breathing becomes heavier. You sweat and experience flashes of heat because your hormones are confused about why you aren't listening to them. Why are you standing still when they are telling you to run? Sometimes in a state of true panic, you forget everything you know—you blank out—because you aren't supposed to be thinking when a tiger is after you.

If Stress Is a Survival Tool, Then Why Does It Make Us Feel Awful?

Good old Sam and Zelda had few choices when the tiger chased them. Either the tiger ate them or they escaped. As sick as it sounds, if they'd been eaten, they wouldn't have much to worry about anymore, right? If they lived, you can be sure their burst of energy allowed them to outrun the tiger or at least outrun Zok (their slower friend whom the tiger devoured instead of them). In their run for survival, Sam and Zelda used up every drop of their hormone burst and then took a well-deserved nap.

In the modern world, our biggest worries are not usually about life or death. We don't really have to run away from our problems. But those same stress hormones stay in our bodies because, unlike Sam and Zelda, we don't use them up by running. Instead, those hormones continue to hang around, unused and confused. They seem to be asking, "Why did my body stand still when that 'tiger' attacked?"

Even when there are no real emergencies, our emotions can make our bodies act like there's a huge crisis because the brain controls both emotions and stress hormones. If your brain thinks something terrible is happening, your body will react as if it really is. Even a little bit of stress that never seems to go away can confuse the body. It makes the body work harder to prepare for an emergency that may not really be there.

A tiger running at you is a real crisis. If you believe a mild stress (like a math test) is an emergency, you will not be able to study. Your body will be preparing to deal with a real tiger, and you won't be able to concentrate on anything but escaping. The trick is to figure out when something is really an emergency and when your emotions are only treating it like one.

A lot of kids treat the college admissions process as if it's a ferocious tiger ready to lunge. This is not surprising considering how much pressure parents, teachers, counselors, coaches, school principals, and sometimes even your friends put on you. If your brain treats this college admissions process as a crisis, you will panic your way through it—you won't even be able to think clearly.

The truth is, whichever college you attend will not determine your success. It is more important that you find the right match for you personally—a college or university where you will feel comfortable, be challenged, develop new interests, and make new friends. It's not necessarily "the best" (whatever that means) college in someone else's estimation.

What will determine your success in college and in life? Your optimism, perseverance, integrity, and love of learning. You can make wonderful friends and broaden your intellectual horizons wherever you go—if you maintain a positive attitude, intellectual curiosity, and a commitment to live your life with integrity.

A Review

- Stress is an important tool that can help us survive.
- The body reacts to stress when the brain, nervous system, and hormones tell the body to prepare for an emergency.
- Emotions play an important role in how we experience stress. How we think about stress and what we choose to do about it affect how stress makes us feel.

How Do People Deal With Stress?

Nobody can avoid all stress, but you can learn ways to deal with it. When you are stressed, it is normal to want to feel better. Anything that makes you feel better is called a coping strategy. Negative strategies are easy, quick fixes, but they are harmful and make stress worse in the long run. Think about some of the ways people cope with stress that can really mess them up:

Drugs
Cigarettes
Alcohol
Bullying
Fighting
Sex
Cutting/self-mutilation

Skipping school
Eating disorders
Running away
Isolation
Gangs

These harmful choices may help you feel good for a little while, but they can be dangerous. They end up messing up your life by creating a cycle of increasing stress. They're especially dangerous if they are the major ways you deal with stress because you will turn to these behaviors more often during tough times, setting you up for an addiction. If you are doing some of these things, ask yourself, "WHY?" If it is to deal with problems, you should learn to deal with these pressures in a healthier, safer manner.

Healthy coping strategies sometimes take more work than the quick fixes, but the investment is well worth it. These strategies are safe, help you feel better, and end up making you happy. They offer relief rather than entrance into the hopeless cycle of stress, quick fixes, and greater stress. Many positive ways to cope are described in the following stress-management plan that you can personalize for yourself.

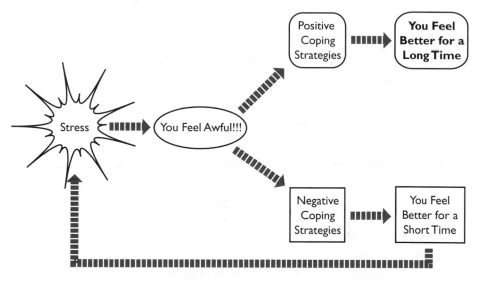

Creating Your Personal Stress-Management Plan

The following plan can help you manage stress. All of these ideas can lower stress without doing any harm. None of them are quick fixes, but they will lead you toward a healthy and successful life. The plan has 10 points that are grouped in the following 4 sections:

1. Tackling the problem
2. Taking care of my body
3. Managing my emotions
4. Making the world better

When you read over the plan, you'll notice that you can come up with a bunch of ideas for each point. PLEEEEEEEEASE do not think you should try them all. This plan is supposed to help you manage stress, not give you more. You probably have more than enough people in your life telling you what you should be doing to impress others. This plan is about what works for you, not about what looks good for anyone else. Try out some ideas and then stick to one or two ideas for each point.

You might notice that this plan is almost like building a college or career resumé. It's the healthy, sane way to build a resumé because you are doing it to manage your life and remain happy and prepared for success—not to cram in as many activities as possible to impress someone else. It will ensure you are healthy and balanced, and it just so happens that it encourages you to do some of the things that are very attractive to colleges and employers.

Tackling the Problem

Point 1: Figure out what the problem is and make it manageable.

- A lot of people cope by ignoring problems. This does not make problems go away; usually they just get worse.

- People who cope by trying to fix problems tend to be emotionally healthier.

- When it comes to studying, chores, jobs, or extracurricular activities, the best way to enjoy yourself is to get the work done first. Because work and studies can produce stress, many people put it off and choose to do fun things first. But the problem with that is they're having less fun because they're worrying about the work they're ignoring. And the longer they put it off, the more they worry. The cycle is endless.

   Two ideas can help you manage a lot of work.

1. Break the work into small pieces. Then do one small piece at a time, rather than look at the whole huge mess. As you finish each piece, the work becomes less overwhelming. The college application is a good example to use here. When you look at the whole pile of papers, you might feel overwhelmed and you'd just rather take a nap. But if

you organize it and develop a strategy to take it one task at a time, it is doable. Some people find that tackling the most difficult part first is a good approach because the rest is downhill.

2. Make lists of what you need to do. This will help you sleep because your head won't spin with worry about whether you can finish everything. At the end of the day, you'll have less to worry about as you check off the things you have completed. You will look at the same huge amount of work and say to yourself "I CAN do this!"

■ Fights with parents and friends don't go away unless you deal with what upset you in the first place, or unless everyone apologizes and decides to forgive each other.

Point 2: Avoid things that bring you down.

Sometimes we know exactly when we are headed for trouble. Avoiding trouble from a distance is easier than avoiding it up close. You know the people who might be a bad influence on you. You know the places where you're likely to get in trouble, and you know the things that upset you. Choose not to be around those people, places, and things that mess you up.

Point 3: Let some things go.

It's important to try to fix problems, but sometimes there's nothing you can do to change a situation. For example, you can't change the weather, so don't waste your energy worrying about it. You can't change the fact that teachers must give tests, so start studying instead of complaining about how unfair they are. You can't control what admissions committees do behind closed doors, so after you've sent in your applications, just let it go. People who waste their energy worrying about things they can't change don't have enough energy left over to fix the things they can.

Taking Care of My Body

Point 4: Exercise.

When you are stressed, your body is saying RUN, so do it. Exercise every day to control stress and build a strong, healthy body. Exercise is the most important part of a plan to manage stress. You may think you don't have time to exercise when you are most stressed, but that is exactly when you need it the most. If you are stressed about an assignment, but too nervous to sit down and study, exercise! You will be able to think better after you have used up those stress hormones.

Point 5: Learn to relax your body.

You can fool your body into thinking you're relaxed. Remember that your
body can only use the relaxed nervous system or the emergency system at
any one time. Turn on the relaxed system! You do this by doing the opposite
of what your body does when it is stressed. Here are 2 ideas.

1. Breathe deeply and slowly. Of all of the things your body does to
   prepare you to run, breathing is the easiest one to change. Slow, deep
   breathing turns on the relaxed system. Take a big deep breath until
   your chest and your belly fill with air. Then let it out slooooooowly.
   Do this 10 times and you will feel much more relaxed.

   Yoga, meditation, and Tai Chi also teach great breathing skills. At the
   end of this section, you will see detailed instructions on mindfulness
   meditation, a technique for learning to use breath as a means to relax
   and become more comfortable with your thoughts. It was written for
   you by Dr Amit Shah. If it intrigues you, there are several books written
   about this type of meditation as well as other relaxation techniques.

2. Put your body in a relaxed position. Your body knows when you're
   nervous. If you sit down to take a test and your legs are shaking, you
   are saying, "I want to run!" Remember, you can't concentrate and run
   at the same time, so you are making it harder to take the test. Take it
   one question at a time. When you don't know an answer, don't panic
   because that can make you draw a blank even when you are well prepared. Instead take deep breaths, lean back, and remind yourself that
   you are quite capable. Tell your body there's no emergency.

   When you're angry, the natural thing to do is stand up and face
   someone shoulder-to-shoulder, chest-to-chest. You do this without
   even thinking, but this tells the other person that you're angry and
   ready to fight. It also may prevent you from thinking clearly because
   it turns on your fighting hormones. Do the *opposite* of what you would
   do if you were really going to fight—sit down, take deep slow breaths,
   and tell your body there is no danger. Then use your brain to get out
   of the situation or turn it in a better direction.

Point 6: Eat well.

Everyone knows good nutrition makes you healthier. But only some people
realize that it also keeps you alert through the day and keeps your mood
steady. People who eat mostly junk food have highs and lows in their energy
level, which harms their ability to manage stress.

Point 7: Sleep well.

Most kids don't get the sleep they need to grow and think clearly. Tired people can't learn as well and can be much crankier. Here are some ideas to improve your sleep.

- Go to sleep about the same time every night.

- Avoid caffeinated drinks, especially in the afternoon and evening.

- Exercise 4 to 6 hours before bedtime. Your body falls asleep most easily when it has cooled down. If you exercise right before bed, you will be overheated and won't sleep well. A hot shower *1 hour before* bedtime also helps your body relax to fall asleep.

- Use your bed only to sleep.

- Don't solve your problems in bed. If you think about all the things that bother you, you'll have trouble falling asleep and wake up in the middle of the night to worry more. Instead, have another spot to think—like a "worry chair." Give yourself plenty of time to think things through, make a list if you need to, *and then set it aside!* Go to bed to sleep.

- Don't do homework, watch television, read, instant message, or use the phone while in bed.

Managing My Emotions

Point 8: Take instant vacations.

Sometimes the best way to de-stress is to take your mind away to a more relaxing place.

1. **Visualize.** Have a favorite place where you can imagine yourself relaxing. The place should be beautiful and calm. When you're stressed, sit down, lean back, take deep breaths, close your eyes, and imagine yourself in your calm place.

2. **Take time out for yourself.** Everyone deserves time for himself or herself: a walk, a bath, something special every day; time to think. (Try a warm bath with your ears just under water; listen to yourself take deep, slow breaths. Feel your body rise and fall with each breath. Take your pulse and count as your heart rate goes down.)

3. **Enjoy hobbies** or creative art. Use it as an instant vacation.

4. **Take pleasure from the small things.** Look at the beauty around you that you may have stopped noticing.

5. **Read.** A good book is an escape from reality. You have to imagine the sights, sounds, and smells—you are somewhere else for a while.

Point 9: Release emotions.

Sometimes feelings become so overwhelming that we cram them all away in an imaginary box and think we'll deal with them later. But later, there's so much stuff in the box that there's too much to deal with. This can make your head feel like it's spinning. Sometimes you get angry or frustrated without even knowing why. You just know there is too much stuff going on in your head. Pick one problem to work on and forget the rest for the moment. When you decide to deal with only one problem at a time, the thought of opening the box is not as overwhelming.

Here are some ideas to release your thoughts or worries one at a time.

- **Creativity:** People who express themselves don't need to hold their emotions inside. Outlets like art, music, poetry, singing, dance, and rap are powerful ways to let your feelings out.

- **Talking:** Every young person deserves adults to talk to and some friends to trust. Hopefully, you can talk to your parents. But if you do not want to tell your parents everything, find an adult you can get advice from and choose wisely among your friends. Make sure the friends are invested in your success, and not in having you mess up alongside them.

- **Journaling:** Write it out!

- **Prayer:** Many young people find prayer or meditation a helpful way to express themselves and decompress.

- **Laughing or crying:** Give yourself permission to feel your emotions fully.

Making the World Better

Point 10: Contribute to the world.

Young people who work to make the world better have a sense of purpose, feel good about themselves, and handle their own problems better. It's important to understand that you really can make a difference in other people's lives. The role of teenagers is to recognize the mistakes adults have made and build a better world.

■ ❖ ■ ❖ ■ ❖ ■ ❖ ■

Mindfulness Meditation: An Ancient Technique

Not only does stress make us feel bad, but it also makes us forget the good people that we are. Deep down inside we have a core of goodness (an inner voice that tells us to eat right, do our homework, not steal or cheat, and help other people, for example). This voice is our "conscience."

When we are stressed, we are deaf to this inner voice. We feel bad, but we may do things that our conscience doesn't tell us to do, like procrastinate on our homework or eat too much junk food. Because we're too stressed to listen to our conscience, we don't finish our homework and we have a stomachache. This makes the situation even worse—a seemingly endless cycle!

Mindfulness meditation is an ancient technique developed in India called *Vipassana* that was developed to make us feel good again and remember our goodness by removing the earplugs of stress. It helps us stop reacting to stress in negative ways. Instead it gives us the strength to deal with it peacefully and effectively. As you read and follow the instructions below, keep in mind that this technique will only work if you approach it with a feeling of curiosity, not expectation. If you *expect* it to help, you may *create more stress* if it does not fulfill your expectations. This technique focuses on turning on your relaxed nervous system and letting the full power of your brain take control of those emotions that make your head spin.

1. Sit in a dignified posture—Sit on a chair or on the floor with your legs crossed, your back straight, and your head directly balanced on top of your spine. Relax your arms and legs so that you are not struggling. Ask yourself, "How would someone with dignity or a feeling of pride sit?" Try sitting in that position and feeling its power. If it is difficult to feel, slouch first by sitting hunched over your lap and then straighten your back again to notice the difference.

2. Breathe—Now that you are in good posture, your body is positioned to hold more air inside. In mindfulness meditation, it is important to breathe with your belly so you can move air in and out more easily. To belly breathe, place your hand on your stomach and push out with your belly as you breathe in air. Then as you breathe out, push air out by bringing your belly in, and watch your hand move as your belly rises and falls. Continue breathing with your belly, but take your hand off your belly and rest it in a comfortable position. As you breathe in, feel the pressure in your belly and your chest. Then as you breathe out, feel yourself letting go of the tension and air. Notice this feeling of relief. Make the experience more powerful by breathing in air over 4 seconds, holding for 4 seconds, breathing out for 4 seconds, and holding again for 4 seconds. Do this for 10 cycles and count the seconds in your head.

3. Separate your thoughts and emotions from yourself. Just as our conscious-ness makes good thoughts, stress causes our brains to make bad thoughts. Many of us automatically listen to these thoughts or react to the emotions, which causes us to make bad decisions. In mindfulness, we hear voices and feel emotions, but when we are being "breathers," we can separate

ourselves from the parts of us that are "thought-makers." As a breather, look at the thoughts or emotions that arise in your head. Don't try to make them go away, just watch them. Because we spend our whole lives trying to make these thoughts and emotions go away, this can be difficult at first. It may be possible, however, to recognize them only as thoughts that do not need to control us or even to sway our emotions. If we do this, they drift away like smoke from a chimney. On the other hand, fighting and wrestling with the thoughts can cause them to stay and get worse.

The Mountain and the Whirlpool

This analogy can help you experience the benefits of this technique. First, try to see your thoughts and emotions as a whirlpool: Not only do they bring about confusion and cause you to lose your "goodness," but they also can make you drown in misery. But as you use the breathing technique with

good posture, you can arise from the whirlpool like a tall, dignified mountain. The constant feeling of breathing will help you remain still and resilient. Just notice the whirlpool. Don't fight it. Imagine the whirlpool becoming calm as you release your breath— you are letting the turmoil go. Let the whirlpool be, and see what happens. After much practice, you may notice that the whirlpool actually becomes a still lake.

Illustration by Amit Shah, MD

Extend the Technique Beyond Sitting Meditation

The spinning sensation of the whirlpool can be caused by stress or other feelings and thoughts: hunger, jealousy, desire, greed, and fear. Over time, extend your use of breathing and learn to "be a dignified mountain" with each emotion. Because you are always breathing, you can do it any time while doing anything—lying down, sitting, standing, or even walking. In addition to noticing your thoughts and emotions, notice your surroundings and appreciate the world around you. With practice and patience, you can learn to experience each moment in a fuller, more mindful way. You will earn the ability not only to deal better with stress, but also to make the most of your life by being a peaceful, dignified observer of every moment. An observer notices and appreciates but can be still—like a mountain—rather than becoming caught up in all the swirling emotions that can capture so much of our energy.

■ ❖ ■ ❖ ■ ❖ ■ ❖ ■

My Personal Stress Plan

Now that you have read about the kinds of things you can do to manage stress, you may be ready to create a plan for yourself. Just check off the ideas you think would work best for you. You don't have to do everything! There are spaces to write down your own ideas.

Tackling the Problem

Point 1: Figure out what the problem is and make it manageable.

When I have too many problems, I will work on just one at a time. As an example, I am going to pick one huge problem and break it into smaller pieces.

_____

_____

_____

_____

Point 2: Avoid the things that bring me down.

I know that everyone has stress, but I could stay away from things that really stress me out. I will learn to trust my instincts when they give me clues that I might be headed for trouble. I will

☐ Avoid certain people, like _____

☐ Avoid certain places, like _____

☐ Avoid certain things, like _____

Point 3: Let some things go.

I realize that I waste some of my energy worrying about things I can't fix. Here are some things that I will try to let go so I can focus on the problems I can change:

☐ _____

☐ _____

☐ _____

Taking Care of My Body

Point 4: Exercise.

I will do something that makes my body work hard for at least 20 minutes every other day. (More often is better.) I know that strong bodies help people better deal with stress, and this will keep me in shape. The kinds of things I like to do include

☐ _____

☐ _____

☐ _____

I know that a really hard physical workout will help me calm down when I am feeling most worried, nervous, or fearful. This is especially true when I can't concentrate on my homework because it feels too overwhelming. The kinds of things I might do include

☐ _____

☐ _____

☐ _____

Point 5: Learn to relax my body.

I will try to teach my body to relax by using

☐ Deep breathing

☐ Yoga

☐ Meditation

☐ Warm, long baths or showers

☐ Imagine I am someplace peaceful and relaxing
　 The place I could imagine myself being is _____

☐ _____

Point 6: Eat well.

I know that having a healthy body helps people deal with stress better. I have already agreed to exercise more. I understand that good nutrition also makes a big difference in my health and how well I deal with stress. The changes I am ready to make include

☐ Eating a good breakfast

☐ Skipping fewer meals

☐ Drinking fewer sodas and sugary drinks

☐ Drinking more water

☐ Eating smaller portions

☐ Eating less greasy meals or snacks

☐ Eating more fruits and vegetables

☐ _____

☐ _____

Point 7: Sleep well.

I know that people who get a good night's sleep do a better job of dealing with stress and do better in school. For me to get the sleep I need, I will try to go to bed at ___:___ on weeknights and ___:___ on weekends.

I will use my bed only for sleeping. I will use someplace other than my bed to do the things I now do in bed. I will

☐ Stop doing homework in bed

☐ Stop reading in bed

☐ Stop watching television in bed

☐ Stop talking to my friends or instant messaging in bed

☐ Stop worrying in bed

☐ Learn to deal with the things that stress me out by having a time to let go of my thoughts and feelings in a place other than my bed

☐ _____

Managing My Emotions

Point 8: Take instant vacations.

Everyone needs to be able to escape problems for a while by taking an "instant vacation." I will

☐ Read a book.

☐ Imagine I am someplace peaceful and relaxing.
The place I could imagine myself being is _____

☐ Watch television.

☐ Listen to music.

☐ Play video games that are not violent or stressful.

☐ Take a warm bath.

☐ Work on my hobby, which is _____

☐ _____

Point 9: Release emotions.

I will try to let my worries go, rather than letting them build up inside.

☐ I will talk to a friend I have chosen wisely because I know he or she will give good advice and support me.

☐ I will talk to my

    ☐ Mother

    ☐ Father

    ☐ Teacher

    ☐ _____

☐ I will ask my parents, a teacher, a clergyperson, or my health care provider to help me find a counselor to help me work out my problems.

☐ I will use prayer to gain strength.

☐ I will meditate.

☐ I will write out my thoughts in a diary or journal.

☐ I will let myself laugh more.

☐ I will let myself cry more.

☐ I will make lists to help me get organized.

☐ When it seems that I have too many problems and they seem like more than I can handle, I will work on one at a time.

☐ I will express myself through art.

☐ I will express myself through music.

☐ I will express myself through creative writing.

☐ I will express myself through poetry.

☐ I will express myself through rap.

☐ _____

☐ _____

Making the World Better

Point 10: Make the world a better place.

I know that people who realize they are needed feel better about themselves because they can make a difference in other people's lives. I plan to

☐ Help a member of my family by _____

☐ Volunteer in my community by _____

☐ Help the environment (or animals) by _____

■❖■❖■❖■❖■

When to Turn for Help

Even with the best ways of coping, there may be times when stress feels like it's getting to you. You are not alone. This doesn't mean you're crazy or a failure. Strong people turn to others for support when they have too much to handle. It's OK to turn to wise friends for advice, but it is also important to turn to your parents or a professional.

Remember: **You deserve to feel good.**

You should seek some extra guidance if

■ Your grades are dropping.

■ You worry a lot.

■ You easily get moody or angry.

■ You feel tired all the time.

■ You have headaches, dizziness, chest pain, or stomach pain often.

■ You often feel sad or hopeless.

■ You feel bored all the time and are less interested in being with friends.

■ You think your life is out of control and/or are doing something unhealthy to feel in control.

■ You are using alcohol or drugs to try to feel better.

■ You ever think about hurting yourself.

Remember that one of the best ways to be happy and successful is to manage stress well. You CAN do it if you commit yourself to a plan that you design for yourself.

■❖■❖■❖■❖■

Epilogue:
Carrots, Eggs, and Coffee

As we were completing this book, one of those many e-mail stories floating through cyberspace landed in our in-box. Like so much material on the Internet, the origin of this story has been impossible to nail down. Some versions use a mother, others a father. Either way, we appreciate the parable's wisdom and thought that it was an appropriate way to end.

A young woman went to her mother and told her about her life and how things were so hard for her. She did not know how she was going to make it and wanted to give up. She was tired of fighting and struggling. It seemed as one problem was solved, a new one arose.

Her mother took her to the kitchen, filled 3 pots with water, and placed each on a high fire. Soon the pots came to a boil. In the first pot she placed carrots, in the second she placed eggs, and in the last she placed ground coffee beans. She let them boil, without saying a word.

After about 20 minutes she turned off the burners, fished out the carrots, and placed them in a bowl. She scooped out the eggs and put them in a bowl. Then she ladled the coffee into a bowl. Turning to her daughter, she asked, "Tell me what you see."

"Carrots, eggs, and coffee," she replied.

Her mother brought her closer and asked her to feel the carrots. She did and noted that they were soft. The mother then asked her daughter to take an egg and break it. After peeling off the shell, she observed the hard-boiled egg. Finally the mother asked the daughter to sip the coffee. The daughter smiled as she savored its rich aroma.

The daughter then asked, "What does it mean, Mother?"

Her mother explained that each of these objects had faced the same adversity—boiling water. Each reacted differently. The carrots went in strong, hard, and unrelenting. After being subjected to the boiling water, however, they softened and became weak. The eggs had been fragile. Their thin outer shells had protected their liquid interior, but after sitting in the boiling water, their insides became hardened. The ground coffee beans were unique, however. After they were in the boiling water, they had changed the water.

"Which are you?" she asked her daughter. "When adversity knocks on your door, how do you respond? Are you a carrot, an egg, or a coffee bean?"

Think of this: Which am I? Am I a carrot that seems strong, but with pain and adversity do I wilt, become soft, and lose my strength?

Am I an egg that starts with a malleable heart, but changes with the heat? Did I have a fluid spirit, but after a hardship, a death, a breakup, or some other trial, have I become hardened and stiff? Does my shell look the same, but on the inside am I bitter and tough with a stiff spirit and hardened heart?

Or am I like the coffee beans? The beans actually change the hot water, the very circumstance that brings the pain. When the water gets hot, the coffee beans release fragrance and flavor. If you are like the beans, when things are at their worst, you get better and change the situation around you.

When the hour is the darkest and trials are greatest, do you elevate yourself to another level? How do you handle adversity? Are you a carrot, an egg, or a coffee bean?

May you have enough happiness to make you sweet, enough trials to make you strong, enough sorrow to keep you human, and enough hope to make you happy.

The happiest of people don't necessarily have the best of everything; they just make the most of everything that comes their way.

■ ❖ ■ ❖ ■ ❖ ■ ❖ ■

Resources

The following resources are offered as an opportunity to explore particular concerns. Resources are grouped by areas of interest. The list is by no means exhaustive; many fine resources are not included. While we cannot endorse every point made in every listed resource, they all are of high quality.

Generations

Smith JW, Clurman A. *Rocking the Ages: The Yankelovich Report on Generational Marketing.* New York, NY: HarperBusiness; 1997

Strauss W, Howe N. *Generations: The History of America's Future, 1584 to 2069.* New York, NY: Morrow; 1991

Strauss W, Howe N. *The Fourth Turning: An American Prophecy.* New York, NY: Broadway Books; 1997

College Admissions

Thacker L, ed. *College Unranked: Ending the College Admissions Frenzy.* Cambridge, MA: Harvard University Press; 2005

Resilience

Wolin SJ, Wolin S. *The Resilient Self: How Survivors of Troubled Families Rise Above Adversity.* New York, NY: Villard Books; 1993

The Search Institute. At the heart of the institute's work is the framework of "40 Developmental Assets," which are positive experiences and personal qualities that young people need to grow up healthy, caring, and responsible. To see the listed assets go to www.search-institute.org/assets/. The assets are modified for each developmental level.

Parenting Books With a Focus on Resilience

Brooks RB, Goldstein S. *Raising Resilient Children: Fostering Strength, Hope, and Optimism in Your Child.* Lincolnwood, IL: Contemporary Books; 2001

Cohen-Sandler R. *Stressed-Out Girls: Helping Them Thrive in the Age of Pressure.* New York, NY: Viking; 2005

Ginsburg KR, Jablow MM. *A Parent's Guide to Building Resilience in Children and Teens: Giving Your Child Roots and Wings.* Elk Grove Village, IL: American Academy of Pediatrics; 2006

Free Time

Hallowell EM. *The Childhood Roots of Adult Happiness: Five Steps to Help Kids Create and Sustain Lifelong Joy.* New York, NY: Ballantine Books; 2002

Hirsh-Pasek K, Golinkoff RM, Eyer DE. *Einstein Never Used Flash Cards: How Our Children Really Learn—And Why They Need to Play More and Memorize Less.* Emmaus, PA: Rodale Books; 2003

Child Development

The American Academy of Pediatrics publishes authoritative books to help parents understand and support healthy development through a child's lifespan. These books can be previewed at www.aap.org/bookstore.

Unhealthy Thinking/Promoting Optimism and Resilience

Reivich K, Shatté A. *The Resilience Factor: 7 Essential Skills for Overcoming Life's Inevitable Obstacles.* New York, NY: Broadway Books; 2002

Seligman MEP, Reivich K, Jaycox L, Gillham J. *The Optimistic Child: A Proven Program to Safeguard Children Against Depression and Build Lifelong Resilience.* Boston, MA: Houghton Mifflin; 1995

Flow

Csikszentmihalyi M. *Flow: The Psychology of Optimal Experience.* New York, NY: Harper Perennial; 1991

Emotional Intelligence

Goleman D. *Emotional Intelligence: Why It Can Matter More Than IQ.* London: Bloomsbury; 1996

Gottman JM, DeClaire J. *The Heart of Parenting: Raising an Emotionally Intelligent Child.* New York, NY: Simon and Schuster; 1997

Over-scheduled, Overstretched Children

Elkind D. *The Hurried Child: Growing Up Too Fast Too Soon.* 3rd ed. Cambridge, MA: Perseus Pub; 2001

Hallowell EM. *The Childhood Roots of Adult Happiness: Five Steps to Help Kids Create and Sustain Lifelong Joy.* New York, NY: Ballantine Books; 2002

Hirsh-Pasek K, Golinkoff RM, Eyer D. *Einstein Never Used Flash Cards: How Our Children Really Learn—And Why They Need to Play More and Memorize Less.* Emmaus, PA: Rodale Books; 2003

Rosenfeld AA, Wise N. *The Over-Scheduled Child: Avoiding the Hyper-Parenting Trap.* New York, NY: St. Martin's Griffin; 2001

Warner J. *Perfect Madness: Motherhood in the Age of Anxiety.* New York, NY: Riverhead Books; 2005

Stress and the Mind-Body Connection

Kabat-Zinn J. *Wherever You Go, There You Are: Mindfulness Meditation in Everyday Life.* New York, NY: Hyperion; 1994

Sapolsky RM. *Why Zebras Don't Get Ulcers: A Guide to Stress, Stress-Related Diseases, and Coping.* New York, NY: W.H. Freeman; 1994

> This classic book translates scientific evidence to help the reader understand the intricate connections between the mind and body.

Sterling P. Principles of allostasis: optimal design, predictive regulation, pathophysiology and rational therapeutics. In: Schulkin J, ed. *Allostasis, Homeostasis, and the Costs of Physiological Adaptation.* Cambridge, England: Cambridge University Press; 2004

> This chapter is written for a scientific audience. If you can survive some of the jargon, it brilliantly and clearly makes the connection between the mind, emotions, and the body's response.

Weiss A. *Beginning Mindfulness: Learning the Way of Awareness.* Novato, CA: New World Library; 2004

Stress Reduction for Teenagers

Hipp E, Espeland P. *Fighting Invisible Tigers: A Stress Management Guide for Teens.* Minneapolis, MN: Free Spirit Publishing; 1995

> This book offers teenagers easily digestible information and concrete skills for stress reduction. It uses the same metaphor of tigers chasing us that we use in Chapter 18 and Part Four.

Seaward BL, Bartlett L. *Hot Stones & Funny Bones: Teens Helping Teens Cope with Stress & Anger.* Deerfield Beach, FL: Health Communications; 2002

> This book may be particularly helpful for teenagers who feel isolated and may not know how common stress is among their peers.

Perfectionism

Elliott M, Goldberg J. *Perfectionism: What's Bad About Being Too Good?* Minneapolis, MN: Free Spirit Publishing; 1999

Greenspon TS. *Freeing Our Families from Perfectionism.* Minneapolis, MN: Free Spirit Publishing; 2002

Mental Health

The American Academy of Child and Adolescent Psychiatry offers information for psychiatrists and families about developmental, behavioral, emotional, and mental disorders affecting children and adolescents: www.aacap.org/.

The American Psychological Association Web site offers information for psychologists and families on a wide variety of mental health concerns and special circumstances such as dealing with death, terrorism, or natural disasters: www.apa.org/.

Finding a Mental Health Professional

Your child's pediatrician or other health care provider, school counselor, or clergyperson can help you find a mental health professional who would be the right match for your child and family. If this is difficult, however, most mental health professional organizations have online referral networks.

United States

American Academy of Child and Adolescent Psychiatry
www.aacap.org/ReferralDirectory/index.htm

American Mental Health Counselor's Association
www.amhca.org

American Psychiatric Nurses Association
www.apna.org

American Psychological Association
locator.apahelpcenter.org

National Association of Social Workers
www.socialworkers.org

American Association for Marriage and Family Therapy
www.aamft.org/TherapistLocator/index.asp

Canada

Canadian Academy of Child and Adolescent Psychiatry
www.canacad.org

Canadian Association of Social Workers
www.casw-acts.ca

Canadian Psychiatric Association
www.cpa-apc.org

Canadian Psychological Association
www.cpa.ca

Index

A

ABC technique of cognitive behavioral therapy,
113–114
Additional information for applications,
193–194
Admitted-student events, 194
Adolescents. *See also* Children; Students
attention-seeking behaviors, 132
authenticity of, 6–7, 15, 43, 127, 191
disappointments, 15, 30, 198
emotional intelligence of, 9
failing well, 198
failure, 15, 30, 61–64
independence and interdependence,
121–122, 175, 178
independence of, 6, 8, 38, 170
initiation into adulthood, 39–40, 43, 47, 55
and integrity, 52, 190, 191, 197
leaving home, 169–178
managing parents and friends, 196–197
moodiness and irritability in, 75, 83
over-scheduling of, 5
privacy protection, 53, 197
reasons for stress, 27–34
self-discovery in, 4, 32
socialization of, 9
and success, 9, 14
Adrenaline, 79–81, 148–149
Adult development, 55–56
Adult relationships, 175–178
Adults outside the family, 125–126
Adversity and resilience, 6, 30
American Academy of Pediatrics, recommen-
dation for sleep, 29
Anger, 123, 168
in fighting, 208
releasing, 150–151, 158, 159
Anxiety, 83, 123, 146, 181
management for parents, 49–50
Artistic expression, 161–162, 210
Athletic event analogy, 42–44
Athletics, 19, 149–150
Attention-seeking behaviors, 132
Authenticity, 6–7, 15, 43, 127, 191
Authoritarian parenting style, 131, 174
Authoritative parenting style, 132

B

Baby Boomers, 21–23, 33, 36
and college admissions process, 7–8
size of, 17
"Barbie Time," 31–33. *See also* Free time
Baths and showers, 105, 209
Beliefs, inaccurate, 113
Bicycling, 150
Big Lies, 13–15
keeping up with other students, 15
sacrificing free time now for the future,
14, 77, 78
successful adults are good at everything,
13–14, 60
top-tier college is a must, 14
Blogging and privacy, 53, 163–164
Body and stress, 149–153, 202, 203–204
Body language, 103
Body position as relaxation technique,
152, 208
Boredom, 83, 140, 217
Boundaries, 8, 22
Breathing to relax, 151–152, 208
Bullying, 84, 140
Burn out, 62, 71, 106, 195

C

Caffeine, 106, 209
Campus visits, 186–187
parents asking all the questions on, 42, 51
Carrots, eggs, and coffee, 219–220
Catastrophizing, 112–113, 135, 145
Celebrating with parents, 46–47
Cell phones, 122, 178
Character, 14, 126–128
and the college admissions process,
127, 128
development of, 126
negative traits, 126
and resilience, 90–91
and values, 127–128
Child care, 25
Child development, 222
Children. *See also* Adolescents; Students
chronic medical conditions, 69
comparing to others, 66, 98
finding help for, 75–76
health of, 51, 52

W

Y